The Collected Courses of the Academy of European Law
Series Editors: Professor Marise Cremona,
Professor Bruno de Witte, and
Professor Francesco Francioni,
European University Institute, Florence
Assistant Editor: Anny Bremner, *European University Institute, Florence*

VOLUME XX/1

Securing Human Rights?

The Collected Courses of the Academy of European Law
Edited by Professor Marise Cremona,
Professor Bruno de Witte, and Professor Francesco Francioni
Assistant Editor: Anny Bremner

This series brings together the Collected Courses of the Academy of European Law in Florence. The Academy's mission is to produce scholarly analyses which are at the cutting edge of the two fields in which it works: European Union law and human rights law. A 'general course' is given each year in each field, by a distinguished scholar and/or practitioner, who either examines the field as a whole through a particular thematic, conceptual, or philosophical lens, or who looks at a particular theme in the context of the overall body of law in the field. The Academy also publishes each year a volume of collected essays with a specific theme in each of the two fields.

Securing Human Rights?

Achievements and Challenges of the UN Security Council

EDITED BY BARDO FASSBENDER

OXFORD
UNIVERSITY PRESS

OXFORD
UNIVERSITY PRESS

Great Clarendon Street, Oxford, OX2 6DP,
United Kingdom

Oxford University Press is a department of the University of Oxford.
It furthers the University's objective of excellence in research, scholarship,
and education by publishing worldwide. Oxford is a registered trade mark of
Oxford University Press in the UK and in certain other countries

First Edition published in 2011

Published in the United States of America by Oxford University Press
198 Madison Avenue, New York, NY 10016, United States of America

British Library Cataloguing in Publication Data
Data available

Library of Congress Control Number: 2011034967

ISBN 978-0-19-964149-9

Contents

List of Contributors

Annalisa Ciampi is Professor of International Law at the University of Verona, where she was also Professor of European Union Law (2005–09). She holds an LLM from Harvard Law School (1996) and a PhD in International Law from the University of Rome *La Sapienza* (1998). She has taught at the Universities of *Magna Graecia* (Catanzaro), Macerata, Trento, and Florence. In 2008, she was a Visiting Professor of International Law at the *Institut des Hautes Etudes Internationales* of the University *Panthéon-Assas (Paris II)*. Annalisa Ciampi has worked as an external counsel for the Legal Department of the Italian Ministry of Foreign Affairs, was a member of the European Committee of Social Rights (2008–09), and has been an ad hoc judge of the European Court of Human Rights. She is an assistant editor of the *Rivista di diritto internazionale* and member of the Editorial Board of *The Law and Practice of International Courts and Tribunals*. She has published extensively in the field of international criminal law and human rights. Among her recent publications is the book *Sanzioni del Consiglio di sicurezza e diritti umani* (2007).

Erika de Wet is Co-director of the Institute for International and Comparative Law in Africa, as well as Professor of International Law at the Faculty of Law, University of Pretoria (South Africa). She also retains an appointment as Professor of International Constitutional Law at the Faculty of Law, University of Amsterdam, where she was employed full time between 2002 and 2010. She completed her basic legal training (BIur, LLB) as well as her doctoral thesis (LLD) at the University of the Free State (South Africa). She also holds an LLM from Harvard University and completed her *Habilitationsschrift* at the University of Zurich in 2002. It was published under the title *The Chapter VII Powers of the United Nations Security Council* (2004). Professor de Wet is Co-editor in Chief of the *Oxford Reports on International Law in Domestic Courts (ILDC) Online*.

Bardo Fassbender is Professor of International Law at the Bundeswehr University in Munich. He studied law, history, and political science at the University of Bonn (Germany) and holds an LLM from Yale Law School (1992) and a Doctor iuris from the Humboldt University in Berlin (1997), where he also completed his *Habilitation* in 2004 and became *Privatdozent* for the disciplines of public law, international law, European law, and constitutional history. He has been a Ford Foundation Senior Fellow in Public International Law at Yale University and a Jean Monnet Fellow at the European University Institute in Florence. Before joining the Bundeswehr University, he taught in Berlin, Sankt Gallen, and Munich (Ludwig Maximilians University). His principal fields of research are international law, United Nations law, German constitutional law, comparative constitutional law and theory, and the history of international and constitutional law. Among his many publications are the books *UN Security Council and the Right of Veto: A Constitutional Perspective* (The Hague/London/Boston, 1998), *Der offene Bundesstaat: Studien zur auswärtigen Gewalt und zur Völkerrechtssubjektivität bundesstaatlicher Teilstaaten in Europa* (Tübingen, 2007), and *The United Nations Charter as the Constitution of the International Community* (Leiden/Boston, 2009).

Vera Gowlland-Debbas is Emeritus Professor of Public International Law at the Graduate Institute of International and Development Studies in Geneva and a Visiting Professor at University College London. She has also been a Visiting Fellow at All Souls College, Oxford, and a Visiting Professor at Ritsumeikan University, Kyoto, the Institut des Hautes Etudes Internationales of the Université Panthéon-Assas, Paris II, and the University of California at Berkeley. Her publications include *Collective Responses to Illegal Acts in International Law* (1990), *Law-making in a Globalized World*, Bancaja Euromediterranean Courses of International Law, Vol. VIII/IX (2004–05), and *Revisiting the Role of UN Sanctions in the International Legal System*, in *Thesaurus Acroasium*, Vol XXXVI (2005). Publication of the course given at the Hague Academy of International Law in 2007 on *The Security Council and Issues of Responsibility under International Law* is forthcoming. Edited works include *National Implementation of United Nations Sanctions* (2004), and *United Nations Sanctions and International Law* (2001). She acted as Counsel for the Arab League in the ICJ *Wall* Opinion and advises governments and international organizations.

Daphna Shraga is a Principal Legal Officer, Office of the Legal Counsel, Office of Legal Affairs, United Nations. She holds an LLB and LLM from Tel-Aviv University, and a PhD from the Graduate Institute of International and Development Studies, Geneva, where she wrote her dissertation on 'Justice in the Distribution of the World's Resources'. Her main areas of work have included the establishment of the legal framework for UN-based judicial and non-judicial accountability mechanisms, the UN Administrations in Kosovo and East Timor, and questions of human rights and international humanitarian law. She is the author of articles on the international criminal tribunals for the former Yugoslavia and for Rwanda, the second generation UN-based tribunals, the applicability of international humanitarian law to UN peacekeeping operations, and the applicability of the laws of occupation to UN transitional administrations. In 2009 she was a guest lecturer at the Melbourne University School of Law.

Salvatore Zappalà is Professor of International Law at the University of Catania (Italy). He currently serves as Legal Adviser to the Permanent Mission of Italy to the United Nations. He holds a PhD in Law from the European University Institute (2000). He has previously taught at the Universities of Pisa (2001–04) and Florence (2004–06). He was a member of the Italian Delegation at the 2010 Review Conference of the International Criminal Court Statute held at Kampala, in Uganda, and at the VI and VII Assembly of States Parties to the ICC Statute. He is the author of various publications on international law and international criminal law, and is Managing Editor of the *Journal of International Criminal Justice*.

Tables of Cases

COURT OF JUSTICE OF THE EUROPEAN UNION

General Court (Court of First Instance)

Court of Justice

EUROPEAN COURT OF HUMAN RIGHTS

HUMAN RIGHTS COMMITTEE

INTERNATIONAL COURT OF JUSTICE

INTERNATIONAL CRIMINAL COURT

INTERNATIONAL CRIMINAL TRIBUNAL FOR RWANDA

INTERNATIONAL CRIMINAL TRIBUNAL FOR THE FORMER YUGOSLAVIA

NATIONAL COURTS

Belgium

Canada

Netherlands

Switzerland

United Kingdom

Tables of Legislation

NATIONAL LEGISLATION

UN General Assembly Resolutions

UN Security Council Resolutions

List of Abbreviations

AMIS	African Union Mission in Sudan
AU	African Union
CAHDI	Committee of Experts of Public International law of the Council of Europe
CFI	Court of First Instance of the European Communities
CTC	Counter Terrorism Committee of the Security Council
CTED	Executive Directorate of the CTC
DRC	Democratic Republic of the Congo
ECHR	European Convention of Human Rights
ECJ	Court of Justice of the European Communities
ECOSOC	Economic and Social Council
ECOWAS	Economic Community of West African States
ECtHR	European Court of Human Rights
EGC	General Court
EU	European Union
GOS	Government of Sudan
HLP	High Level Panel on Threats, Challenges and Changes
HRC	Human Rights Committee
HRC	Human Rights Council
ICC	International Criminal Court
ICCPR	International Covenant on Civil and Political Rights
ICISS	International Commission on Intervention and State Sovereignty
ICJ	International Court of Justice
ICTR	International Tribunal for Rwanda
ICTY	International Tribunal for the former Yugoslavia
IHL	International Humanitarian Law
ILC	International Law Commission
IWG	Informal Working Group on Documentation and Other Procedural Questions
JEM	Justice and Equality Movement
MINURSO	United Nations Mission for the Referendum in Western Sahara
NAM	Movement of Non-Aligned Countries
OAS	Organization of American States
OMPI	Organisation des Modjahedines du peuple d'Iran
PACE	Parliamentary Assembly of the Council of Europe
POAC	Proscribed Organizations Appeal Commission
POC	Protection of Civilians
RPF	Rwandese Patriotic Front
SADC	Southern African Development Community
SIAC	Special Immigration Appeals Commission
SLM/A	Sudan Liberation Movement/Army
SPLM/A	Sudan People's Liberation Movement/Army
UDI	Unilateral Declaration of Independence

UNAMET	United Nations Mission in East Timor
UNAMID	AU/UN Hybrid Operation in Darfur
UNAMIR	United Nations Assistance Mission for Rwanda
UNCIO	United Nations Conference on International Organization
UNITA	Uniao Nacional para a Indipendencia Total de Angola
UNMIK	UN Interim Administration in Kosovo
UNPROFOR	United Nations Protection Force
UNTAET	United Nations Transitional Administration in East Timor
UNTAG	United Nations Transition Assistance Group

1

Introduction

Bardo Fassbender

Today, a book dealing with the issue of human rights and the UN Security Council does not come as a big surprise. Readers familiar with developments in international law and international relations have become accustomed to a Security Council that tries to promote and protect fundamental human rights in situations of war and internal conflict, as well as to prevent and punish (by means of ad hoc criminal tribunals) grave violations of human rights and international humanitarian law, such as acts of genocide and war crimes.[1] By the same token, it has become a matter of general knowledge that in certain circumstances action taken by the Security Council has given rise to human rights concerns. In particular, the comprehensive economic sanctions against Iraq and the so-called targeted sanctions imposed on individuals in the fight against international terrorism have been sharply criticized as detrimental to the internationally recognized human rights of the affected persons. The ensuing academic discussion resulted in widespread agreement that the Security Council is bound by international human rights, even though authors have used different reasoning to reach this conclusion.

An international lawyer or UN specialist who some 20 years ago had been told about these later developments would have been taken aback. He or she would have wondered: What happened to the concept of domestic jurisdiction, enshrined in Article 2(7) of the UN Charter, which for decades had been invoked by UN member states against involvement of the Organization in human rights affairs? Has the Charter allocation of competences to the different principal organs, according to which human rights remained the business of the General Assembly and Economic and Social Council (ECOSOC) but not the Security Council, been given up? And how can the United Nations, which has not ratified a single human rights treaty, be legally bound by human rights?

Based on the experience of the Hitler regime in Germany and other dictatorships in Europe and elsewhere, the founders of the United Nations regarded national governments and administrations as the main threat to human rights and fundamental freedoms. Accordingly, the preamble of the Universal Declaration of

[1] A first comprehensive record of the Security Council's handling of human rights issues was presented by SD Bailey in his book *The UN Security Council and Human Rights* (1994). See also BG Ramcharan, *The Security Council and the Protection of Human Rights* (2002).

Human Rights of 1948 recalled that 'disregard and contempt for human rights have resulted in barbarous acts which have outraged the conscience of mankind'. The General Assembly proclaimed the Universal Declaration 'as a common standard of achievement for all peoples and all nations'. Article 1(3) of the UN Charter assigned to the United Nations the task 'to achieve international co-operation' among member states 'in promoting and encouraging respect for human rights and for fundamental freedoms for all without distinction as to race, sex, language, or religion'. Human rights was understood as a matter of international economic and social cooperation. For that reason, the subject was placed in Chapters IX and X (see Articles 55 lit. c, 62(2) and 68), whereas the notion of human rights does not appear once in Chapters V, VI, VII, and VIII, which address the Security Council and its functions and powers.

This cautious treatment of human rights in the UN Charter let most governments and international lawyers of the time draw the conclusion that all the Charter was asking for was the voluntary cooperation of states (coordinated by the General Assembly and ECOSOC) with the objective of promoting human rights. However, right from the start some voices in politics and in the legal literature claimed that the provisions of the UN Charter on human rights established binding obligations on both UN member states and the United Nations as an international person. Perhaps the most authoritative and, in view of later developments, influential of those voices was that of Sir Hersch Lauterpacht.[2] In his book *International Law and Human Rights* of 1950, Lauterpacht rejected the view that the respective Charter provisions were a mere declaration of principle. The provisions of the Charter on the subject of human rights, he wrote, 'figure prominently in the statement of the Purposes of the United Nations'. 'Members of the United Nations are under a legal obligation to act in accordance with these Purposes. It is their legal duty to respect and observe fundamental human rights and freedoms. They were adopted . . . as part of the philosophy of the new international system and as a most compelling lesson of the experience of the inadequacies and dangers of the old . . . The legal character of these obligations of the Charter would remain even if the Charter were to contain no provisions of any kind for their implementation.'[3] Any construction of the Charter, Lauterpacht added, according to which members of the UN are, in law, entitled to disregard and to violate human rights and fundamental freedoms 'is destructive of both the legal and the moral authority of the Charter as a whole'.[4]

As regards the human rights obligations of the United Nations itself and its organs, Professor Lauterpacht held that the provisions of the Charter 'imply a comprehensive legal obligation upon the United Nations as a whole': 'They not only authorise the various organs of the United Nations to take steps for encouraging and promoting the realisation of that crucial purpose of the Charter . . . There is

[2] For a brief account of Lauterpacht's life and work, see Scobbie, 'Sir Hersch Lauterpacht (1897–1960)', in B Fassbender and A Peters (eds), *The Oxford Handbook of the History of International Law* (forthcoming, 2012).

[3] H Lauterpacht, *International Law and Human Rights* (1950) 147 *et seq.*

[4] Ibid 149.

laid down here a clear duty of collective action.'[5] Lauterpacht described the General Assembly and ECOSOC as the principal organs of the UN competent to implement the provisions of the Charter in the matter of human rights.[6] But he also envisaged a role for the Security Council in the protection of human rights, namely in cases 'when the degree and scope of their violation are such as to constitute a threat to international peace and security'.[7]

> The Security Council is not the normal instrument of the United Nations in that sphere [of the protection of human rights]. It cannot, as a rule, be concerned with isolated violations of human rights. It is not within its province to frame general policies for implementing that objective of the Charter. But... it constitutes an unlimited reservoir of power—a power not confined to recommendation and not impeded by the reservation of domestic jurisdiction—for the protection of human rights and freedoms when their violation results in situations or disputes which might lead to international friction or endanger the maintenance of international peace and security or constitute a threat to peace. Situations of disputes of this nature may arise in relation to States which by reason of a systematic and flagrant denial of human rights become a source of international friction and of an actual or potential danger to peace; or they may originate in isolated outrages of such magnitude or cruelty as to shock the conscience of civilised mankind and impose an intolerable strain upon peaceful relations... The correlation between peace and observance of fundamental human rights is now a generally recognised fact. The circumstance that the legal duty to respect fundamental human rights has become part and parcel of the new international system upon which peace depends, adds emphasis to that intimate connexion.[8]

However, as Daphna Shraga recalls in her contribution to the present volume, it took a long time for these progressive views to be generally accepted. With the exception of the cases of Southern Rhodesia (1966) and South Africa (since 1977), which were situated in the special context of the fight against colonialism and racial discrimination, action of the Security Council against serious violations of human rights and international humanitarian law had to await the end of the Cold War. '[F]or more than four decades, the Security Council did its best to avoid taking up human rights issues.'[9] The first monograph about the Security Council and human rights was published as recently as 1994.[10] Yet, since the 1990s, as Shraga points out, the Security Council 'has carved itself a role in the protection of human rights'.[11]

It was in the same post-Cold War era, and against the background of the Council's new activism after the East–West antagonism had been overcome, that the Security Council was first perceived as a possible threat to human rights. The idea that the work of the UN Security Council could interfere or come into conflict with internationally protected human rights had surely not been contemplated by the founders of the United Nations. If they had seen a relationship at all between the work of the Council and the issue of human rights, it was a positive one: the Council would promote human rights by promoting international peace. That idea was expressed in the first draft of the Universal Declaration, the 'Humphrey

[5] Ibid 159. See also ibid 221. [6] Ibid 221. [7] Ibid 147.
[8] Ibid 185 *et seq*. [9] Bailey (n 1 above) x. [10] See Bailey (n 1 above).
[11] See D Shraga, in the present volume at 11.

Draft',[12] which suggested that the Declaration's preamble proclaims two related principles—'that there can be no peace unless human rights and freedoms are respected' and 'that there can be no human freedom or dignity unless war and the threat of war are abolished'.[13] But only the first principle was included in the final text of the Declaration, which opened with the words: 'Whereas recognition of the inherent dignity and of the equal and inalienable rights of all members of the human family is the foundation of freedom, justice and peace in the world.'[14] It was only in 1984, when the General Assembly proclaimed the 'right of peoples to peace', that the second principle was officially declared. 'Life without war', the General Assembly then said, 'serves as the primary international prerequisite . . . for the full implementation of the rights and fundamental human freedoms proclaimed by the United Nations'.[15]

Broadly speaking, the view that the Security Council would almost automatically advance the protection of human rights by maintaining international peace was upheld throughout the years of the Cold War, years in which the Council had little chance to detrimentally affect human rights. It was only after the end of the long stalemate that the Council was considered to be a force with the potential of doing harm to the cause of human rights, or of even violating the rights of concrete individuals. The two principal cases in which this fear arose were, first, the sanctions imposed on Iraq since 1991, which were harshly criticized because of the harm they inflicted on the Iraqi civil population[16] and, secondly, the 'targeted sanctions' directed against the Taliban and members or supporters of the al-Qaida network since the terrorist attacks of September 2001.

The contributions to the present volume, which are based on lectures delivered in the session on human rights law of the Academy of European Law in the summer of 2009, take a closer look at these two sides of the Security Council's involvement in human rights—its efforts to promote and enforce human rights on the one hand, and the imperilling of those same rights by action of the Council meant to maintain or restore international peace and security, on the other hand.

In her chapter 'The Security Council and Human Rights—from Discretion to Promote to Obligation to Protect' Daphna Shraga analyses how the role of the Council in the promotion and protection of human rights has developed since 1945: an organ not endowed with any specific powers in the field of human rights

[12] Named after John Humphrey, a Canadian law professor who in 1946 had been appointed as Director of the Division of Human Rights of the UN Secretariat. In this role he produced a first draft of the Universal Declaration. See MA Glendon, *A World Made New: Eleanor Roosevelt and the Universal Declaration of Human Rights* (2001) 47 *et seq*.

[13] The text of the draft is reprinted in Glendon, ibid 271 *et seq*.

[14] In the same vein, the Security Council declared in 2006: 'The Security Council attaches vital importance to promoting justice and the rule of law, including respect for human rights, as an indispensable element for lasting peace.' See Statement by the President of the Security Council, UN Doc S/PRST/2006/28, 22 June 2006.

[15] Declaration on the Right of Peoples to Peace, UNGA Res 39/11, 12 November 1984, preamble, para 4.

[16] See Fassbender, 'Uncertain Steps into a Post-Cold War World: The Role and Functioning of the UN Security Council after a Decade of Measures against Iraq' (2002) 13 EJIL 273, 282 *et seq*.

became the 'centre-piece of the human rights protection system' of the international community. The author describes the place of the Security Council in the framework of the UN human rights institutions, and how the Council came to regard human rights violations as a threat to international peace, making it possible for the Council to take action against such violations with measures provided for in Chapter VII of the UN Charter. Daphna Shraga identifies three human rights, or clusters of human rights, which have attracted most of the Council's attention: the right of peoples to self-determination, the right to democratic governance, and the fundamental rights (arising under international human rights law and international humanitarian law) of civilian populations and minorities during war and internal conflict. One section of the chapter is devoted to the Council's obligation to prevent and punish the crime of genocide. In a concluding section, the author addresses the Council's reaction to criticism levelled against a number of 'legitimacy deficits' in its procedure and in peacekeeping operations endorsed by the Council.

The issue of a qualification of violations of human rights and humanitarian law as threats to the peace within the meaning of Chapter VII of the UN Charter also figures prominently in the chapter by Vera Gowlland-Debbas on 'The Security Council as Enforcer of Human Rights'. Taking a different approach to Daphna Shraga, Professor Gowlland-Debbas focuses her attention on the legal issues of the Council's actions in favour of human rights. In particular, the author addresses the legal problems of a qualification of human rights violations as a threat to international peace, problems which in the past aroused an intensive debate among international lawyers: Was the Council competent to broaden the notion of a threat to the peace to include human rights violations? Is the Council authorized to act in internal matters of a state? Can the Council hold responsible for human rights violations not only states but also de facto governments and non-state entities? Who can legally review such qualifications made by the Security Council? In a subsequent section of her chapter, the author distinguishes five major categories of measures applied by the Council in order to enforce fundamental norms of international human rights and humanitarian law: (i) the sanction of nullity and non-recognition, (ii) non-military measures, in particular economic sanctions, (iii) military force, (iv) measures in the context of criminal law, and (v) monitoring and fact-finding. Further sections of the chapter address the effects of the enforcement of human rights by the Security Council on the development of international law (for instance, its sources) and on human rights treaties and domestic law. The author concludes that today human rights form 'a component part of the security fabric' the preservation of which has been entrusted to the Security Council.

Procedural questions take centre stage in the contribution by Bardo Fassbender on 'The Role for Human Rights in the Decision-making Process of the Security Council'. The chapter addresses questions of safeguarding human rights in the course of Council action directed towards 'other' goals rather than the direct protection of human rights, ie mainly 'classical' goals of maintaining and restoring international (inter-state) peace. In particular, the chapter evaluates how human rights considerations and concerns can be better integrated in the decision-making processes of the Security Council. The chapter takes as its starting point the idea of an 'international rule of law' as a concept expressing, inter alia, certain expectations regarding the place of human rights in the work of the Council. It then addresses the foundation and the extent of the human rights obligations of the Council in the present international legal order. In a following section, the decision-making process of the Council is analysed with a view to the problems of a lack of transparency and legitimacy. Subsequently, an effort is made to identify types of Security Council action in which the problem of safeguarding human rights is acute. In the final section, the author explores different options for enhancing the role for human rights in the decision-making of the Council.

The chapter by Annalisa Ciampi on 'Security Council Targeted Sanctions and Human Rights' then turns to a practice of the Council which has been sharply criticized because of its negative effects on human rights—'targeted sanctions' imposed on individuals in the form of travel bans, arms embargoes, and the freezing of financial assets. In no other area of its work has the Security Council been so vulnerable to attack by human rights activists and lawyers. Paradoxically, the Council only intensified the use of this particular form of non-military sanction because of the harsh criticism levelled against its 'conventional' sanction regimes, ie sanctions imposed on the entire population of a country, as provided for in Article 41 of the UN Charter. Such criticism was especially strong in the case of the sanctions against Iraq upheld after the liberation of Kuwait. Many humanitarian organizations and governments disapproved of those sanctions as mainly hurting the general population (and in particular its most vulnerable parts) without influencing the policies of the Iraqi government and military leadership. After setting out the general legal framework of targeted sanctions, Annalisa Ciampi focuses on the most significant case of such sanctions, the measures imposed on al-Qaida and the Taliban in Security Council Resolution 1267 (1999) and subsequent resolutions. She critically analyses the absence of any *ex ante* protection of individuals and entities placed on the list of the 1267 Committee of the Security Council, as well as the deficiencies of the available *ex post* remedies. Following sections of the chapter deal with the legal challenges brought against the 1267 sanctions regime before national and regional (EU) courts as well as international human rights bodies (the Human Rights Committee and the European Court of Human Rights). A final section is devoted to possible improvements of the system of targeted sanctions with a view to an effective review of listing and de-listing decisions made by the 1267 Committee. In conclusion, the author warns against 'the potentially devastating consequences of a continuous failure to take into account the law's limits' in the Security Council's fight against international terrorism.

In her contribution entitled 'Human Rights Considerations and the Enforcement of Targeted Sanctions in Europe: The Emergence of Core Standards of Judicial Protection', Erika de Wet analyses decisions of European courts pertaining to the targeted sanctions provided for in Security Council Resolutions 1267 (1999) and 1373 (2001). The focus of her attention are the *Kadi* and the *OMPI* cases decided by the courts of the European Union. In addition, she also takes into account decisions rendered by courts of the United Kingdom and views of the Human Rights Committee. Erika de Wet's analysis focuses on the right to a fair hearing and the right to judicial review of the individuals and entities who were made the addressees of sanctions by their being placed on the respective lists. She seeks to identify the legal standards for listing and de-listing that would satisfy the requirements of effective judicial protection before courts in the European Union. The author reaches the conclusion that 'after a cautious start', characterized by a deferential attitude towards the Security Council, courts have become more assertive with respect to their own jurisdiction over targeted sanctions cases, the applicability of national (constitutional), European, and international human rights law, and the requirements to be met by national administrative organs and the European Commission when they exercise their discretion in determining whether a particular person is listed or de-listed. However, many open questions remain, not least with respect to the effectiveness of the judicial decisions and the interplay of domestic courts, EU courts, and international institutions (in particular the Sanctions Committees of the Security Council and the Ombudsperson established by Security Council Resolution 1904 (2009)).

The final chapter of the book, 'Reviewing Security Council Measures in the Light of International Human Rights Principles', contributed by Salvatore Zappalà, is a very critical account of the Security Council's involvement in human rights matters since the early 1990s from a legal perspective. The author maintains that the Council has often operated outside the original framework of the UN Charter, taking measures not provided for in the text of the Charter and probably not even anticipated by its drafters. He argues that the action of the Council has produced positive effects for human rights when the Council limited itself to measures of a general character and the establishment of autonomous bodies (such as the ad hoc criminal tribunals for the former Yugoslavia and Rwanda) able to balance contradictory interests in specific cases. On the other hand, action of the Council directly interfering with individual rights, as in the case of targeted sanctions, is assessed as likely to have resulted in violations of human rights. Accordingly, the author advises the Council against imposing such individualized sanctions.

As this brief review of the chapters indicates, this book does not claim to cover all aspects of the responsibilities and the practice of the Security Council in the area of human rights. Nor is it a systematic review of the Council's work. Rather, the book offers a collection of individual views and appraisals, presented by experts in international law, of how the Council has dealt with human rights issues in the post-Cold War phase of its life and of possible avenues for improvement. Thus, no effort shall be made here by the editor to harmonize those views or to come up with general findings shared by all authors. Evaluating the human rights work of the Council in light of the different perspectives and views presented by each of the authors contributing to this volume, readers will draw up their own balance sheet. However, I personally believe that the efforts of the Council, though still inconsistent and in most cases inadequate, can be described as significant steps towards an international order of the kind Sir Hersch Lauterpacht referred to as an 'organised *civitas maxima*, with the individual human being in the very centre of the constitution of the world'.[17]

[17] Lauterpacht (n 3 above) 463.

2

The Security Council and Human Rights—from Discretion to Promote to Obligation to Protect

*Daphna Shraga**

1. Introduction

The role of the Security Council in the promotion and protection[1] of human rights has developed in time and space. In time, as it shifted throughout the second half of the 20th century from an organ endowed with no Charter-based powers in the field of human rights to the centrepiece of the human rights protection system; and, in space, as it expanded to fill the 'protection gap' left by all other human rights institutional mechanisms combined.

By the end of the century, a combination of seemingly unrelated developments—the emergence of the human rights movement, the end of the cold war, and the exponential growth in the Security Council activities in areas not traditionally within its purview—created the expectation that the Council would assume its responsibility for the protection of civilian populations at risk, a role none of the existing human rights monitoring mechanisms could assume, or assume with any degree of success.

In examining the Security Council's actions—its successes but also its dramatic failures—this inquiry begins with a discussion of other human rights institutional mechanisms, for it is only in relation to the protection space they occupy, that the 'protection gap' filled by the Security Council can be fully appreciated.

* The views expressed in this contribution are those of the author and do not necessarily reflect the opinion of the UN Office of Legal Affairs, or of the United Nations.

[1] Ramcharan, 'The Concept of Protection in the International Law of Human Rights', in Y Dinstein (ed), *International Law at a Time of Perplexity, Essays in Honour of Shabtai Rosenne* (1989) 593.

2. The Human Rights Protection System – the 'Protection Gap'

The human rights provisions in the UN Charter are both skeletal and lofty.[2] At the time of its adoption, when many states considered human rights to be subject to Article 2(7) reservation of 'domestic affairs', there was little support for an active role for the United Nations, let alone the Security Council, in the field of human rights. Since the adoption of the Charter, the human rights protection system has developed in the practice of states and the UN organization along two parallel tracks: (i) UN-mandated or Charter-based organs (the General Assembly, ECOSOC, and the Trusteeship Council[3]); and (ii) Treaty-based organs established under specific human rights treaties.[4]

A. UN-based organs

1. The General Assembly

Of the three UN organs, the General Assembly was endowed with the most extensive, all-embracing mandate, among others, to discuss any matter concerning human rights, initiate studies, make recommendations, and draft conventions for the promotion of international cooperation and the realization of human rights and fundamental freedoms. Throughout the years, as the balance of power within the UN membership shifted, so did the philosophy of human rights it advocated: from civil and political rights promoted by a Western-dominated Assembly, to economic and social rights reflecting the political philosophy of a socialist or Eastern European Group, to the so-called 'third generation' human rights espoused by the Third World and newly independent de-colonized states.[5] In its standard-setting activities in the field of human rights, as in all other fields, the General Assembly acts through resolutions whose legal effect is that of a recommendation.

2. The Economic and Social Council (ECOSOC)

The second UN principal organ, ECOSOC, like the General Assembly, was mandated to initiate studies, make recommendations for the promotion of human rights and fundamental freedoms, prepare draft conventions, and convene international conferences. While, in theory, ECOSOC was to have a key role in the promotion, standard-setting, and coordination of human rights activities, in reality, it made little contribution in any of these respects. ECOSOC was an organ in

[2] Articles 1(3), 55, and 56 of the Charter.

[3] Articles 13(1)(b) and 60, 62(2) and 76(c) of the Charter, respectively. With the independence of the last Trust Territory in 1994, the Trusteeship Council suspended its operations.

[4] G Alfredsson, J Grimheden, BG Ramcharan, and A Zayas (eds), *International Human Rights Monitoring Mechanisms, Essays in Honour of Jakob Th. Möller* (2009).

[5] Cassese, 'The General Assembly: Historical Perspective 1945–1989', in P Alston (ed), *The United Nations and Human Rights, A Critical Appraisal* (1992) (hereinafter: Alston, *The United Nations and Human Rights*) 25.

decline almost from the start, and over time it found itself 'squeezed' between a prominent General Assembly and a very active Commission on Human Rights, its subsidiary organ.[6]

3. *The Commission on Human Rights—and its successor the Human Rights Council*

A subsidiary organ of ECOSOC, the Commission on Human Rights[7] has been the most important UN organ in the field of human rights in standard-setting, monitoring, and protection of human rights through a combined procedure of the so-called *1235* and *1503 Procedures,* and a system of country or thematic Special Rapporteurs (*Special Procedures*).[8] In 2006 it was succeeded by the Human Rights Council, established by General Assembly Resolution 60/25 with an enhanced status—of a subsidiary organ of the General Assembly—but with virtually the same mandate.[9]

UN-mandated bodies of all kinds are universal in scope; their mandate is general, all-inclusive and, in principle, extends to monitoring the compliance of all states with all human rights obligations. The resolutions and decisions of all three organs are of a recommendatory value and thus devoid of a legally binding effect. Comprising representatives of member states, these are political, quite often politicized bodies, whose monitoring of human rights in countries and situations is almost inherently selective.

[6] O'Donovan, 'The Economic and Social Council', in Alston, *The United Nations and Human Rights*, ibid 107.

[7] Alston, 'The Commission on Human Rights', in Alston, *The United Nations and Human Rights*, ibid 126; MN Shaw, *International Law* (2008) 304–7.

[8] The *1235 Procedure*, named after ECOSOC Res 1235 (XLII), 6 June 1967, authorized the consideration of human rights violations brought to its attention by individuals or groups of individuals ('complainants'), which reveal a 'consistent pattern of gross violations'. Throughout the years, the public consideration of the complaint has developed into annual debates, at the end of which the Commission may adopt recommendations, provide 'advisory services', establish commissions of inquiry, condemn states for their violations of human rights, or call upon UN organs to take further action. Unlike the *1235 Procedure*, the *1503 Procedure* established by ECOSOC Res 1503 (XLVIII), 27 May 1970, as modified in 2000, is confidential. The Commission examines (behind closed doors) individual complaints (communications) which, like those considered under the *1235 Procedure*, reveal a consistent pattern of gross violations of human rights. Unlike the former, however, it allows for discrete discussions to take place with the governments concerned. The outcome of its deliberations will become public only if the Commission decides to refer the 'situation' to ECOSOC. *Special Procedures* consist of appointing a country-specific Special Rapporteur, or thematic Rapporteur on a specific subject. See, HJ Steiner, P Alston, and R Goodman (eds), *International Human Rights in Context, Law, Politics, Morals* (2008) (hereinafter: Steiner et al, *International Human Rights in Context*) 754–91.

[9] GA Res 60/25, 15 March 2006, para 5(e). The Council's most distinctive feature is its universal periodic review mechanism by which the human rights record of all countries is to be examined systematically and in an equal manner ('peer review') (Human Rights Council Res 5/1, 18 June 2007, *United Nations Human Rights Council: Institution Building*; Steiner et al, ibid, 791–823. See also Fassbender, 'Architectural Clarity or Creative Ambiguity? The Place of the Human Rights Council in the Institutional Structure of the United Nations', in U Fastenrath, R Geiger, D-E Khan, A Paulus, S von Schorlemar, and C Vedder (eds), From Bilateralism to Community Interest: Essays in Honour of Judge Bruno Simma (2011) 443.

B. Treaty bodies

The human rights treaty bodies are committees established on the strength of specific human rights treaties, both universal and regional.[10] Unlike UN-mandated bodies their monitoring mechanism is limited in scope and subject matter to states parties and their human rights treaty obligations. The monitoring system of all Human Rights Committees, with variations, consists of states' reporting systems, individual complaints, and inter-state complaints. Regional human rights conventions, with the exception of the Arab Human Rights Convention, have, in addition, established judicial institutions[11] to adjudicate in inter-state and individual applications against states for violation of any of their human rights treaty obligations.

In setting human rights standards, monitoring their observance, publicly deliberating, adjudicating complaints, and putting moral and political pressure to bear on governments in breach of their human rights obligations, protection mechanisms of all kinds contributed in their own distinctive way to the promotion of human rights. The acts of all human rights monitoring mechanisms, however, both UN and treaty-based organs, have no legally binding effect. And while Regional Courts are the exception, the legally binding effect of their judgments is limited to the parties to the litigation, and their implementation within states' territories is left to the national authorities of the state concerned. With no exception, none of the existing mechanisms have any enforcement powers, not at least directly applicable within the territories of member states of the regional organization or system, and none are empowered to prevent the violations or to protect individuals or collectivities at risk. Understanding the limitations of the existing human rights protection system, therefore, is understanding the 'protection gap' that, as of the 1990s, the Security Council was called upon to fill. In so doing it had first to establish the missing link, or the legal and political justification for action.

3. Human Rights Violations as a Threat to the Peace—the Missing Link

In the absence of a Charter-specific mandate to promote, protect, and enforce respect for human rights, the Security Council—the foremost political organ and the one primarily responsible for the maintenance of international peace and security—has carved itself a role in the protection of human rights, depending on

[10] Notably, the International Covenants on Civil and Political Rights and on Economic, Social and Cultural Rights, 1966, the International Convention on the Elimination of All Forms of Racial Discrimination, 1965, the Convention on the Elimination of All Forms of Discrimination against Women, 1979, the Convention Against Torture and Other Cruel, Inhumane or Degrading Treatment or Punishment, 1987 and the Convention on the Rights of the Child, 1989. For a review of the human rights treaty organs, see Alston, *The United Nations and Human Rights* (n 5 above), 339 *et seq*; Steiner et al, *International Human Rights in Context* (n 8 above), 844–923; Shaw (n 7 above) 311 *et seq*.

[11] On the regional human rights protection system see, Steiner et al, ibid 779–874 and 920–37; Shaw, ibid 347–95.

its preliminary determination that violations of any such human rights in any given case constitute a threat to international peace and security. A conceptual link was thus established between human rights and international peace and security, or between their serious, systematic, and massive violations and the existence of a threat to the peace; a link which was both a legal basis for the Council's intervention and a limitation on its powers to intervene at its political discretion.

Article 39 of the Charter confers upon the Council the power to determine the existence of a 'threat to the peace, breach of the peace, or act of aggression'. The authority conferred is sole, exclusive, and inherently political. It is also broad, if not virtually unfettered or unlimited, other than by the 'Purposes and Principles of the Charter',[12] themselves broadly defined. And while few would argue that the Security Council is unbound by international law, or that as a 'creature' of the Charter it may act in violation of its constituent instrument or in disregard of its provisions, the question of what legal limitations are put on the political discretionary power of the Security Council to determine the 'existence of a threat'—as part of the more general question of the legal limitations on its Chapter VII powers—remains debatable.[13] In the practice of the Security Council, however, its determinations of a 'threat to the peace' and the proliferation of enforcement measures prescribed in an ever-growing number and diversity of situations and circumstances have never been seriously challenged.

More than six decades after the adoption of the UN Charter, the concept of 'peace' and of what constitutes a 'threat to the peace', have fundamentally changed. From an international armed conflict—the classic concept of a 'threat to the peace' in the immediate aftermath of the Second World War—it had, by the end of the century, expanded to include situations as diverse as a Unilateral Declaration of Independence by a white minority regime (Rhodesia 1966),[14] the apartheid regime and its military build-up (South Africa since 1977),[15] civil wars (Congo 1961, Liberia 1992),[16] humanitarian crises and the flow of refugees (Somalia 1992, Haiti

[12] Article 24(2) of the Charter; Frowein and Krisch, 'Article 39', in B Simma, H Mosler, A Randelzhofer, C Tomuschat, and R Wolfrum (eds), *The Charter of the United Nations, A Commentary,* Volume I (2002) 717–29; I Österdahl, *Threat to the Peace, The Interpretation by the Security Council of Article 39 of the UN Charter* (1998) 85–6.

[13] Österdahl, ibid 85–98; Franck, 'The Security Council and "Threats to the Peace": Some Remarks on Remarkable Recent Developments', in R-J Dupuy (ed), *The Development of the Role of the Security Council,* Workshop, The Hague, 21–3 July 1992, Hague Academy of International Law (1993) 83; D Sarooshi, *The United Nations and the Development of Collective Security, The Delegation by the UN Security Council of its Chapter VII Powers* (1999); Lamb, 'Legal Limits to United Nations Security Council Powers', in GS Goodwin-Gill and S Talmon, *The Reality of International Law, Essays in Honour of Ian Brownlie* (1999) 361; E de Wet, *The Chapter VII Powers of the United Nations Security Council* (2004); Bianchi, 'Assessing the Effectiveness of the UN Security Council's Anti-terrorism Measures. The Quest for Legitimacy and Cohesion' (2007) 17 EJIL 881, 885–6; Gowlland-Debbas, 'Security Council Enforcement Action and Issues of State Responsibility' (1994) 43 ICLQ 55, 90–8; Angelet, 'International Law Limits to the Security Council', in V Gowlland-Debbas (ed), *United Nations Sanctions and International Law* (2001) 71.

[14] SC Res 217 (1965).

[15] SC Res 418 (1977).

[16] SC Res 161 (1961) and SC Res 788 (1992).

1994, Kosovo 1998),[17] repression of civilian population, and minorities in particular (Iraq 1991–2),[18] serious violations of human rights and international humanitarian law (the former Yugoslavia 1991, Rwanda 1994, Liberia, the Democratic Republic of the Congo (DRC) and Sudan (throughout the 2000s)),[19] an overthrow of a democratically elected government (Haiti 1993, Sierra Leone 1997),[20] disintegration of states and breakdown of governmental authority, law and order, and economic strife (Albania 1997),[21] and acts of terrorism (Libya 1992).[22] In its pursuit of justice and accountability, the Security Council determined that *impunity* constitutes a threat to international peace and security, including impunity for serious violations of international humanitarian law (in the former Yugoslavia and Rwanda);[23] Libya's failure to hand over the alleged perpetrators of the bombing of the Pan Am flight over Lockerbie to the US and the UK;[24] Sudan's failure to extradite to Ethiopia for prosecution the suspects in the assassination attempt of Egyptian President, Mubarak, in Addis Ababa,[25] and the failure of the Taliban to cooperate with efforts to bring indicted terrorists to justice, and to hand over Usama bin Laden to the appropriate authorities for arrest and prosecution.[26] Other 'non-military sources of instability in the economic, social, humanitarian and ecological fields' were likewise recognized as threats to international peace and security.[27]

By the end of the 20th century, the recognition of human rights as a quintessential element of a stable world order and their massive violation as a 'threat to the peace', and the consequential diminishing scope of states' *domaine reservé*, placed the Security Council at the centre of the human rights protection system. In the intersection between human rights and international world order, a number of collective human rights were singled out by the Council for promotion and protection. They include the right of peoples to self-determination, to democratic

[17] SC Res 794 (1992), 940 (1994), and 1199 (1998).

[18] SC Res 688 (1991).

[19] Security Council resolutions on the former Yugoslavia: SC Res 808 (1993) and 827 (1993); on Rwanda: SC Res 929 (1994) and 955 (1994); on Liberia: SC Res 1509 (2003); on the DRC: SC Res 1291 (2000), 1493 (2003), 1756 (2007), and 1856 (2008); on Sudan: SC Res 1590 (2005) and 1706 (2006). In its SC Res 1674 (2006) on the Protection of Civilians in Armed Conflict, the Security Council noted 'that the deliberate targeting of civilians and other protected persons, and the commission of systematic, flagrant and widespread violations of international humanitarian law and human rights law in situations of armed conflict, may constitute a threat to international peace and security'.

[20] SC Res 841 (1993), 875 (1993), 917 (1994), and 1132 (1997).

[21] SC Res 1101 (1997).

[22] SC Res 1822 (2008) and 731 (1992).

[23] SC Res 827 (1993) and 955 (1994), respectively.

[24] SC Res 748 (1992).

[25] SC Res 1054 (1996) and 1070 (1996).

[26] SC Res 1214 (1998), 1267 (1999), and 1333 (2000).

[27] At the conclusion of the Security Council Meeting held on 31 January 1992 at the level of heads of state and government, members of the Council made the following statement: 'The absence of war and military conflicts amongst States does not in itself ensure international peace and security. The non-military sources of instability in the economic, social, humanitarian and ecological fields have become threats to peace and security' (Note by the President of the Security Council, S/23500, 31 January 1992).

governance, and the protection of minorities and civilian populations at large from serious violations of human rights and international humanitarian law.

4. Human Rights Promoted and Protected by the Council

A. The right to self-determination: the cases of Southern Rhodesia, the Portuguese Territories, Namibia, East Timor, and Western Sahara

The right of peoples under colonial domination to self-determination, to freely determine their political status and to pursue their economic, social, and cultural development, and the correlative obligation of the colonial power to withdraw its forces and administration from the territory, were enshrined in the 1960 General Assembly Resolution 1514 (XV) on the Granting of Independence to Colonial Countries and Peoples.[28] Ever since, the process of decolonization has played out primarily in the General Assembly—whose composition was fundamentally transformed by the time the decolonization process was over—but it was in the Security Council that enforcement action was taken to give the principle of self-determination practical effect.[29]

In all but one non-self governing territory (Western Sahara), the Security Council determined that obstructing the right of the people to self-determination constitutes a threat to international peace and security, a determination which paved the way for Chapter VII enforcement measures.[30] In Southern Rhodesia, the Portuguese Territories, and Namibia, it imposed military and economic sanctions to prevent the flow of arms, military equipment, and other assistance which would enable the colonial power (or the white minority regime in the case of Southern Rhodesia) to continue its repression of the people under its domination. Other non-enforcement measures were resorted to as well. In Namibia,[31] East Timor,[32] and Western

[28] GA Res 1514 (XV), 14 December 1960, Declaration on the Granting of Independence to Colonial Countries and Peoples, paras 2, 4, and 5.

[29] SD Bailey, *The Security Council and Human Rights* (1994) 1–58.

[30] In the case of Southern Rhodesia, it was the consequence of the Unilateral Declaration of Independence by the white minority regime (SC Res 217 (1965), 232 (1966), and 253 (1968)). In the Portuguese Territories, it was the military operations and other measures of repression undertaken by the Portuguese forces against the African population concerned (SC Res 180 (1963), 183 (1963) and 218 (1965), 290 (1970), and 312 (1972)). In Namibia, it was the illegal continued presence of South Africa (SC Res 276 (1970)), and in East Timor—a Portuguese colony until 1975 and an Indonesian occupied territory until 1999—it was the outbreak of violence following the results of the 1999 popular consultation, a deteriorating security situation, and widespread and systematic violence (SC Res 1264 (1999)).

[31] In Namibia, the United Nations Transition Assistance Group (UNTAG) was established to ensure the early independence through free elections under the supervision and control of the United Nations (SC Res 435 (1978) and 629 (1989)).

[32] In East Timor, two consecutive operations were established: the United Nations Mission in East Timor (UNAMET) to organize the popular consultation, and, following the outbreak of violence, the UN Transitional Administration in East Timor (UNTAET) with overall responsibility for the administration of the territory pending independence (SC Res.1236 (1999) and 1272 (1999)).

Sahara,[33] the Security Council established UN peacekeeping operations to assist in the transition to independence. And in the case of Namibia only, having declared the continued presence of South Africa in the territory illegal and all acts taken by it on behalf of Namibia invalid, the Security Council requested an Advisory Opinion from the ICJ on the legal consequences for states of the continued presence of South Africa in Namibia notwithstanding Resolution 276 (1970).

For all of its condemnations of the policies of colonial powers, the political pressure it brought to bear and the enforcement measures it imposed, the role of the Security Council in the decolonization process has not always been decisive. In the Portuguese Territories, it was not necessarily a decade-long engagement of the Security Council which brought about the withdrawal of the Portuguese armed forces from its administered territories in Africa, but rather the 1974 coup d'état in Lisbon which overthrew the Salazar regime and paved the way for a force withdrawal and a hasty handover of power to the leaders of the respective African national liberation movements. Similarly, the question of Namibia was finally resolved through diplomatic process outside the framework of the Council. By a series of agreements between the US, Angola, Cuba, and South Africa the withdrawal of South Africa from Namibia was linked to the withdrawal of Cuban forces from Angola—a linkage to which the Council had, in principle, objected, but to which, once established, it promised its full support.[34]

The case of Western Sahara remains, in many ways, the exception. Two decades after the establishment of the Mission for the Referendum in Western Sahara to organize a referendum for self-determination of the people of Western Sahara, no referendum was held, Morocco still administers the territory, Western Sahara is still a non-self-governing territory,[35] and a divided Council continues to be seized of the matter. Its approach to the right of self-determination and its application in the circumstances of Western Sahara, however, has changed. Since 2000, the Security Council has favoured a political process where the options of autonomy under Moroccan sovereignty, independence from Morocco, or maintaining the status quo, have dominated the discussions.

While striving to find an agreed political solution to the question of Western Sahara, the Security Council described the political process of self-determination as 'a just, lasting, and *mutually acceptable political solution*, which will provide for self-determination of the people of Western Sahara in the context of arrangements consistent with the principles and purposes of the Charter of the United Nations, and noting the roles and responsibilities of the parties in this respect'.[36]

[33] In Western Sahara, a United Nations Mission for the Referendum in Western Sahara (MINURSO) was established to organize, under the supervision of the United Nations, a referendum for self-determination of the people of Western Sahara (SC Res 690 (1991)).

[34] Compare SC Res 566 (1985) to Res 628 (1989).

[35] For a legal analysis of the status of Western Sahara in the United Nations, see Letter dated 29 January 2002 from the Under-Secretary-General for Legal Affairs, the Legal Counsel, addressed to the President of the Security Council, S/2002/161, 12 February 2002.

[36] Emphasis added. SC Res 1754 (2007), 1783 (2007), 1813 (2008), 1871 (2009), and 1920 (2010).

In the political realities of the Security Council, the right of the people of Western Sahara to self-determination is thus no longer a people's right to determine *freely* its own political future, in the spirit of General Assembly Resolution 1514, but rather a right conditional upon the *agreement* of the parties and qualified by the outcome of the political process.[37]

B. The right to democratic governance

The right to democratic governance, as a post-colonial manifestation of the right to self-determination, is understood as a right to governance expressive of the people's will, based on a regular, genuine, and fair election accountable to the electorate and based on the respect for human rights and the rule of law.[38] Beyond its promise of full participation in the political process of determining a people's system of governance, democracy is conceived as the ultimate guarantee for the respect of all other human rights and the rule of law within and among states. It is conducive to economic, social, and cultural progress and a condition necessary, though not sufficient, for durable, sustainable peace, security, and world order.

In its pursuit of an 'agenda for democratization', the United Nations system as a whole has, since the early 1990s, supported emerging democracies in post-conflict countries or in countries in transition from a single to a multi-party system of governance. It provided technical, financial, and electoral assistance, contributed to building or rebuilding of state and government institutions, and supported capacity building and the establishment of transitional justice mechanisms of all kinds.[39] For the Security Council, however, advocating democratic governance was part of a broader context of its responsibility for the world peace, security, and conflict resolution.[40] In enforcing respect for democratic institutional order, the Council defended an *existing* democratic order or its restoration when its reversal was brought about through unconstitutional means.

The Council's reaction to unconstitutional changes of government varied throughout the decades depending on the political context, both in the region and at the Security Council, and more importantly, perhaps, on whether the unconstitutional change had ousted a democratically elected government (in particular,

[37] On the right to self-determination as a 'free and genuine expression of the will of the people of the territory', see *Western Sahara, Advisory Opinion*, ICJ Reports (1975) 12, 31–3, paras 54–9.

[38] Article 21 of the Universal Declaration of Human Rights; Art 25 of the International Covenant on Civil and Political Rights, and para 135 of the World Summit Outcome (GA Res 60/1, 16 September 2005), see also GA Res 61/226, 22 December 2006 and 62/7, 8 November 2007. On the human right to democracy, see Franck, 'The Emerging Right to Democratic Governance' (1992) 86 AJIL 46; Steiner et al (n 8 above), *International Human Rights in Context*, 980–1001.

[39] Report of the Secretary-General, *Support by the United Nations System of the Efforts of Governments to Promote and Consolidate New or Restored Democracies*, A/50/332, 7 August 1995, and its *Supplement*, Letter dated 17 December 1996 from the Secretary-General addressed to the President of the General Assembly, A/51/761, 20 December 1996.

[40] LA Sicilianos, *L'ONU et la démocratisation de l'état, Systèmes régionaux et ordre juridique universel* (2000); Fox, 'Democratization', in DM Malone (ed), *The UN Security Council from the Cold War to the 21st Century* (2004) 69.

one elected with UN electoral assistance), or a government similarly instituted through unconstitutional means.[41]

In Burundi,[42] Guinea Bissau,[43] and Mauritania,[44] the Council's condemnation of the *coup d'état* against the democratically elected government was immediate. In all three cases, it expressed its opposition to any attempt to change the government through unconstitutional means, and demanded an immediate restoration of democratic institutions and return to constitutional order and legality through free, fair, and transparent elections.

The 2008 *coup d'état* in Guinea triggered little reaction from the Council, partly because Guinea had a history of *coups d'état* and military takeover of power, and partly because of the joint engagement of the Economic Community of West African States (ECOWAS)—the African Union and President Compaoré's mediation—in bringing about a political solution to Guinea.[45]

The *coups d'état* in Liberia, Sierra Leone, and Haiti took place in a broader context of civil war and a history of violent succession of power. The Council's intervention to impose military, economic, and targeted sanctions to induce the military junta and coup leaders to return to constitutional order or restore the democratically elected government, was thus part of a more general effort to bring an end to the civil war through a peaceful conflict resolution process.[46]

Haiti was the only case where the Security Council resorted to the ultimate measure of military force for the purpose of restoring democracy, removing the military junta and coup leaders, and reinstating the ousted democratically elected president. Having determined that the 'exceptional circumstances' of Haiti (ie the refusal of the military junta leaders to reinstate the democratically elected president, their failure to fulfil their obligations under the Governor Island Agreement, and to

[41] In its Presidential Statement of 5 May 2009, the Council expressed its 'deep concern over the resurgence of unconstitutional changes of Government in a few African countries', and stressed 'the importance of expeditiously restoring constitutional order, including through open, transparent elections'. Acknowledging the link between unconstitutional changes and a threat to international peace and security, it welcomed the relevant decision of the African Union condemning the resurgence of *coups d'état*, and its conclusion that such 'not only constitute a dangerous political downturn and serious setback to the democratic processes, but could also pose a threat to the peace, security and stability of the continent' (Statement by the President of the Security Council, PRST/2009/11). See also d'Aspremont, 'La Liceité des coups d'état en droit international', in *L'Etat de droit en droit international*, Société française pour le droit international, Colloque de Bruxelles (2009) 123; Sicilianos, 'Le respect de l'état de droit comme obligation internationale', ibid 143.

[42] Statement by the President of the Security Council, S/PRST/1996/32; SC Res 1072 (1996).

[43] Statement by the President of the Security Council, S/PRST/2009/2; SC Res 1876 (2009).

[44] Statement by the President of the Security Council, S/PRST/2008/30.

[45] Statements by the President of the Security Council, S/PRST/2009/27 and S/PRST/2010/3.

[46] In the Liberian civil war, the Security Council intervened in 1992 to impose a complete embargo on all deliveries of weapons and military equipment (SC Res 788 (1992)), and in 2003, to authorize a Multinational Force to support the ceasefire agreement and maintain security in the period after the departure of President Taylor and the instauration of the successor authority (SC Res 1497 (2003)). In Sierra Leone in 1997, sanctions were imposed—both on members of the military junta and the country as a whole—as a punitive measure with the purpose of inducing the military junta and coup leaders to relinquish power, restore the democratically elected government, and return to constitutional order (Statements by the President of the Security Council: S/PRST/1997/29, S/PRST/1997/36, and SC Res 1132 (1997)).

comply with relevant Security Council resolutions) constituted a threat to peace and security in the region,[47] the Security Council imposed a comprehensive regime of military and economic sanctions, including a travel ban on the participants in the *coup d'état* of 1991, and a freeze on their funds and financial assets abroad. When the measures failed, it authorized member states to form a multinational force and use all necessary means to facilitate the departure from Haiti of the military leadership, the prompt return of the democratically elected president, and the restoration of the legitimate authorities of the government of Haiti.[48]

Not all *coups d'état*, however, triggered a reaction by the Security Council. In the cases of Niger,[49] Madagascar,[50] and Honduras,[51] where the deposed president or government were not democratically elected, or did not otherwise respect the existing constitutional order, and where regional organizations—the African Union (AU), ECOWAS, the Southern African Development Community (SADC), or the Organization of American States (OAS)—were actively engaged in steering the authorities to return to constitutional order, the Security Council was disinclined to react, or to react with sufficient force.

C. Protection of civilian population and minorities from serious violations of human rights and international humanitarian law

The conflicts in the former Yugoslavia and Rwanda in the mid-1990s, where war crimes, crimes against humanity, and genocide were committed on a scale unseen since the Second World War, have shaped the Security Council's action in the protection of civilian populations for decades to come. In places as diverse as Georgia,[52] Armenia and Azerbaijan,[53] Afghanistan,[54] the former Yugoslavia

[47] SC Res 841 (1993), 875 (1993), and 917 (1994).

[48] SC Res 940 (1994); Corten, 'La résolution 940 du Conseil de sécurité autorisant une intervention militaire en Haïti; L'émergence d'un principe de légitimité démocratique en droit international?' (1995) 6 EJIL 116, 128–33.

[49] In Niger, the military *coup d'état* of February 2010 and the arrest of President Tanja was a (direct) consequence of his decisions in June 2009 to dissolve the Parliament and the Constitutional Court, and to conduct a controversial referendum to amend the Constitution to extend his term of office.

[50] In Madagascar, following the *coup d'état* by Andry Rajoelina in March 2009, members of the Security Council expressed their support for the Joint Mediation Team composed of the AU, SADC, the UN and the Francophonie, and called for a rapid return to the constitutional order through an inclusive election process. The situation in Madagascar, however, was not inscribed on the agenda of the Security Council, and the sanctions adopted by the African Union were not endorsed by the Council (S/2010/149, 23 March 2010).

[51] In Honduras, a battle over a proposed referendum, which President Zelaya hoped would allow him to defy the Constitution's limit of a presidential four-year term, led to a political-constitutional crisis and eventually to a *coup d'état* in which the president was arrested and forced out of the country. The General Assembly condemned the *coup d'état*, demanded the immediate and unconditional restoration of the legitimate and constitutional government of the president and called 'firmly and unequivocally upon States to recognize no Government other than that of the Constitutional President, Mr. José Manuel Zelaya Rosales' (GA Res 63/301, 30 June 2009). All this time, however, the Security Council was conspicuously silent.

[52] SC Res 1036 (1996).

[53] SC Res 822 (1993).

[54] Statement by the President of the Security Council, S/PRST/2000/2; SC Res 1333 (2000).

(including Bosnia and Herzegovina),[55] Angola,[56] Liberia,[57] Rwanda,[58] Burundi,[59] Côte d'Ivoire,[60] Sudan,[61] and the DRC,[62] the Security Council condemned a litany of serious, systematic, and widespread violations of human rights and international humanitarian law committed against the civilian population, in general, and minorities and other vulnerable groups—women, children, refugees, and internally displaced—in particular.[63] In condemning the violations, the Security Council called upon the parties to comply with their human rights and international humanitarian law obligations, put an end to the violations, and bring those responsible to account.[64] Since 1999, it held, in addition to country-specific debates, thematic debates on the protection of civilians in armed conflict,[65] on children and armed conflict,[66] and on women, peace, and security,[67] in which protection strategies, for the most part through the deployment of peacekeeping operations, were devised.

But beyond the thematic debates and condemnations in specific cases and situations, the protection of civilian population in imminent physical danger demanded action. In establishing the two International Tribunals for the former Yugoslavia (ICTY) and Rwanda (ICTR) as a judicial response to serious violations of human rights and international humanitarian law, the Security Council set the bar for its action and the expectations that in future similar cases, it would do no less. But it would be in its ability and willingness to prevent or arrest the violations,

[55] SC Res 771 (1992), 808 (1993), and 827 (1993), 941 (1994) and 1034 (1995).

[56] SC Res 834 (1993), and Statement by the President of the Security Council, S/PRST/1999/26.

[57] SC Res 1509 (2003); Presidential Statements: S/PRST/1997/34 and S/PRST/1997/38.

[58] SC Res 912 (1994), 918 (1994), 925 (1994), and 955 (1994).

[59] Statement by the President of the Security Council, S/PRST/1996/31; SC Res 1791 (2007) and 1902 (2009).

[60] SC Res 1933 (2010).

[61] SC Res 1547 (2004) and 1769 (2007).

[62] Statement by the President of the Security Council, S/PRST/1998/26; SC Res 1341 (2001), 1355 (2001), 1468 (2003), 1794 (2007), 1856 (2008), 1906 (2009), and 1925 (2010).

[63] They included: mass killing, acts of genocide, large scale disappearances, forcible expulsion, displacement, deportation of civilians or 'ethnic cleansing', imprisonment, arbitrary detention, torture, rape and all forms of sexual violence, discrimination against women and girls, forced labour, deliberate attacks on civilians and non-combatants, on hospitals, ambulances, and humanitarian workers, and impeding food and medical supplies, wanton devastation and destruction and looting of property, recruitment, training and use of child soldiers, and incitement to violence and ethnic hatred. See also SC Res 1019 (1995) on the Serb population in Croatia; SC Res 688 (1991) on the Iraqi civilian population, and in Kurdish populated areas, in particular; and Presidential Statement, S/PRST/2000/12, condemning all human rights violations committed by the Taliban, in particular, the 'grave violations of human rights of women and girls'.

[64] Nolte, 'Practice of the UN Security Council with Respect to Humanitarian Law', in *Weltinnenrecht, Liber Amicorum Jost Delbrück* (2005) 487.

[65] SC Res 1265 (1999), 1296 (2000), and 1674 (2006); *Aide Memoire for the consideration of issues pertaining to the protection of civilians in armed conflict*, Statement by the President of the Security Council, Annex, S/PRST/2009/1, and SC Res 1894 (2009).

[66] SC Res 1460 (2003), 1612 (2005); Statement by the President of the Security Council, S/PRST/2008/6 and SC Res 1882 (2009).

[67] SC Res 1325 (2000), 1820 (2008); Report of the Secretary-General on women, and peace and security, S/2005/636 (10 October 2005), annex (*System-wide action plan for the implementation of Security Council Resolution 1325 (2000)*); SC Res 1888 (2009) and 1889 (2009).

by force if necessary, that its success or failure to protect civilian population would ultimately be measured.

5. From Humanitarian Intervention to Responsibility to Protect—the Role of the Security Council

A. Humanitarian intervention

The debate over the use of force in the protection of civilian population at risk, reignited by the NATO air campaign in Kosovo, was an old debate over sovereignty and non-interference in states' domestic affairs, the protection of human rights, the Charter prohibition on the use of force and its exceptions, and the Security Council legal monopoly over the use of force—a debate which in the post-Second World War era began with the doctrine of 'humanitarian intervention'. The question at the heart of the debate was the legality of a military intervention in a third state to protect its population from massive violations of human rights without the consent of the target state or an authorization of the Security Council. It was a question to which the legal, the political, and the moral provided very different answers.[68]

In the 'humanitarian interventions' of the 1970s, and notably, the Indian intervention in East-Pakistan,[69] the Vietnamese intervention in Cambodia,[70] and the Tanzanian intervention in Uganda,[71] the 'humanitarian' was hardly the only, not even the decisive motive. While it is a fact that in all three interventions the lives of hundreds of thousands of people were saved, it is also a fact that their outcome was a 'regime change' in the target state, and in the case of Bangladesh (the then East Pakistan), an emergence of a new state.

[68] Verwey, 'Humanitarian Intervention', in A Cassese (ed), *The Current Legal Regulation of the Use of Force* (1986) 57; S Chesterman, *Just War or Just Peace? Humanitarian Intervention and International Law* (2001) 65–87.

[69] In 1971, India intervened in what was then East Pakistan to stop massive human rights violations committed by the Pakistani army against the Bangladeshi population, many of whom had been imprisoned, killed, and forced to flee to India. Motivated by humanitarian concerns to rescue the Bengali population and alleviate its suffering, India was equally motivated by its interest to enable the return of over 10 million Bengali refugees in its territory to East Pakistan, and its political interest in the secession of East Pakistan, under the Awami League. Franck and Rodley, 'After Bangladesh: The Law of Humanitarian Intervention by Military Force' (1973) 67 AJIL 275.

[70] The Vietnamese intervention in Cambodia in 1978–79 ended the four-year brutal regime of the Khmer Rouge which had, by then, exterminated between 1.8 and 2 million Cambodians. Its intervention might have saved the lives of millions. It also brought about the overthrow of the Pol Pot regime, and its replacement, in Phnom Penh, with a pro-Vietnamese government. On the background and circumstances of the Vietnamese intervention, see Heder, 'The Kampuchean-Vietnamese Conflict', *Southest Asian Affairs* (1979) 157.

[71] Tanzania's intervention in Uganda in March 1979 in response to a previous Ugandan attack on its territory, and in reaction to the bloody regime of Idi Amin Dada, during which thousands of civilians were killed, tortured, or disappeared, ended two months later with the overthrow of Idi Amin and the institution of a new government, recognized shortly thereafter by many states. See, Chatterjee, 'Some Legal Problems of Support Role in International Law: Tanzania and Uganda' (1981) 30 ICLQ 755.

The humanitarian interventions of the 1990s, in Iraq (1991–92) and in Kosovo (1999)—the 'second generation' humanitarian interventions—changed the parameters of the debate. Like the military interventions of the 1970s, the imposition of the 'no-fly zones' in Northern and Southern Iraq to protect the Kurds and Shiia communities,[72] and the 78-day NATO air campaign to protect the Kosovo-Albanian population,[73] were unauthorized operations, and thus illegal. Unlike the former interventions, however, they were conducted in circumstances of a divided Security Council, by *members* of the Council, individually or in the framework of a regional organization. And while legally impermissible and politically controversial, both operations enjoyed broad moral support. In the world public opinion they were perceived as morally legitimate, or in the words of the Kosovo Report 'illegal, yet legitimate'.[74]

In the decade that followed, there was general agreement that an unauthorized military intervention in a territory of a third state—for any reason, including humanitarian—is prohibited under Article 2(4) and (7) of the Charter. There was also an agreement that the Charter ban on the use of force is all-inclusive and absolute in character, with only two exceptions of self defence (Article 51) and a Security Council authorization (Articles 39 and 42). There was no agreement, however, on the implications of the moral imperative, and its consequences for the legality or legitimacy of humanitarian intervention. For some, humanitarian

[72] Following the brutal repression of the Kurdish and Shiia uprisings in the Northern and Southern provinces of Iraq in the aftermath of the first Gulf War, the Security Council adopted Resolution 688 (1991). Having determined that the magnitude of the human suffering and massive flow of refugees constituted a threat to international peace and security, it demanded that Iraq end the repression, ensure respect for the human and political rights of all Iraqi citizens, and allow access by international humanitarian organizations to population in need. The resolution fell short, however, of authorizing military action in support of the threatened population, and its call on the Iraqi government went unheeded. As attacks against the ethnic groups continued, members of the coalition forces decided to establish 'safety zones' or 'enclaves' in Northern Iraq under Allied military protection, and allow for humanitarian relief and the eventual return of Kurdish refugees. In April 1991 and August 1992, respectively, two 'no-fly zones' were unilaterally imposed by the US, UK, and France in the North (above the 36th parallel) and South of Iraq (below the 32nd parallel) to protect Kurdish and Shiite populations within the security zones. The 'safe havens' were effective in averting further repression, stemming the flow of refugees, and allowing the return of almost half-a-million Kurdish refugees to relative safety. See Schachter, 'United Nations Law in the Gulf Conflict' (1991) 85 AJIL 452; Alston, 'The Security Council and Human Rights: Lessons to be Learned From the Iraq-Kuwait Crisis and its Aftermath' (1990–1991) 13 *Australian Yearbook of International Law* 107; Malanczuk, 'The Kurdish Crisis and Allied Intervention in the Aftermath of the Second Gulf War' (1991) 2 EJIL 114; Gray, 'After the Ceasefire: Iraq, the Security Council and the Use of Force' (1994) *65 British Yearbook of International Law* 135; Chesterman (n 68 above) 196–206.

[73] With the collapse of the talks at Rambouillet between Kosovo-Albanians and Serbia on the autonomous status of Kosovo, and in the light of intensified Serb military operations in Kosovo, the displacement of over 800,000 Kosovo-Albanians within and outside Kosovo and the execution of hundreds of civilians, a NATO 78-day air campaign against targets in Kosovo, Serbia and Montenegro was launched in the spring of 1999. The NATO operation succeeded in stemming the massive flow of refugees and internally displaced, protecting the Kosovar population and creating the conditions for the establishment of a UN Administration to administer the territory in the spirit of the Rambouillet Accord. See 'Editorial Comments: NATO's Kosovo Intervention' (1999) 93 AJIL 824 *et seq*; Chesterman, ibid 206–18.

[74] The Independent International Commission on Kosovo, *The Kosovo Report, Conflict, International Response, Lessons Learned* (2000) 186.

intervention is, and should in all circumstances remain prohibited; for others, in extreme circumstances of serious and massive violations of human rights amounting to genocide or crimes against humanity, where the Council fails to act or is otherwise paralysed, the use of force as a last resort—albeit illegal—could 'occasionally' be 'tolerated' on the condition, though, that it remains an isolated case or the rare exception. For others, still, in extreme circumstances, the humanitarian imperative legitimizes the military intervention—its illegality under the Charter notwithstanding.[75]

In the early 2000s, the doctrine of 'responsibility to protect' emerged as an alternative to the largely discredited doctrine of 'humanitarian intervention'. It shifted the focus from the right to intervene to responsibility to protect, or from the right of the intervening states to the needs of the populations at risk. It did, however, little to resolve the dilemma at the heart of the debate—of how to protect civilian population in imminent threat in case of a paralysed, divided, or otherwise indifferent Council. A dilemma put by the then UN Secretary-General in an oft-quoted passage in his Millennium Report thus: 'If humanitarian intervention is, indeed, an unacceptable assault on sovereignty, how *should* we respond to a Rwanda, to a Srebrenica—to gross and systematic violations of human rights that offend every precept of our common humanity?'[76]

In the passage from humanitarian intervention to responsibility to protect, there was no avoiding the real debate over the role of the Security Council. In the renewed debate over the limitations of sovereignty, the Charter prohibition on the use of force, and the 'responsibility to protect' as an 'obligation to intervene', the Security Council no longer operated as a political forum for debate over the legality of humanitarian intervention, but as an active participant in a debate over its own role in the protection of civilians. The responsibility to protect doctrine thus placed the legal-political-moral debate squarely before the Security Council, and challenged it to act.[77]

B. Responsibility to protect (R2P)

The concept of responsibility to protect was first articulated in the Report of the International Commission on Intervention and State Sovereignty (ICISS).[78] It was

[75] For the divergence of views see, Simma, 'NATO, the UN and the Use of Force: Legal Aspects' (1999) 10 EJIL 1; Cassese, 'Ex iniuria ius oritur: Are We Moving towards International Legitimation of Forcible Humanitarian Countermeasures in the World Community?' (1999) 10 EJIL 23; Cassese, 'A Follow-Up: Forcible Humanitarian Countermeasures and Opinio Necessitatis' (1999) 10 EJIL 791; Roberts, 'The So-called 'Right' of Humanitarian Intervention' (2000) 3 *Yearbook of International Humanitarian Law* 3.

[76] Report of the Secretary-General, *We the Peoples: the role of the United Nations in the twenty-first century*, A/54/2000, 27 March 2000 para 217.

[77] See generally, Bellamy, 'Whither the Responsibility to Protect? Humanitarian Intervention and the 2005 World Summit' (2006) 20 *Ethics & International Affairs* 143; Stahn, 'Responsibility to Protect: Political Rhetoric or Emerging Legal Norm?' (2007) 101 AJIL 99; G Evans, *The Responsibility to Protect. Ending Mass Atrocity Crimes Once and for All* (2008).

[78] Report of the International Commission on Intervention and State Sovereignty, *The Responsibility to Protect* (2001).

later endorsed by the High Level Panel on Threats, Challenges and Changes (HLP)[79] and the Secretary-General in his Report *In Larger Freedom*,[80] and was finally embraced by the wider UN membership in the 2005 World Summit Outcome.[81] Its main distinctive features consist of the following: (i) a concept of 'shared responsibility' between the sovereign state and the international community, where the primary responsibility to protect its civilian population falls to the state, and when it fails—through inability or ill-will—a secondary responsibility to protect then falls to the broader community of states; (ii) a three-pronged continuum of obligations: *to prevent* in addressing the root causes of the conflict, *to react* in response to the humanitarian imperative, by force if necessary, and to *rebuild* in the wake of the military intervention through assistance in the recovery, reconstruction, reconciliation, and the restoration of the rule of law; and (iii) when all peaceful means have failed and the use of force is contemplated as a last resort, an authorization of the Security Council should first be sought. A proposed set of so-called 'threshold' or 'legitimacy criteria' to guide the Security Council in its discretionary power to authorize, or not, the use of force[82] was not endorsed by the Secretary-General. It was later rejected by member states either for fear that it would pre-commit them to military action at a time and circumstances not of their choosing, or for the potential of abuse that such criteria may hold.[83]

In embracing the R2P doctrine at the 2005 World Summit, an assembly of heads of state and government affirmed that each individual state has the responsibility to protect its population from genocide (ethnic cleansing[84]), war crimes, and crimes against humanity, with the assistance of other states, and the support of the United Nations. With the shifting of the residual 'responsibility to protect' to the entire UN membership, however, their preparedness to take action to arrest the violations, when all peaceful means have failed, was qualified, conditional, and non-committal. In paragraph 139 of the World Summit Outcome they affirmed their preparedness 'to take collective action, in a timely and decisive manner, through

[79] Report of the High Level Panel on Threats, Challenges and Change, *A More Secure World: Our Shared Responsibility*, A/59/565 (2 December 2004).

[80] Report of the Secretary-General, *In Larger Freedom: Towards Development, Security and Human Rights for All*, A/59/2005, 21 March 2005.

[81] GA Res 60/1, 16 September 2005, endorsed by the Security Council in Res 1674 (2006), para 4 and 1706 (2006) preambular para 2.

[82] They include: (a) just cause (or seriousness of threat); (b) proper purpose; (c) last resort; (d) proportional means; (e) reasonable prospects of success (or balance of consequences); and (f) the right or legitimate authority.

[83] Both the ICISS and the HLP argued that their task is not to identify alternative sources of authority to the Security Council, but rather to make the Council work better. But while the ICISS did not exclude the possibility that if the Security Council fails to act, others, ie the General Assembly, regional organizations, or states, would assume this responsibility to meet the gravity and urgency of the situation, the HLP endorsed the concept of collective international responsibility to protect exercisable *only* by the Security Council, and thus avoided the dilemma of a Security Council deadlock. Joyner, '"The Responsibility to Protect": Humanitarian Concern and the Lawfulness of Armed Intervention' (2006–2007) 47 *Virginia Journal of International Law* 693, 710–16.

[84] Considered as one of the so-called 'R2P crimes', ethnic cleansing is not a stand-alone crime, but a manifestation of any of the other 'heads of crimes' (war crimes, crimes against humanity, and genocide).

the Security Council, in accordance with the Charter, including Chapter VII, on a case-by-case basis, and in cooperation with relevant regional organizations as appropriate'.

The R2P doctrine, as conceptualized in the World Summit, was of little normative value, not only because like all other General Assembly resolutions, Resolution 60/1 is recommendatory in character, but also, and more importantly, because states' preparedness to shoulder their residual responsibility to protect and take collective action 'on a case-by-case basis' was a political commitment. A legally binding obligation would have required a systematic approach to all R2P situations, and a commitment to treat all similar cases—provided they meet the same conditions—alike. A legally binding obligation would have also entailed legal consequences for non-compliance, none of which were envisaged under the doctrine of R2P.

But while a legal obligation 'to protect' or 'to intervene to protect' has not emerged on the strength of the R2P concept, the Security Council has, since 1999, mandated peacekeeping operations to protect, by force if necessary, civilian population in imminent threat of physical violence. In Sierra Leone,[85] Liberia,[86] Côte d'Ivoire,[87] Haiti,[88] Chad and the Central African Republic,[89] the DRC,[90] and the Sudan,[91] peacekeeping operations were mandated, with variations, to protect civilians in imminent threat, within the limitations of their areas of operation, capabilities, and available resources, and without prejudice to the government's responsibilities.[92]

For the first time, however, during what has come to be known as the Arab Spring, Responsibiliy to Protect was invoked—though not by name—as a basis for a Security Council authorized military operation in Libya—one of half-a-dozen Arab States shaken by popular uprising and bloody crackdown in the spring of 2011. Security Council Resolution 1973 (2011) was the Council's first 'R2P reaction' to an 'R2P situation'. It reiterated the responsibility of the Libyan authorities to protect the Libyan population, and qualified the wide-spread and

[85] SC Res 1270 (1999), para 14.

[86] SC Res 1509 (2003), para 3(j).

[87] SC Res 1528 (2004), paras 6(i) and 16, and SC Res 1933 (2010), para 16(b).

[88] SC Res 1542 (2004), para 7 I(f).

[89] SC Res 1778 (2007), para 6(a) authorized the deployment of the EU Operation with a mandate (among others) 'to contribute to protecting civilians in danger, particularly refugees and displaced persons'; SC Res 1861 (2009), para 7(a)(i) and SC Res 1923 (2010).

[90] SC Res 291 (2000), para 8; SC Res 1484 (2003) authorized an Interim Emergency Multinational Force in Bunia in coordination with MONUC to protect civilians following the atrocities in Bunia, Ituri; SC Res 1493 (2003), para 25, SC Res 1565 (2004), para 4(b), SC Res 1756 (2007), para 2(a), SC Res 1794 (2007), paras 5 and 8, SC Res 1856 (2008), para 3(a), SC Res 1906 (2009), paras 5 (a), 7, 22–3, and SC Res 1925 (2010), para 12(a) and (c). See also, Månsson, 'Use of Force and Civilian Protection: Peace Operations in the Congo' (2005) 12 *International Peacekeeping* 503.

[91] SC Res 1590 (2005), para 16, SC Res 1706 (2006), para 12(a), SC Res 1769 (2007), para 15, SC Res 1919 (2010), para 4 and SC Res 1935 (2010), para 2.

[92] For a comparative study of peacekeeping operations mandated to protect civilians, see Holt and Taylor with Kelly, *Protecting Civilians in the Context of UN Peacekeeping Operations, Successes, Setbacks and Remaining Challenges*, independent study jointly commissioned by the Department of Peacekeeping Operations and the Office for the Coordination of Humanitarian Affairs (2009).

systematic attacks against civilians as crimes against humanity—one of the three 'R2P crimes'. When measures short of use of force (ie military and financial sanctions, travel ban and referral to the International Criminal Court) failed to arrest the violations, member states, in the words of paragraph 139 of the Outcome Summit, took a collective action in accordance with Chapter VII of the Charter, through the Security Council. Using a formula routinely used in peacekeeping operations mandates, Resolution 1973 authorized member states 'to take all necessary measures . . . to protect civilians and civilian populated areas under threat of attack . . . '. The question of what measures are 'necessary' to protect civilians was left to be determined by the military and political leadership of the states conducting the operation. As the NATO air-campaign, however, intensified and expanded beyond securing a 'no fly zone', disagreements over whether all measures taken were necessarily to protect civilians only, divided members of the Council and of the NATO-led coalition.

But if Responsibility to Protect has not emerged as a legally binding obligation for states or the Security Council, the question at the end of a decade which witnessed the Council's inaction in Rwanda, Srebrenica, and Darfur, was whether in the particular case of genocide, the international law obligation 'to prevent', binding on all states, should also be deemed to be binding upon the Security Council, and what, if any, are the consequences of non-compliance.

6. The Case of Genocide and the Security Council Obligation to Prevent and Punish

The record of the Security Council in the prevention and punishment of the crime of genocide has been uneven. While it has never been conceivable, not at least at the time of the adoption of the Genocide Convention, that the Security Council would have any role to play in the prosecution of genocide, its engagement in establishing international criminal tribunals of all kinds is perhaps its greatest contribution to the eradication of impunity, to the prosecution of those most responsible for the crimes of genocide, war crimes, and crimes against humanity, and indirectly, to the revival and development of international criminal law and jurisprudence.

It is in the prevention of genocide, however, where all other measures have failed or not been resorted to, that the Security Council has dramatically failed. In learning the lessons of its inaction, the reasons for the Council's failure in Rwanda, Srebrenica, and Darfur must first be examined.

A. Rwanda, Srebrenica, and Darfur—the failure to prevent

The chronology of the genocide in Rwanda and Srebrenica, and the failure to prevent or arrest it is by now well documented. The criminal responsibility of individuals and states for the commission of the crimes and for failing to prevent them was the subject of international jurisprudence of the two ad hoc tribunals for the former Yugoslavia and Rwanda (the ICTY and ICTR),[93] and the International Court of Justice (ICJ),[94] respectively. The responsibility of the UN Secretariat, the Security Council, and the collectivity of member states was the subject of three separate international investigations.[95]

1. Rwanda—the preventable genocide

The systematic, large scale mass killing in Rwanda in 1994 was unprecedented in scope and pace. On 6 April 1994, only a few hours after the plane carrying the two Presidents of Rwanda and Burundi crashed while approaching Kigali, the carnage began. When it ended 100 days later it had left an estimated number of 800,000 Tutsis and moderate Hutus dead.

At the time of the genocide, the United Nations Assistance Mission for Rwanda (UNAMIR), established under Security Council Resolution 872 (1993), had already been deployed with a mandate to contribute to the security of the city of Kigali. At the time of its establishment and for its duration, UNAMIR was a traditional, so-called Chapter VI operation, with no enforcement powers or a mandate to use force. The killing of the ten Belgian soldiers of UNAMIR at the start of the genocide and the decision of the Belgian government to withdraw its contingent which followed suit triggered the collapse of the military capability of UNAMIR.

The Security Council reaction to the unfolding events was erratic at best. In April 1994, when the scale and horror of the atrocities had already been apparent, it authorized a reduced force level of 270 military observers to monitor the situation, and the withdrawal of the remainder of UNAMIR personnel.[96] In May 1994, when the genocide was at its peak, the Council reversed its decision, and, on the recommendation of the Secretary-General, decided to expand UNAMIR's mandate and authorize the increase in force level to 5,500, with a mandate 'to contribute to the security and protection of displaced persons, refugees and civilians at risk'.[97] The Security Council call for troop contribution, however, went unheeded. During

[93] Case No IT-95-10-T, *The Prosecutor v Goran Jelisic*, Judgment, 14 December 1999; Case No IT-98-33-T, *The Prosecutor v Radislav Krstić*, Judgment, 2 August 2001; Case No ICTR-96-4-T, *The Prosecutor v Jean-Paul Akayesu*, Judgment, 2 September 1998; Case No ICTR-95-1-T, *The Prosecutor v Clément Kayishema and Obed Ruzindana*, Judgment, 21 May 1999.

[94] Case *Concerning the Application of the Convention on the Prevention and Punishment of the Crime of Genocide (Bosnia and Herzegovina v Serbia and Montenegro)*, Judgment, 26 February 2007 (the '*Genocide* case'), ICJ Reports (2007).

[95] Report of the Independent Inquiry into the actions of the United Nations during the 1994 Genocide in Rwanda (the Carlsoon Commission), S/1997/1257, 16 December 1999; Report of the International Panel of Eminent Personalities to Investigate the 1994 Genocide in Rwanda and the Surrounding Events, *Rwanda: The Preventable Genocide*, available at www.africa-union.org/Official_documents/reports/offreports.htm (last accessed 3 March 2011); Report of the Secretary-General pursuant to General Assembly Resolution 53/35, *The Fall of Srebrenica*, A/54/549, 15 November 1999.

[96] SC Res 912 (1994).

[97] SC Res 918 (1994); an expanded Mission was recommended by the Secretary-General in his Report on the situation in Rwanda, S/1994/565, 13 May 1994.

the darkest hours of the Rwandan genocide, a derisory force of 550 troops—a tenth of the authorized strength—was left to protect the hundreds of thousands of displaced persons, refugees, and other civilians at risk.

It was the advance of the Rwandese Patriotic Front (RPF) into South-Western Rwanda and the massive movement of over 1.5 million people, for the most part Hutus, towards Zaire (now the DRC), that ultimately forced the Security Council to react. On 22 June, it authorized by Resolution 929 (1994) the deployment of a temporary operation under national command and control (Operation Turquoise), with the aim of contributing 'in an impartial way, to the security and protection of displaced persons, refugees and civilians at risk'. In Rwanda, however, Operation Turquoise was perceived largely as one designed to protect the Hutu refugee population, many of whom were believed to be *genocidaires*.

In assessing the international response to the genocide in Rwanda and the failure to prevent and stop it, both the Carlsoon Commission established by the Secretary-General and the Independent Panel of Eminent Personalities established by the Organization of African Unity attributed responsibilities to the Secretary-General, the Secretariat, the Security Council, UNAMIR, and the membership of the United Nations at large. The Security Council, they concluded, was responsible for reducing the already inadequate UNAMIR force to a mere 270 military observers, at a time when it was needed the most; for failing to adjust, or to adjust in time, its mandate to the fast-changing realities on the ground; and for failing to acknowledge and qualify the events as genocide, for fear, however misplaced, that such qualification would call it for action.[98] Above all, however, the Security Council and the entire UN membership were responsible for lack of political will 'to act or to act with enough assertiveness' in face of mass atrocities, and for lack of commitment to provide the necessary troops and material resources to stop the genocide.[99]

2. *The genocide at Srebrenica*

On 6 July 1995, the Bosnian-Serb Army launched its attack on Srebrenica—one of the six Security Council declared 'safe areas' in Bosnia and Herzegovina.[100] Within six days of the attack, Srebrenica fell. On 12 July, roughly 25,000 Bosnian Muslims were forcibly deported from Srebrenica; some 8,000 men, for the most part of military age, were separated from the women, children, and the elderly and later executed. It was a massacre qualified by the ICTY in the cases of *Krstić* and *Jelisic*, and by the ICJ in the *Genocide* case, as genocide.

In its judgment in the *Genocide* case, the ICJ held that the acts committed in Srebrenica with a specific intent to destroy the group of Muslim Bosnians, as such,

98 For the first time in its Resolution 925 (1994), the Security Council noted 'with gravest concern the reports indicating that *acts of genocide* have occurred in Rwanda', and 'that genocide constitutes a crime punishable under international law' (emphasis added).

99 R Dallaire, K Manocha, and N Degnarain, 'The Major Powers on Trial' (2005) 3 *Journal of International Criminal Justice* 861.

100 SC Res 819 (1993) and 824 (1993).

amounted to acts of genocide, and that having had the power to influence effectively the actions of those likely to commit, or already committing genocide, and failing to employ all means reasonably available to it to prevent it, Serbia had violated its international obligation to prevent the crime of genocide.[101] The single most important contribution of the judgment to the development of international criminal law and the law of state responsibility, however, was in attributing a definitional content to the international obligation of states to prevent genocide. Accordingly, a state in whose territory genocide is committed is bound to prevent it—unless the state itself commits the crime, in which case it entails direct criminal responsibility. A state is also responsible, 'within the limits permitted by international law',[102] to prevent genocide in a third state if it has control, however loose, or influence over those engaged in the commission of the crime. The question of whether states are obligated to prevent genocide in the absence of any kind of control or influence over those who commit the crime was not decided by the Court. There is no basis to assume, therefore, that states are legally bound to prevent and arrest genocide wherever it occurs, and to employ to that end 'all means reasonably available to them so as to prevent genocide, as far as possible', or that failure to do so would entail for them a secondary international obligation to make reparation for a breach of an international obligation.

Like UNAMIR in Rwanda, the United Nations Protection Force (UNPROFOR) in Bosnia and Herzegovina had been deployed in the surroundings of Srebrenica at the time of the genocide, and like the former it was lightly armed, under resourced, outnumbered, and incapable of protecting the civilian population in an area designated 'safe'. Unlike the derisory strength of UNAMIR at the time of the Rwandan genocide, however, UNPROFOR in Bosnia and Herzegovina—although not in the surroundings of Srebrenica itself—was 30,000 troops strong, with the UK and France providing the largest troop contributions. Unlike Rwanda in 1994 also, in Srebrenica in 1995, the Security Council adopted a range of Chapter VII enforcement measures to respond to Bosnian-Serb attacks—from arms embargo, humanitarian aid, deployment of peacekeeping force, and the threat of NATO air power—all of which, however, were 'half measures' or, in the words of the Secretary-General's Report on the Fall of Srebrenica, 'poor substitutes for more decisive and forceful action to prevent the unfolding horror'.[103] When by Resolution 836 (1993), the Security Council had finally authorized NATO air power to protect the safe areas, none of its 15 member states, including the sponsors of the resolution, committed additional troops to implement the resolution. It was

[101] The *Genocide* case (n 94 above) paras 430 and 438; Cassese, 'On the Use of Criminal Law Notions in Determining State Responsibility for Genocide' (2007) 5 *Journal of International Criminal Justice* 875; Gaeta, 'On What Conditions Can a State be Held Responsible for Genocide' (2007) 18 EJIL 631; Schabas, 'Genocide and the International Court of Justice: Finally a Duty to Prevent the Crime of Crimes' (2007) 2 *Genocide Studies and Prevention* 101.

[102] A qualification no doubt added by the ICJ to avoid the conclusion that the use of force may be implicitly authorized on the strength of the Genocide Convention in disregard of the Charter prohibition on the use of force (*Genocide* case (n 94 above), para 430).

[103] Report of the Secretary-General, *Fall of Srebrenica*, (n 95 above) 490.

no surprise, therefore, that when the Bosnian-Serb forces overran the enclave, neither the Security Council's authority, nor UNPROFOR presence, not even NATO air power were able to deter them and protect the inhabitants of Srebrenica. Like Rwanda in 1994, in Srebrenica in 1995, the Security Council and the UN membership at large, lacked the political will and thus the military means to confront the threat and use a decisive force, whether air power or ground troops, to repel the Serb attacks on the 'safe area'.

But the lessons of Rwanda and Srebrenica were not learned. When a decade later millions of black Africans in Darfur were at the risk of decimation, there was little political will to intervene, or intervene decisively with all necessary means.

3. Darfur—in the seam between genocide and crimes against humanity

The conflict in Darfur, often described as a racial conflict between Arab and black African tribes, originated in a conflict over scarce resources between Arab nomadic groups and black Africans, the traditional cultivators of pastures and livestock. In 2003, the conflict between government forces and the Sudan Liberation Movement/Army (SLM/A) and the Justice and Equality Movement (JEM) rebels seeking redress for decades of political marginalization, discrimination and socio-economic neglect, broke out. Government-backed Janjaweed militia attacked the black African tribes, mostly the Zaghawa, Masaalit, and Fur. They burned and raided towns and villages, murdered, tortured, and raped, and in a coordinated campaign of scorched-earth 'ethnic cleansing' triggered a massive flow of refugees into Chad. By 2008, well over a quarter of a million people were killed and more than 2.5 million were displaced.

At the United Nations, just as it was in Rwanda in 1994, qualifying the crime has given rise to much debate. The Secretary-General, who was asked in June 2004 whether genocide was committed in Darfur, said: 'we don't need a label to propel us to act'. The US Congress, in its resolution 467 of 2004 declared that 'the atrocities unfolding in Darfur, Sudan are genocide', and urged the Security Council to declare the same. The UN Commission of Inquiry established to investigate reports of violations of international humanitarian law and human rights in Darfur concluded that the government of the Sudan had not pursued a policy of genocide, and that while war crimes and crimes against humanity were committed on a massive scale, they did not amount to genocide within the meaning of the Genocide Convention.[104] In the International Criminal Court, the Prosecutor's Application for a Warrant of Arrest against Omar El-Bashir, the President of Sudan on charges of war crimes, crimes against humanity, and genocide, was denied in

[104] Report of the International Commission of Inquiry on Darfur to the Secretary-General Pursuant to Security Council Resolution 1564 (2004) of 18 September 2004, S/2005/60, 1 February 2005, paras 663–42. For a critical view of the Commission's findings see, Schabas, 'Darfur and the "Odious Scourge": the Commission of Inquiry's Findings on Genocide' (2005) 18 *Leiden Journal of International law* 871.

2009 by the Pre-Trial Chamber I with respect to the crime of genocide.[105] On appeal, the decision was reversed to that extent,[106] and a second Warrant of Arrest for El-Bashir was issued in 2010 on charges of genocide.[107]

Unlike Rwanda and Srebrenica at the time of the genocide, there was no international presence in Darfur in 2003 when the conflict broke out and atrocities unfolded. The African Union Mission in Sudan (AMIS), deployed in 2004 lacked sufficient troop capacity, logistics, and funding. Unable to confront the highly mobile and relatively well-armed Janjaweed militia, it soon lost any credible deterrent power.

In July 2007, the Security Council decided to establish an AU/UN Hybrid Operation in Darfur (UNAMID). UNAMID was mandated, in the areas of its deployment and as it deems within its capabilities, to 'protect civilians, without prejudice to the responsibility of the Government of Sudan', and was authorized under Chapter VII to take to that effect 'the necessary action'—a code word for the use of force.[108] Like AMIS before it, however, UNAMID's capability to fulfil its mandate effectively to defend itself and protect civilians was hampered by insecurity, lack of significant troops, logistical and operational challenges, the refusal of the government of the Sudan to allow deployment of non-African troops, and the lack of contributions of means of transportation and critical aviation capabilities from member states in a position to do so—yet another manifestation of the lack of political will and resolve of the international community to engage and stop the killing.[109]

The criminal responsibility for the genocide in Rwanda and Srebrenica, and for the crimes against humanity in Darfur, was that of the Hutus, the Bosnian-Serbs, and the Janjaweed militia supported by the government of Sudan, respectively. It was largely facilitated, however, by a Security Council in denial, unwilling to engage, or to engage with a decisive force. Unable to prevent the genocide and unwilling to commit the necessary resources to arrest mass killings, both the Security Council and member states opted, as a 'second-best remedy',[110] for the punishment of those most responsible for genocide, crimes against humanity, and war crimes.

[105] Case No ICC-02/05-01/09, *The Prosecutor v Omar Hassan Ahmad Al Bashir ('Omar Al Bashir')*, Decision on the Prosecution's Application for a Warrant of Arrest against Omar Hassan Ahmad Al Bashir, Pre-Trial Chamber I, 4 March 2009.

[106] Case No ICC-02/05-01/09-OA, *The Prosecutor v. Omar Hassan Ahmad Al Bashir*, Judgment on the appeal of the Prosecutor against the 'Decision on the Prosecution's Application for a Warrant of Arrest against Omar Hassan Ahmad Al Bashir', 3 February 2010.

[107] Case No ICC-02/05-01/09, *The Prosecutor v. Omar Hassan Ahmad Al Bashir ('Omar Al Bashir')*, Second Warrant of Arrest for Omar Hassan Ahmad Al Bashir, 12 July 2010.

[108] SC Res 1769 (2007), para 15(a).

[109] Abass, 'The United Nations, The African Union and the Darfur Crisis. Of Apology and Utopia' (2007) 54 *Netherlands International Law Review* 415; De Waal, 'Darfur and the Failure of the Responsibility to Protect' (2007) 83 *International Affairs* 1039.

[110] Reisman, 'Acting Before Victims Become Victims: Preventing and Arresting Mass Murder' (2008) 40 *Case Western Reserve Journal of International Law* 57.

B. The obligation to punish

The obligation 'to punish' within the meaning of Article 6 of the Genocide Convention, ie an obligation to prosecute within a state's own judicial system or surrender an accused to an international tribunal having jurisdiction in the matter, is attributable to states alone.[111] And while not, strictly speaking, bound by the Conventional obligation 'to punish', the Security Council has, since the early 1990s, been engaged in the establishment of all, but two, international criminal tribunals for the prosecution and punishment of those responsible for genocide, crimes against humanity, and war crimes. The two ad hoc international criminal tribunals for the former Yugoslavia and for Rwanda were the first judicial accountability mechanisms established by the Security Council in 1993 and 1994, respectively, as an enforcement measure under Chapter VII of the Charter.[112] They were the model upon which all subsequent international jurisdictions were established, whether by the Security Council, the General Assembly, member states, or the Secretary-General by agreement with the State of the Tribunal.[113] In the case of Darfur where conditions were not conducive to the establishment of any kind of UN-based tribunal, the Security Council decided, under Chapter VII and consistently with Article 12 of the Rome Statute, to refer the situation in the Sudan to the International Criminal Court;[114] a referral recommended by the Commission of Inquiry for Darfur, and made possible by the abstention from vote of the United States, the strongest opponent of the ICC.

The emerging pattern of establishing UN-based tribunals in the former Yugoslavia, Rwanda, Sierra Leone, Cambodia, Lebanon, and elsewhere was for the most part a political response in recognition of the Security Council's inability and unwillingness to commit the necessary military troops to stop the massacres, rather than an indication of a sense of legal obligation 'to punish' within the meaning of Article 6 of the Convention. It has nevertheless created legitimate expectations that where mass atrocities are committed, and where the government is unwilling or unable to prevent, stop, or prosecute them in its failed or non-existent administration of justice, or worse still, where it is actually committing them or tacitly encouraging their commission, the Security Council would establish or facilitate the establishment of a credible international criminal jurisdiction.

[111] The *Genocide* case (n 94 above) paras 448–50; Ben-Naftali and Sharon, 'What the ICJ did not Say About the Duty to Punish Genocide' (2007) 5 *Journal of International Criminal Justice* 859.

[112] Report of the Secretary-General Pursuant to Paragraph 2 of Security Council Resolution 808 (1993), S/25704, 3 May 1993; SC Res 827 (1993) and SC Res 955 (1994).

[113] Agreement between the United Nations and the Government of Sierra Leone on the Establishment of a Special Court for Sierra Leone, 2002, S/2002/246, 8 March 2002, Appendix II. The Extraordinary Chambers for Cambodia was established by Agreement between the United Nations and the Royal Government of Cambodia Concerning the Prosecution Under Cambodian Law of Crimes Committed During the Period of Democratic Kampuchea, 2003 (approved by the General Assembly in Resolution 57/228, 13 May 2003 (Annex)). The Special Tribunal for Lebanon was established by Agreement between the United Nations and the Lebanese Republic on the Establishment of a Special Tribunal for Lebanon (annexed to SC Res 1757 (2007)).

[114] SC Res 1593 (2005).

The relative success of the Security Council in prosecuting those most responsible for genocide, crimes against humanity, and war crimes in the former Yugoslavia, Rwanda, and Sierra Leone tends to obscure its failure to prevent the mass atrocities in the first place. More importantly, perhaps, it entails the risk of blurring the distinction between the 'two distinct yet connected obligations',[115] or of conveniently substituting the legally and politically more difficult obligation 'to prevent' for the relatively easy obligation, 'to punish'.

C. The obligation to prevent

That the Security Council failed to prevent the genocide in Rwanda and Srebrenica, and the first presumed genocide of the 21st century in Darfur, is a fact of history. That it was also legally, and not only morally or politically obliged to do so, depends on the customary international law nature of the obligation—for a Conventional obligation would be binding on states parties only—and the definitional content attributable to it by analogy and *mutatis mutandis*.

The customary international law nature of the principles underlying the Genocide Convention was recognized by the ICJ already in its 1951 Advisory Opinion on the *Reservations to the Genocide Convention*,[116] and the application *erga omnes* of the rights and obligations enshrined by the Convention was recognized in its 1996 Decision on *Preliminary Objections* in the *Genocide* case.[117] In its 2007 Judgment in the *Genocide* case, however, the Court declined to pronounce itself on the customary international law nature of the obligation 'to prevent', not even in the relationship between the state having the capacity to influence the events, and the state where genocide is committed.[118]

For all its ambiguities, the customary international law obligation to prevent genocide—to the extent of its applicability to states and within the limitations attributed to it in the *Genocide* case—must be deemed to be applicable also to the United Nations, and in particular, the Security Council, uniquely placed to exert influence over peoples and events, and to take or impose enforcement measures to prevent or arrest the crime. Its application to the Security Council, however, is application by analogy and *mutatis mutandis*, taking into account the nature and specificity of the Council and its powers and responsibilities under the Charter. Accordingly, 'all means reasonably available' to the Security Council, in the words

[115] The *Genocide* case (n 94 above) para 425.

[116] *Reservations to the Convention on the Prevention and Punishment of the Crime of Genocide*, ICJ Reports (1951) 15, at 23.

[117] *Case Concerning Application of the Convention on the Prevention and Punishment of the Crime of Genocide (Bosnia and Herzegovina v Yugoslavia)*, Preliminary Objections, ICJ Reports (1996) 595, at 616, para 31.

[118] The Court expressly declined to address the question of whether 'there is a general obligation on States to prevent the commission by other persons or entities of acts contrary to certain norms of general international law', and confined itself 'to determining the specific scope of the duty to prevent in the Genocide Convention, and to the extent that such a determination is necessary to the decision to be given on the dispute before it' (the *Genocide* case (n 94 above) para 429).

of the ICJ, are those spelled out in Articles 41 and 42 of the Charter, including the authorization to use force. Their effectiveness, however, is subject to two important limitations: first, the *power* to authorize the use of force is not a *duty* to do so, but a discretion exercised within the political constraints of the Council and its individual member states, and secondly, and more importantly, a decision to authorize the use of force, in itself, does not compel states to contribute the necessary troops for the formation of an intervention force. An authorizing resolution would still depend on the ability and willingness of states to implement and carry it out.

In the final analysis, the Responsibility to Protect has not given rise to an obligation 'to prevent', and the obligation to prevent genocide has not given rise to an obligation to *intervene* to prevent genocide absent a Security Council authorization, or, in the case of the Security Council, to an obligation to *authorize* intervention 'to prevent'.

7. Trends and Challenges

The Council's choice of human rights for promotion and protection was selective, but not necessarily exhaustive. For over six decades, the rights to self-determination, to democratic governance, and to freedom from serious violations of human rights and international humanitarian law were protected by the Council because of their perceived link to international peace, security, and stability of world order. As other human rights are perceived to be essential to the peace, or rather that their massive violation is determined to constitute a threat, additional human rights would be selected by the Council for promotion and protection, by force if necessary. The humanitarian operations in Somalia (1992–93)[119] and Albania (1997),[120] mandated to secure humanitarian aid and food distribution to populations affected by famine or financial crisis, respectively, are an indication that economic rights, and notably the right to food, are just as essential to peace, security, and stability of world order.

The expectation that the Security Council will promote human rights, prevent their serious violations, protect civilian population at risk of annihilation, and in its activities be bound by human rights standards was a challenge to its legitimacy. Respect for human rights in all of these respects was a standard—one perhaps among others—by which nations will have judged its 'compliance pull'—that which makes nations obey, not because of fear of sanctions or out of self-interest, but out of a deep sense that the rule, decision, or institution is intrinsically fair, just

[119] UNOSOM-I was established by SC Res 751 (1992), and UNOSOM II was established, under Chapter VII, by SC Res 814 (1993).

[120] SC Res 1101 (1997). The multinational protection force was mandated 'to facilitate the safe and prompt delivery of humanitarian assistance, and to help create a secure environment for the missions of international organizations in Albania' (para 2). For a detailed description of 'Operation Alba', see *the Eleventh and final report to the Security Council on the operation of the multinational protection force in Albania*, S/1997/632, 12 August 1997, Appendix.

and thus must be obeyed.[121] A 'legitimacy deficit' is what prompted the then Secretary-General, Kofi Annan, in his 1999 address to the General Assembly, to warn that '[T]he Charter requires the Council to be the defender of the common interest, and unless it is seen to be so—in an era of human rights, interdependence and globalization—there is a danger that others could seek to take its place'.[122] A 'legitimacy deficit' is what threatened also the integrity of the Security Council's sanctions regime against presumed terrorists on the al-Qaida/Taliban 1267-list, whose conformity with the right to due process of law has been challenged for nearly a decade now before national and regional courts.[123]

The Security Council's response to the challenge was both limited and selective. While it is probably premature to draw conclusions from the Council's one-time authorization of military action in Libya to protect civilians—either as a precedent for future cases or an indication of the need better to define the scope and limitations of the 'necessary measures to protect'—an emerging practice of mandating peacekeeping operations to protect civilians in physical danger has, for over a decade, been its response, however limited, to the R2P challenge. The Council's instruction to the UN operation in the DRC that it condition its support for government-led military operations against armed groups posing threat to the civilian population, on their compliance with human rights, international humanitarian law, and refugee law,[124] was in recognition of the risk that support for those who commit serious violations of human rights and international humanitarian law may implicate the UN operation, if not entail the international responsibility of the United Nations.[125] The establishment of the institution of the Ombudsperson to review the fairness of the de-listing procedure from the al-Qaida/Taliban

[121] T Franck, *The Power of Legitimacy Among Nations* (1990) 16–26. ('. . . legitimacy exerts a pull to compliance which is powered by the quality of the rule or of the rule-making institution and notably coercive authority. It exerts a claim to compliance in the voluntarist mode', ibid at 26); Caron, 'The Legitimacy of the Collective Authority of the Security Council' (1993) 87 AJIL 552.

[122] Secretary-General Presents his Annual Report to the General Assembly, Press Release, SG/SM/7136, GA/9596, 20 September 1999.

[123] The 'Kadi jurisprudence' developed in the Court of First Instance (Case T-315/01 of 21 September 2005), the European Court of Justice (Joined Cases C-402/05 and C-415/059 of 3 September 2008), and the General Court of the European Union (Case T-85/09 of 30 September 2010), tested the legitimacy of Security Council resolutions, the legality of EU Regulations, and the relationship between the international and the Community legal orders.

[124] By Res 1906 (2009), the Security Council reiterated that 'the support of MONUC to FARDC-led military operations against foreign and Congolese armed groups is strictly conditioned on FARDC's compliance with international humanitarian, human rights and refugee law and on an effective joint planning of these operations', and called upon MONUC 'to intercede with the FARDC command if elements of a FARDC unit receiving MONUC's support are suspected of having committed grave violations of such laws, *and if the situation persists, calls upon MONUC to withdraw support from these FARDC units*' (emphasis added).

[125] Article 13 of the ILC draft Articles on the Responsibility of International Organizations adopted at its First Reading, provides:

> An international organization which aids or assists a State or another international organization in the commission of an internationally wrongful act by the State or the latter organization is internationally responsible for doing so if:
> a) That organization does so with knowledge of the circumstances of the internationally wrongful act.

1267-list,[126] may not have fully guaranteed 'due process' to individuals and entities directly targeted by its sanctions; it was nonetheless an acknowledgement that whether legally bound by them or not, the Council's failure to abide by human rights standards, might lead national and regional courts to decline to give its sanctions resolutions, within their respective jurisdictions, legally binding effect.

As the foremost political organ, however, the Security Council acts in the promotion and protection of human rights, as in all other fields of its activities, in pursuit of its political choices. Understanding the political nature of the Security Council and the role politics played in shaping its response to violations of human rights and international humanitarian law is understanding the risk or inevitability of selectivity and inconsistency of its actions. 'Politics' is what explains why only in Haiti military intervention was authorized to restore democracy, why only in Western Sahara the right to self-determination is subject to a politically agreed solution, and why, of half-a-dozen Arab States in the spring of 2011, only in Libya did the Security Council authorize a military intervention to protect civilians. 'Politics' is also the explanation for the Council inaction in Iraq, Kosovo, but also in Rwanda, Srebrenica, and Darfur, although in the latter cases there is little indication that had it not been for its reluctance to authorize the use of force, states would have provided the necessary troops.

[126] SC Res 1904 (2009).

3

The Security Council as Enforcer of Human Rights

Vera Gowlland-Debbas

1. Introduction

The Security Council was established as an elitist political body with primary responsibility for the maintenance of international peace and security. It was never intended to play a role in the field of human rights, one of the purposes of the UN Charter, a strict delineation of functions between it and the General Assembly having been initially instituted. The latter, as the plenary organ, was entrusted under Article 10 with broad powers of discussion and recommendation over any question or matter within the scope of the Charter, including human rights, with ECOSOC charged with coordination, inter alia, in this field, and the focus of human rights activities found in the UN human rights bodies.

A first linkage between human rights and enforcement action under Chapter VII was made, however, in 1965, in relation to the crisis in Southern Rhodesia arising from the unilateral declaration of independence of a white minority regime contrary to the right to self-determination of the African majority. Under the pressure from a number of states from Africa and the rest of the developing world, the Security Council in 1965 declared the illegality and invalidity of the UDI and, the following year, determined under Article 39 that the situation was a threat to international peace and security, thereby opened the way for the application of first select and then comprehensive sanctions under Article 41 of the Charter, the first textual application of such enforcement action. Today, this link between human rights and enforcement action has become a commonplace part of the Security Council's activities.

I propose to review the way in which the Security Council's functions, along with its competence and powers, have developed under external pressures to encompass enforcement of human rights, as well as, taking a broader view, of international humanitarian law. This evolution can be seen within a systemic framework, in the light of an emerging international public policy and of the linkages which are being forged between different functional areas of international law, in particular between regimes of responsibility and collective security. Within a Charter framework, the Council's recent enforcement action must also be set against a more contemporary reading of collective security as laid down in Article 1 (1) of the Charter, resulting in part from the pressures of UN reform proposals calling for the application of such concepts as human security, a so-called responsibility to protect or the rule of law.

A. The systemic framework

The evolution of the international legal system has included certain contradictory trends: on the one hand, a certain fragmentation and compartmentalization of international law, on the other, the construction of unifying, universalizing elements—the development of what may be viewed as an international public policy or *ordre public*, leading to a hierarchization of rules due to a growing value-oriented or public-interest oriented international law. While this development is contested and the content of such an international public policy is as yet undetermined, certain norms which have vital functions in the system have been singled out: these include at the minimum, certain survival rules—such as the maintenance of international public order—and the incorporation into the legal system of a certain universal moral or ethical foundation—such as human rights law or humanitarian law.

Along with this hierarchization of norms, we have seen the construction of bridges between and the permeability of different areas of law, due in part to the fact that the values and interests of the international community need to be addressed and protected through coherent, across-the-board, holistic responses.

Many international organizations have internalized such community values and interests often under pressure from international society—NGOs, tribunals, and other external entities—leading to a teleological interpretation of their own constituent instrument, internalization of environmental and human rights norms, auto-limitation, or reformulation of certain essential principles, all this requiring a re-interpretation of mandates. Just to take the example of NATO, that organization has considered that the risks to the security of NATO allies comes less from aggression than from the negative consequences of instability due to a number of factors, including ethnic rivalries and violations of human rights, thus redefining its concept of security to incorporate human security concerns.

B. The Charter framework

These community values and interests are already integrated into Articles 1 and 2 of the UN Charter which is viewed by many as the constitutional document for the international community, though these purposes and principles should now be read in the light of the evolution of the contemporary legal system. The purposes of the UN not only underline the primary goal of peace maintenance, but also reflect human rights, humanitarian, economic, and social concerns. Although the Security Council has the primary responsibility of maintaining or restoring international peace and security, a function which continues to be an important priority of the international community, it has today arraigned on itself also, among others, a human rights protection function. We will see that there has been, in consequence, a shift of priority with human rights now forming a component part of the security fabric rather than perceived as part of the longer-term creation of the conditions conducive to peace and therefore secondary to the Charter's principal goal. Indeed in its Resolution 1674 (2006), the Council declares:

> Acknowledging that peace and security, development and human rights are the pillars of the UN system and the foundations for collective security and well-being, and recognizing in this regard that development, peace and security and human rights are interlinked and mutually reinforcing.

The collective security system has therefore evolved quite markedly in recent decades in response to fundamental changes within the international system and in the light of reform proposals and other external pressures.[1] This trend has been reinforced by the move from a state-oriented to a more individually oriented international legal system reflected in current reform proposals.[2] This has meant that the term security referred to in Article 1(1) can no longer be confined to the security of states, but must ultimately be destined to the protection of individuals in conformity with a new collective duty formulated as the so-called responsibility to protect populations from genocide, war crimes, ethnic cleansing, and crimes against humanity.[3] This has been reflected in a shift in the use of Chapter VII measures to protect populations from the actions of states determined to constitute threats to international peace and security. The re-orientation of the notion of security to include 'human security'—not an entirely novel concept and one to be defined—has nevertheless also meant that collective security measures can no longer aim to be simply 'effective' in the words of Article 1(1), or efficient, but must also be *equitable*, as the High Level Panel Report points out.[4]

This shift in perspective has also led to a linkage between international peace and security and justice. These two concepts can no longer be separated as they once were in the original Charter reading of Article 1(1) which linked justice only to peaceful settlement of disputes and not to collective measures.[5]

[1] See Gowlland-Debbas, 'Collective Security Revisited in Light of the Flurry Over UN Reform: An International Law Perspective', in V Chetail (ed), *Conflits, sécurité et cooperation/Conflict, Security and Cooperation. Liber amicorum Victor-Yves Ghebali* (2007) 251–77.

[2] See among others, *In Larger Freedom: Towards Development, Security and Human Rights for All*, Report of the UN Secretary General Kofi Annan, UN Doc A/59/2005, 21 March 2005; *A More Secure World: Our Shared Responsibility*, Report of the High-level Panel on Threats, Challenges and Change, UN Doc A/59/565, 2 December 2004; World Summit Outcome, UN Doc A/RES/60/1, 24 October 2005.

[3] See ICISS, *The Responsibility to Protect*, Report of the International Commission on Intervention and State Sovereignty, Ottawa, Canada, December 2001; World Summit Outcome Document, paras138–40 and 143; Implementing the Responsibility to Protect, Report of the Secretary-General, A/63/677, 12 January 2009.

[4] Report of the High-level Panel, para 31.

[5] An amendment by Egypt at the San Francisco Conference which would have generally linked the two concepts in Art 1(1) was defeated on the grounds, inter alia, that this would have undermined the effectiveness of the Security Council when dealing with threats to the peace (see discussion in *United Nations Conference on International Organization* (UNCIO), *Selected Documents*, US Department of State, Washington, 1946, Vol VI, 46–57).

Finally the reference to International Law which was likewise originally linked in Article 1(1) of the Charter to peaceful settlement of disputes, must now be read as referring also to collective enforcement measures. The operation of the rule of law both at the national and international levels as a framework for advancing human security has been underlined in all the recent reform proposals, eg the World Summit Outcome Document.[6] Finally, the numerous references to international law by the Security Council, make the traditional separation between collective security and international law also obsolete.

Yet at the same time, ironically, the Security Council's actions have led to clashes between public policy norms which have landed before a number of domestic and judicial organs—I am referring in particular to the current tensions between international public order, on the one hand, as reflected in the decisions taken by the Security Council under Chapter VII, and human rights law, on the other. For the paradox is that effective implementation of Security Council decisions, including those aiming to protect human rights, have challenged in turn the fundamental principles safeguarding individual rights, both modifying states' human rights obligations under international law as well as in certain cases purporting to override them.

C. The link between Chapter VII and the concept of sanctions

The link made by the Security Council in its practice between threats to the peace and violations of international law raises the question as to whether its enforcement action may be viewed from a systemic framework as a form of sanction.

Article 39, which is the trigger to further action under Chapter VII, states:

> The Security Council shall determine the existence of any threat to the peace, breach of the peace, or act of aggression and shall make recommendations, or decide what measures shall be taken in accordance with Articles 41 and 42, to maintain or restore international peace and security.

Such a preliminary finding forming the basis for further Security Council action under Chapter VII has to be made explicitly.

The link between the Charter mechanisms for peace maintenance and the concept of legal sanction may appear to be more tenuous than that in the Covenant, for the League collective security system embedded in Article 16(1) and (2) of the Covenant had sanctioned infringements of Covenant obligations.

Enforcement measures provided for under Articles 39, 41, and 42 of the Charter, were clearly not intended as a response to the violation of a pre-existing obligation in the Charter, though they went further than those instituted by the League in being mandatory, centralized, and collective. The mandatory decisions of the Security Council under Chapter VII, which are triggered by a determination under Article 39, are the outcome of political considerations, not legal reasoning.

[6] Which has reaffirmed this commitment 'to an international order based on the rule of law', para 134(a).

For all these reasons, it has been held that such measures only constitute police measures for the preservation and restoration of the peace.[7] The Council was deliberately given wide discretionary powers in making its preliminary finding under Article 39, a prerequisite for the application of Chapter VII measures, for there is no legal definition of a threat to the peace, although such measures must be adopted within the limits imposed by the Charter (see in particular, Article 24(2) which refers back to the Purposes and Principles of the United Nations).

In its practice, the Security Council has considerably enlarged the notion of threat to the peace by acknowledging that threats to international peace and security can come from all sources of instability, whether in the economic, social, humanitarian, and ecological field or the proliferation of weapons of mass destruction, as well as acts of international terrorism in general. The term 'sanctions' moreover, which appears nowhere in the Charter (although used in the past to designate the measures provided for under Articles 5, 6 and 19) has now become part of the vocabulary to designate Security Council measures under Chapter VII both in its resolutions and the practice of member states.

There has therefore been some support in the doctrine for viewing the mandatory measures under Chapter VII as a sanction in the sense of a response to a prior violation of an international obligation and the infringement of the subjective legal rights of the party against whom they are directed, beginning with the contradictory positions assumed by Hans Kelsen.[8] At any rate, a survey of the major philosophical and legal approaches to the question—natural law theorists, John Austin, Hans Kelsen, Herbert Hart, and beyond—have shown the wide differences of views as regards the concept of sanctions in international law, the central role they play, the form they assume, their content, conditions for their application, and their purpose. Moreover, traditional concepts of sanctions which have been at the core of debates on the nature and function of international law have undergone certain mutations in international law.

The term 'sanctions', as a term of art, was reserved by the International Law Commission for reactive measures adopted inter alia within the framework of the collective security system established by the Charter under Chapter VII.[9] This concept of sanctions also reflects the contemporary notion of community interests which found its way in the ILC Articles on Responsibility of States for Internationally Wrongful Acts, which even after the deletion of former Article 19 on international crimes of states, nevertheless retained a hierarchy of norms in two overlapping though not identical concepts: that of serious breaches of obligations

[7] See, eg, Arangio-Ruiz, 'On the Security Council's Law-making' (2000) 80 *Rivista di diritto internazionale* 609, 694.

[8] See H Kelsen, *The Law of the United Nations* (1950) 294 and Kelsen, 'Collective Security and Collective Self-Defense under the Charter of the United Nations' (1948) 41 AJIL 783, 788.

[9] See Commentary of Roberto Ago on Article 30 of Part I of the Draft Articles on the term countermeasures, in 1979-II YBILC (Part One) 39–66, and ibid (Part Two), 115–22; and Arangio-Ruiz, Third Report, Doc A/CN.4/440 (1991) 1991-II YBILC (Part One) 13. See also: Report of the International Law Commission on the work of its 53rd session (2001), Commentary to Art 1, para (3) in which sanctions were made 'part and parcel' of the law of state responsibility thus going beyond the traditional institution of reparations.

under peremptory norms of international law (Article 40) and that of obligations to the international community as a whole (Article 48) in relation to the invocation of responsibility. The ILC Articles however shelved the question of the relationship between state responsibility and collective measures in Article 59, which has been left to be worked out in practice.

The role which the Security Council, as a political organ, plays in international law enforcement provides an interesting illustration of the mutations to which the concept of sanctions has been subjected. Though the Council is *not required* to react only to a violation of international law, its decisions in numerous cases relating to international peace and security *have undoubtedly functioned* as collective responses to violations of fundamental norms of international law, including enforcement action, as will be illustrated below.[10] I will focus more particularly in this contribution on responses to violations of both human rights and humanitarian law. I will not cover some earlier resolutions adopted outside of Chapter VII calling on states to respect their obligations under these two fields of law.[11] Nor will all the issues arising from such enforcement action be analysed, so as not to overlap with other contributions in this work.

D. Sanctions practice

Pre-1990, the only mandatory economic and financial sanctions adopted under Article 41 of the Charter were those adopted beginning in December 1966 against the white minority regime in Southern Rhodesia following on from the Unilateral Declaration of Independence (UDI) in November 1965 and the arms embargo imposed in 1977 against South Africa. But the reactivation of the powers of the Council in the early 1990s on the basis of a newly found consensus, resulted in a broad quantitative and qualitative expansion of the powers of the Security Council and a proliferation of sanctions measures, although the resulting euphoria was to be short-lived.

The Security Council has to date imposed around 19 sanctions regimes[12] spanning four continents. Sanctions measures have targeted both states, non-state entities, and individuals, and aimed at enforcing an increasingly diverse range of stated purposes, such as putting an end to aggression, to violations of human rights and humanitarian law, and the conditions leading to massive flows of refugees across international borders, as well as restoration of governments emerging from a legitimate UN electoral process, and enforcing peace agreements. In addition, the

[10] See generally, Gowlland-Debbas, 'The Functions of the United Nations Security Council in the International Legal System', in M Byers (ed), *The Role of Law in International Politics* (2000) 305–41.

[11] See, eg, SC Res 237 (1967), with respect to the Six Day War in the Middle East and the series of resolutions calling for the implementation by Israel of its obligations under the Geneva Conventions; and SC Res 540 (1983) in relation to the war between Iraq and Iran.

[12] These relate to Afghanistan (*Taliban/alQaida*), Angola, *Democratic Republic of Congo, Democratic Republic of Korea*, Ethiopia and Eritrea, Haiti, *Iran, Iraq, Côte d'Ivoire, Liberia*, Libya, Rwanda, *Sierra Leone, Somalia*, South Africa, Southern Rhodesia, *Sudan, Syria/Lebanon*, and the Former Yugoslavia. Those in italics are still in force. Sanctions committees were created to monitor each sanctions regime.

Security Council has adopted resolutions which are general in nature and not targeted against specific entities but at combating individual 'acts of terrorism'. Finally, it has adopted a series of 'legislative resolutions' laying down general and abstract obligations.

2. The Qualification of State and Individual Violations of Fundamental Norms of International Law as Threats to Peace

In its practice, as a prelude to the imposition of enforcement measures under Chapter VII of the Charter, the Security Council has determined under Article 39 that not only conduct which breaches the *jus ad bellum*, but also conduct in violation of norms which serve to protect the individual, such as genocide or ethnic cleansing and serious breaches of human rights, including the right to self-determination, as well as grave breaches of humanitarian law, including those encompassed within a state's own borders, constitute threats to international peace and security. It has done so either explicitly, or by parallel determinations in the same resolution, for the purpose of extending to such breaches the special regime of Chapter VII.

In its findings, the Council has, moreover, singled out the kinds of breaches which touch on the very fabric of the international legal order, some of which in the old jargon of the State Responsibility Articles could be said to constitute international crimes.[13] While some of the obligations breached fall outside the scope of the Charter—notably humanitarian law and international criminal law—these may nevertheless be linked to the Council's responsibility for maintenance of international peace and security.

A. Violations of human rights and humanitarian law and threats to the peace

In the case of Southern Rhodesia, the central issue for the Security Council was the consideration that the UDI infringed the right of self-determination of the majority of the people in the territory;[14] while Resolution 418 (1977) stated that 'the acquisition by South Africa of arms and related matériel' constituted the threat to international peace and security, in reality it targeted the practice of apartheid.

[13] 1980-II YBILC (Part Two) 30–4. Article 19: '(a) a serious breach of an international obligation of essential importance for the maintenance of international peace and security, such as that prohibiting aggression; (b) a serious breach of an international obligation of essential importance for safeguarding the right of self-determination of peoples, such as that prohibiting the establishment or maintenance by force of colonial domination; (c) a serious breach on a widespread scale of an international obligation of essential importance for safeguarding the human being, such as those prohibiting slavery, genocide and *apartheid*, and (d) a serious breach of an international obligation of essential importance for the safeguarding and preservation of the human environment, such as those prohibiting massive pollution of the atmosphere or of the seas'.

[14] This is evident from the numerous references to self-determination in both Council (SC Res 423 (1978), SC Res 448 (1979)) and Assembly resolutions (GA Res 2022 (XX), GA Res 2379 (XXIII), GA Res 2383 (XXIII), etc).

Council resolutions on Iraq not only referred to Iraq's liability arising from its unlawful invasion and occupation of Kuwait, the focus of the Council's action, but also to violations of, inter alia, a range of human rights and humanitarian law obligations. Interestingly, this was the first time the Fourth Geneva Convention was expressly cited under Chapter VII in connection with, inter alia, acts of violence, taking of hostages, and unlawful destruction and seizure of public and private property (see, for example, SC Resolutions 664, 667, and 670 (1990)).

While the Council's pronouncements relate to the unacceptability of territorial gains or changes within Yugoslavia brought about by violence, its resolutions were also punctuated by condemnations of the massive and systematic violations of human rights and fundamental freedoms—including those of ethnic minorities—and of the grave breaches of international humanitarian law—including the practice of 'ethnic cleansing' and the deliberate impeding of delivery of food and medical supplies to the civilian population.[15] As for the conflict in Kosovo, although Council concern was triggered by the instability created in the region and the threat of intervention by neighbouring states, considerations relating to violations of fundamental principles of human rights, including respect for minority rights, and humanitarian law also lay at the heart of the crisis.[16]

In the case of Somalia, clearly an internal conflict, Resolution 794 (1992) authorizing 'all necessary means to establish a secure environment for humanitarian relief operations in Somalia', ie the use of force, made a direct reference to a 'strong condemnation of' violations of international humanitarian law 'including in particular the deliberate impeding of the delivery of food and medical supplies essential for the survival of the civilian population'. In the Rwandan crisis, the Council also used the word 'genocide' for the first time—in connection with the massacres in Rwanda—although its fact-finding commission in Darfur abstained from doing so.[17]

Violations of human rights and humanitarian law as elements of the threat to the peace may be discerned in other Council resolutions on Africa. For example in the case of the Democratic Republic of Congo, the Council condemned the massacres and atrocities perpetuated there, deploring the persistence of violations of human rights and international humanitarian law, in particular those carried out by militias and foreign armed groups as well as by elements of the DRC Armed Forces, in North and South Kivu and Ituri and stressed the urgent need for those responsible for these crimes to be brought to justice (SC Resolutions 1493 (2003), 1736 (2006)).

In the case of Darfur, the Council condemned 'all acts of violence and violations of human rights and international humanitarian law by all parties' including 'indiscriminate attacks on civilians, rapes, forced displacements, and acts of violence especially those with an ethnic dimension' (SC Resolution 1556 (2004)). While in

[15] See, inter alia, SC Res 713, 752, 757, 770, 787 (1992), 819, 820 (1993), 836 (1993).

[16] See, eg, Res 1160 (1998) and Res 1199 (1998).

[17] See, eg, SC Res 794 (1992) and Res 837 (1992) on Somalia, Res 925 and Res 935 (1994) on Rwanda.

the case of its early resolutions on Afghanistan, Resolution 1267 (1999) in its preamble recalls not only the Council's deep concern over the continuing violations of IHL and of human rights, but also particularly underlines in this connection discrimination against women and girls, in the context of a threat to international peace and security.

B. Mass exodus and threats to the peace

The Council has considered that particular policies of massive and systematic violations of human rights and grave violations of humanitarian law leading to humanitarian catastrophes which engender mass exodus or refugee flows constitute threats to international peace and security. This linkage between collective security and forced displacement has been a notable development in the regime of international protection of refugees. Refugee issues can now be viewed as a matter of concern to the international community as a whole, giving the latter a broad platform for action.

The Council has thus reacted to imminent movements of populations or addressed their root causes for the purpose of restoration of international peace and security, whether in northern Iraq, Haiti, or Kosovo. It has also given a central place in the framework of a sustainable peace to the solution of the problem of refugees and internally displaced persons in the peace settlements it has helped to conclude and to enforce.

In the case of SC Resolution 688 (1991), the Security Council declared itself:

> gravely concerned by the repression of the Iraqi civilian population in many parts of Iraq, including most recently in Kurdish populated areas, which led to a massive flow of refugees towards and across international frontiers and to cross border incursions which threaten international peace and security.
>
> . . .
>
> 1. *Condemns* the repression of the Iraqi civilian population in many parts of Iraq, including most recently in Kurdish-populated areas, the consequences of which threaten international peace and security in the region.

One can well understand here the threat to regional security of a potential exodus of Kurds, particularly in relation to Iran and Turkey with their Kurdish minorities—in effect it was these countries that called the attention of the Security Council to the situation.

In the case of Haiti, SC Resolutions 841 (1993) and 940 (1994) linked the threat to international peace and security with the humanitarian crisis in Haiti, including mass displacements of population and the desperate plight of Haitian refugees, following on from 'a climate of fear of persecution and economic displacement' as a result of the failure to reinstate the legitimate government of President Aristide.

In SC Resolution 771 (1992) on former Yugoslavia, the Security Council taking into account the large number of refugees and displaced persons, expressed:

grave alarm at continuing reports of widespread violations of international humanitarian law occurring within the territory of the former Yugoslavia and especially in Bosnia and Herzegovina including reports of mass forcible expulsion and deportation of civilians . . . [18]

In SC Resolution 787 (1992) which established economic sanctions against the Federal Republic of Yugoslavia (Serbia and Montenegro), the Council:

2. Reaffirms that any taking of territory by force or any practice of 'ethnic cleansing' is unlawful and unacceptable . . . and insists that all displaced persons be enabled to return in peace to their former homes.

And in SC Resolution 819 (1993), the Security Council referred to the 'tragic humanitarian emergency' in Srebrenica resulting from the 'brutal actions of Bosnian Serb paramilitary units, forcing the large-scale displacement of civilians, in particular women, children and the elderly.'

The Security Council has also promoted the return of refugees and displaced persons based on a right of return which it affirmed, for example, in its Resolutions 361 (1974) concerning Cyprus, and 820 (1993) concerning Bosnia-Herzegovina in which it 'insists' that 'all displaced persons have the right to return in peace to their former homes and should be assisted to do so'. It has also reaffirmed the right of return of refugees and displaced persons in Kosovo and 'the responsibility of the Federal Republic of Yugoslavia for creating the conditions which allow them to do so' including 'an enhanced status for Kosovo, (with) a substantially greater degree of autonomy' (SC Resolution 1199 (1998)). In its Resolution 1244 (1999) it mandated the international security presence and the international civilian presence to establish a secure environment in order to assure 'the safe and unimpeded return of all refugees and displaced persons to their homes in Kosovo'.

Having noted with grave concern in the case of Darfur, that up to 200,000 refugees had fled to the neighbouring Chad, which constituted a serious burden upon that country (SC Resolution 1556 (2004)), it determined in Resolution 1778 (2007) that the situation in the border regions of Sudan, Chad, and the Central African Republic constituted a threat to international peace and security and approved the establishment in the two latter states of 'a multidimensional presence intended to help to create the security conditions conducive to a voluntary, secure and sustainable return of refugees and displaced persons, inter alia, by contributing to the protection of refugees, displaced persons and civilians in danger'.

Similar concern with refugees in East Timor appears in Resolutions 1272 (1999) and 1319 (2000) in which the Council calls on the Indonesian authorities, as well as all parties, 'to take immediate and effective measures to ensure the safe return of refugees who choose to go back to East Timor, and stresses the need for parallel programmes to resettle individuals who choose not to return'.

Finally, it has worked for the political resolution of conflicts and has actively sought to establish a multilateral framework for the conclusion of peace settlements which give a central place to the solution of the problem of refugees and internally

[18] See also SC Res 752 (1992).

displaced persons, through large-scale refugee repatriations, as illustrated by the peace settlements relating to Cambodia, Bosnia-Herzegovina, or Darfur.[19] Such solutions include human rights monitoring by international bodies, embedded, for example, in Annexes 6 on human rights and 7 on refugees and displaced persons which are integral parts of the Dayton Agreement, and include a mechanism for restitution of or compensation for property.[20] In a resolution on the situation in Georgia (Resolution 1781 (2007)), as in SC Resolution 820 (1993) on Bosnia, the Council not only underlined the importance of internally displaced persons being able to return 'to their homes and property' but also stated that 'individual property rights have not been affected by the fact that owners had to flee during the conflict and that the residency rights and the identity of those owners will be respected'.

C. Legal issues arising under such qualifications

The above developments illustrate the broadening of the notion of threat to the peace. Several questions have been raised in this context.

Is the Council competent to act on this broadened notion of a threat to the peace, in other words in what way could human rights violations be deemed to constitute a threat to international peace and security, and are there any limits to be placed on its discretionary powers to make such determinations? Controversy over this had raged at the time of the first imposition of sanctions in the case of Southern Rhodesia.[21] Some sought to show that the activities of the Ian Smith regime could not conceivably be characterized as a threat to the peace, for they contained no element of aggression since confined within the boundaries of Southern Rhodesia. Moreover they were a matter for the United Kingdom, the administering power, and Southern Rhodesia, its 'self-governing' colony. If a threat existed it was only a potential one resulting from the possibility of intervention from external powers. These arguments were rebutted at the time—for example by pointing out that the Charter did not require that some overt act of aggression be committed and that such qualifications of a situation were entirely within the discretion of the Security Council. Moreover, some human rights violations could lead to cross-border effects, in which case the threat to the peace came from these effects rather than from the violations themselves. Finally, it can be argued that while there were limitations imposed by the Charter's purposes and principles of the Charter laid out in

[19] See, eg, Agreements on a Comprehensive Political Settlement of the Cambodia Conflict (1991) endorsed by the Security Council (SC Res 668 (1990), 717 and 718 (1991)) Annex 4; the General Framework Agreement for Peace in Bosnia and Herzegovina, December 1995 between the Republic of Bosnia and Herzegovina, the Republic of Croatia and the Federal Republic of Yugoslavia (FRY) (on behalf of the Republika Srpska) endorsed by SC Res 1031 (1995); Security Council resolutions on Darfur, see, eg, SC Res1590 (2005), welcoming the Comprehensive Peace Agreement between the Government of Sudan (GOS) and the Sudan People's Liberation Movement/Army (SPLM/A) in Nairobi, Kenya on 9 January 2005.

[20] See also Report of the Secretary General on the protection of civilians in armed conflict, UN Doc S/2009/277, 29 May 2009, para 17.

[21] See, eg, for one of the first scholars to pose this question: Fenwick, 'When is there a Threat to the Peace?—Rhodesia' (1967) 61 AJIL 753–5.

Article 24, these were also concerned with human rights although admittedly the Security Council could have been accused of having infringed the allocation of competences laid down in the Charter. But the ICTR has pointed out:

> The Trial Chamber cannot accept the Defence Counsel's argument that the existence of specialized institutions for the protection of Human Rights precludes the Security Council from taking action against violation of this body of the law. Rather to the contrary, the protection of international Human Rights is the responsibility of all United Nations organs, the Security Council included, without any limitation, in conformity with the UN Charter.[22]

At any rate, such arguments have by now been made moot by the practice of the Security Council.

Is the Council authorized to act in internal matters? A common refrain is that since most of the situations relating to human rights violations have taken place within a state's own borders, the Council could not override the barrier of domestic jurisdiction under Article 2(7). The objections to Article 2(7) can easily be overcome. First, that article includes an exception for Security Council enforcement action and it is therefore not inhibited by Article 2(7) when acting under Chapter 7, although it does have to respect the Charter principle of sovereign equality. Its practice has clearly confirmed that the Council has not balked at linking violations of human rights with maintenance of international peace and security, even in the absence of cross-border effects—beginning with the case of Southern Rhodesia. Secondly, the evolution of human rights law itself has ensured that such matters are no longer to be considered a matter of domestic jurisdiction, so no longer fall within that prohibition;[23] while in the relations between states the principle of non-intervention in GA Resolution 2625 (1970) and respect for territorial integrity continues to be insisted upon and strengthened, Article 2(7) of the Charter which delimits the relations between the United Nations and its member states, has on the contrary been seriously and consistently eroded most notably in the field of human rights, thus leading to the expansion of international jurisdiction within a multilateral context. Moreover, respect for fundamental human rights is now considered to be an *erga omnes* obligation, and it is by now accepted that all states can react short of military force to such violations, a fortiori act within a collective context. Thirdly, situations arising from an internal armed conflict are now regulated by international law—the conventional and customary law of armed conflict (Common Article 3 to the Geneva Conventions, Additional

[22] ICTR, Case No ICTR-96-15-T, The Prosecutor v Joseph Kanyabashi, Decision on the Defence Motion on Jurisdiction, 18 June 1997, para 29.

[23] Interestingly at the San Francisco Conference, France had attempted to insert a reservation to Art 2(7) limiting its scope which read:

> à moins que la violation manifeste des libertés essentielles et les droits de l'homme ne constitue par elle-même une menace susceptible de compromettre la paix.

Cited in Cohen-Jonathan, 'Le Conseil de Sécurité et les droits de l'homme', in JF Flauss and P Wachsmann, *Le droit des organisations internationales* (1997) 19, at 22.

Protocol II), or elementary principles of humanitarian law as the ICJ stated in the *Nicaragua* case[24]—hence not a matter of domestic jurisdiction.

A third question arising from such determinations relates to problems of attribution and evidence. The Council has imputed or attributed such violations not only to state entities, but also to de facto governments and non-state entities, such as the white minority in Rhodesia, UNITA in Angola, the Bosnian Serbs, and the Taliban. But it has also pointed to shared responsibility, between for example, the Serbs of Bosnia, as well as the FRY, the Kosovars, as well as Albanians, and sometimes, addressed 'all parties and others concerned', as for example in the Democratic Republic of Congo. This has raised the question of whether non-state entities are bound by international law, including human rights and humanitarian law, and whether by dealing with them in such fashion they were not in fact being granted some form of recognition.

Who can review such qualifications? Weeramantry had pointed out in his dissenting opinion in the case of *Lockerbie*:

> [T]he determination under Article 39 of the existence of any threat to the peace, breach of the peace or act of aggression, is one entirely within the discretion of the Council. It would appear that the Council and no other is the judge of the existence of the state of affairs which brings Chapter VII into operation... Once taken, the door is opened to the various decisions the Council may make under that Chapter.[25]

In the same vein the Counsel for the United Kingdom stated in the Lockerbie case: 'the Court will not allow its jurisdiction to be used as an appeal court from the political assessments made by the Security Council'.[26]

This brings us to the question of judicial review, treated briefly in a later section. What may be said in this context is that whereas the Council's findings under Article 39 in a particular situation are discretionary within the limits we have traced, and could not be contested by the Court because of the particular allocation of competence under the Charter, the Council's separate determinations relating to violations of international law, including human rights law, where these form a constituent element of the threat to the peace, can only be declaratory of the existing situation in international law and therefore where they raise disputed questions of state responsibility could be reviewed by the Court if these are incidentally put before it.

Finally, have violations under international law, such as breaches of human rights or humanitarian law violations, only been considered in the practice of the organization in so far as they may lead to a threat to international peace or are in themselves threats to the peace? This was the position once taken by Rosalyn

[24] *Military and Paramilitary Activities in and Against Nicaragua* (Nicaragua v United States of America) (Merits), ICJ Reports (1986) 23.

[25] *Case Concerning Questions of Interpretation and Application of the 1971 Montreal Convention Arising from the Aerial Incident at Lockerbie* (Libyan Arab Jamahiriya v United Kingdom and Libyan Arab Jamahiriya v United States of America) (Provisional Measures) (Orders of l4 April 1992), ICJ Reports (1992) 66 and l76 respectively.

[26] Ibid, Verbatim Record, CR.92/3, at 74.

Higgins.[27] In the case of Southern Rhodesia, I had contended on the contrary, that such breaches of self-determination and other human rights, had been considered threats to the peace only in order that the mechanisms provided for in the Charter as a response to such threats could be extended to them, the intention being law enforcement. It could be argued therefore that in certain cases, in view of the fundamental nature of the norms in question, a process of collective enforcement of such norms has been sought by linking their violation to the consequences of the Chapter VII regime.

3. The Enforcement of Fundamental Norms of International Human Rights and Humanitarian Law

The mandatory enforcement measures which follow determinations under Article 39, despite their evident political origins, function in many cases as sanctions, in the sense that they may deny all legal effects to the illegal acts of the entity against which they are applied, and result also in the forcible temporary suspension of its subjective legal rights.

Sanctions have covered a wide range of enforcement measures, mandatory under Article 25 of the Charter, which are either explicitly or implicitly provided for under Article 41 of the Charter, or have developed from the practice of the Security Council. There is no pattern of responses dependent on the nature of the threat to or breach of the peace, but the types of measures referred to below illustrate the potential enforcement measures which can be applied in reactions to breaches of human rights and humanitarian law.

A. The sanction of nullity and non-recognition

In some cases the characterization of state conduct as illegal may have a function autonomous from a finding under Article 39 in serving as a ground for determining the absolute nullity of the acts in question. This serves to underline the fundamental nature of the obligation breached.

1. Nature and content of the measures

Acting under Chapter VII, the Security Council has determined, in the cases of Southern Rhodesia, Iraq, and Yugoslavia, the illegality and nullity of certain acts, calling for their collective non-recognition.

Thus the unilateral declaration of independence in Rhodesia was declared to be without legal validity and a similar fate was reserved to all the subsequent acts of the

[27] Higgins, 'The Place of International Law in the Settlement of Disputes by the Security Council' (1970) 64 AJIL 1–18.

illegal regime.[28] SC Resolution 217 (1965), for example: 'Condemns the usurpation of power by a racist settler minority in Southern Rhodesia and regards the declaration of independence by it as having no legal validity', while SC Resolution 445(1979) '[d]eclares any elections held under the auspices of the illegal racist régime and the results thereof null and void'. In SC Resolution 662 (1990), the Council: '1. *Decides* that annexation of Kuwait by Iraq under any form and whatever pretext has no legal validity, and is considered null and void', while the preamble to Resolution 670 (1990) affirms 'that any acts of the Government of Iraq which are contrary to the above-mentioned resolutions or to Articles 25 or 48 of the Charter of the United Nations, such as Decree No. 377 of the Revolution Command Council of Iraq of 16 September 1990 are null and void'. In the case of Bosnia and Herzegovina, the Council reaffirmed 'its endorsement of the principles that all statements or commitments made under duress, particularly those relating to land and property, are wholly null and void' as they contributed to ethnic cleansing (SC Resolution 820 (1993)). In these cases, it will be noted that the Council refused to accept the effects on the international plane of *domestic* public and private acts.

These determinations have also served as the basis for a duty of collective non-recognition.[29] The content of this policy was formulated for the first time since the Manchukuo crisis, in the case of Southern Rhodesia, in which the Council called on states not to recognize the declared state of Rhodesia, despite its evident effectiveness;[30] subsequently, the ICJ outlined the content of non-recognition in relation to South Africa's effective occupation of Namibia in its 1971 Advisory Opinion. It was considerably more extensive than that flowing from ordinary policies of bilateral non-recognition, entailing non-recognition of passports, exclusion from multilateral treaties, non-admission to, or suspension from, international organizations, symbolic acts such as exclusion from participation in international sporting events and suspension of scientific and technical cooperation and cultural exchanges, and non-cognizance of the acts of the regime in municipal law, the Council calling on states to ensure that their courts did not apply the laws or acts of the sanctioned entity, and to deny rights inherent in governmental status, such as the right to sue or to state immunity.

One should also mention in this context, Resolution 777 (1992) which, in paragraph 1:

> *Considers* that the Federal Republic of Yugoslavia (Serbia and Montenegro) cannot continue automatically the membership of the former Socialist Federal Republic of Yugoslavia in the United Nations; and therefore recommends to the General Assembly

[28] For an analysis of nullity and non-recognition in the Rhodesian context, see V Gowlland-Debbas, *Collective Responses to Illegal Acts in International Law. United Nations Action in the Question of Southern Rhodesia* (1990) ch 3 and 4.

[29] In the former Draft Articles on State Responsibility, non-recognition had been considered, inter alia, to be the minimum content of the response to the commission of an international crime (see Art 14(2)(a) of Part 2); in the final Articles, the duty of non-recognition and non-assistance in Art 41 flows from serious breaches of peremptory norms.

[30] In 1965 the purported new state of Rhodesia had serious claims to fulfilling the traditional criteria of statehood (see Gowlland-Debbas, *Collective Responses*, pp.205–16).

that it decide that the Federal Republic of Yugoslavia (Serbia and Montenegro) should apply for membership in the United Nations and that it shall not participate in the work of the General Assembly.

The human rights limitations on such a policy of non-recognition were drawn by the ICJ in its *Namibia* Opinion. Interpreting paragraph 2 of Resolution 276 (1970), the Court held that the obligation on states not to enter into treaty relations with South Africa where it was purporting to act for Namibia, could not be applied to certain general conventions such as those of a humanitarian character, the non-performance of which might adversely affect the people of Namibia. Again it stated that the duty of non-recognition imposed by Resolution 276 of South Africa's administration of the territory should not result in depriving the people of Namibia of any advantage derived from international cooperation.[31]

2. Legal issues raised

Such determinations of illegality and invalidity, with consequent collective non-recognition, have become a part of UN practice even in cases falling outside of Chapter VII, eg the cases concerning Namibia, South African Bantustans, and Israeli-occupied territories, all concerning human rights and humanitarian law issues.[32]

Yet while nullity and non-recognition may be seen as a sanction, its Charter basis is unclear. It certainly cannot be assimilated to the severance of diplomatic relations in Article 41[33] and it is only with respect to the well-established rule regarding non-recognition of territorial acquisitions through the use of force that this can be seen as the natural corollary of Article 2(4).[34]

It is important to underline, however, that the Council's determinations of illegality and invalidity are essentially declaratory and not intended to create the nullity of the acts in question. In his separate opinion in the *Namibia* Opinion, Judge Onyeama emphasized this point by stating:

> The declaration [by the Security Council] of the illegality of the continued presence of South Africa in Namibia did not itself make such presence illegal; it was . . . a statement of the Security Council's assessment of the legal quality of the situation created by South Africa's failure to comply with the General Assembly's resolution . . . it was in fact a judicial determination.[35]

[31] *Legal Consequences for States of the Continued Presence of South Africa in Namibia (South-West Africa) Notwithstanding Security Council Resolution 276 (1970)*, ICJ Reports (1971) 55–6.

[32] See also the case of the Turkish Republic of Northern Cyprus which had more to do with the use of force and secession.

[33] The Court in the *Namibia Opinion* confirms this by implication, in arguing that SC Res 276 calling for the non-recognition of South Africa's hold over Namibia could constitute a decision under Art 25 even though falling outside of Chapter VII (at 53). See UN Doc S/9732, 31 March 1970, in which France questions whether non-recognition spelled out in SC Res 277 (1970) could be considered to fall under Art 41. See also Virally, 'Panorama du droit international contemporain' (1983) 183 RCADI 222–3, who distinguishes nullity as a legal sanction from coercive sanctions taken on the basis of Art 41.

[34] See, eg, Definition of Aggression annexed to GA Res 3314 (XXIX).

[35] *Namibia Opinion* at 147.

As judicial determinations, these are operations of law. They constitute legal determinations, which have what the Court has called 'operational design' in the sense of entailing definitive and far-reaching legal effects, in respect of the particular case concerned, and are aimed at the denial of legal effects to illegal acts.[36] As the ICJ has stated:

> To deny to a political organ of the United Nations . . . the right to act, on the argument that it lacks competence to render what is described as a judicial decision . . . would amount to a complete denial of the remedies available against fundamental breaches of an international undertaking.[37]

For, as stated by the Court:

> A binding determination made by a competent organ of the United Nations to the effect that a situation is illegal cannot remain without consequence . . . 'This decision entails a legal consequence, namely that of putting an end to an illegal situation'.[38]

The Court also maintained that such determinations could not remain without effect under general international law, and 'were opposable to all states in the sense of barring *erga omnes* the legality of a situation which is maintained in violation of international law'.[39]

B. Non-military measures

The Council, this time more clearly on the basis of Article 41, has imposed the severance or reduction of diplomatic and other official relations and closure of representations abroad, as well as restrictions on the movement of persons. The wide range of economic measures taken by the Council under Article 41 include: restrictions on commodities and products (including general or selective embargoes, such as on petroleum, diamonds, arms, or aircraft), as well as prohibitions in their dealings and shipments or transhipments; the freezing of funds and assets, the prohibition of financial and other services; and the severance of air, sea, and land communications and seizure of vessels and aircraft, to name a few. Such measures would ordinarily constitute encroachments on state rights to engage in international trade and communications that are normally protected under international law.[40] The following are some of the issues raised by Article 41 enforcement measures.

[36] *Namibia Opinion* at 50. The French translation is 'procédant d'une intention d'éxecution'.
[37] Ibid 49.
[38] Ibid 54.
[39] Ibid 56.
[40] For select sanctions resolutions, see Iraq: SC Res 661, 670 (1990) and 1137 (1997); Yugoslavia: SC Res 713 (1991), 757, 787 (1992), 820, 942 (1993), and 1160 (1998); Somalia: SC Res 733 (1992); Libya: SC Res 748 (1992) and 883 (1993); Liberia: SC Res 788 (1992); Haiti: SC Res 841 (1993); Rwanda: SC Res 918 (1994); Sudan: SC Res 1054 (1996), 1591 (2005), 1672 (2006); Sierra Leone: SC Res 1132 (1997), DRC: SC Res 1649 (2005).

1. *The evolution of Article 41 since 1945*

Some of the measures prescribed under Article 41 are by now obviously obsolete, such as the severance of postal, telegraphic, and radio communications; some, if applied, have obviously come into conflict with contemporary human rights law, such as the right to life, the right to health, freedom of movement, and freedom of expression. Reservations had already been expressed at the time of the Southern Rhodesian sanctions in relation to freedom of expression, of movement, of communications, and re-entry of nationals into their own state. The United States representative, for example, had vehemently opposed a ban on means of communications, on the basis of a 'profound belief in the free flow of information and communications', others pointing out that means of communication constituted essential human needs and were relied on by numerous health and educational facilities.

On the other hand, in the *Tadić* case the Appeals Tribunal considered that the provisions of Article 41 were not exhaustive and could accommodate such measures as the Council itself could take in the performance of its functions, including the establishment of international criminal tribunals.[41]

2. *The humanitarian fallout of comprehensive sanctions*

Of the post-1990 measures, only three—those relating to Iraq, Haiti, and Yugoslavia—can be considered to have been quasi-comprehensive, covering the whole gamut of economic, financial, diplomatic, and other measures. These far-reaching sanctions have raised grave humanitarian issues with considerable repercussions and have led to disillusionment with comprehensive measures and a turn to other solutions.

Comprehensive sanctions are difficult to end once set in place, since a targeted entity is hostage to the subjective assessment of a single veto-wielding member as to whether the attainment of the objectives of sanctions have been reached, particularly when these objectives have not been clearly defined in the sanctions resolutions, or where, as in Iraq, the goalposts were moved, which resulted in subjecting Iraq to sanctions for over a decade.

The humanitarian and other exceptions which are included in sanctions resolutions (in particular foodstuffs 'in humanitarian circumstances' and medical supplies) have not been easy to interpret and such interpretation has been open to unilateral and often unsubstantiated blockages by member states on the alleged grounds of their 'dual use'. The ludicrous situations this could lead to was illustrated by the refusal to deliver baby milk to occupied Kuwait, or

[41] International Tribunal for the Prosecution of Persons Responsible for Serious Violations of International Humanitarian Law Committed in the Territory of Former Yugoslavia since 1991, *The Prosecutor v Dusko Tadić a/k/a 'Dule'*, Decision on the Defence Motion for Interlocutory Appeal on Jurisdiction, 2 October 1995, paras 32–6.

pencils for Iraqi schoolchildren on account of their purported dual use; moreover, it will be noted that the Iraq sanctions did not include educational materials among the important exceptions to sanctions, thus penalizing an entire generation of schoolchildren for the 12 years or more during which sanctions lasted. The 'Oil for Food' programme designed to redress the humanitarian impact of comprehensive sanctions led ironically to a major scandal within the UN, although one of the worst effects of this programme was not so much the derisory sums that were raked off by UN officials in charge, but the 'appalling disrepair', in the words of the Secretary General, of Iraq's infrastructure, due in part to 'holds' on contract applications imposed by certain permanent members in the sanctions committee on Iraq.

3. The due process problems raised by targeted sanctions

The disillusionment with comprehensive sanctions resulted in targeted sanctions, measures involving, in particular, restrictions on financial and banking operations (asset freezes, blocking of financial transactions or financial services) and travel and aviation bans, including visas, first directed against individual members of targeted regimes or their family, and later against particular individuals suspected of acts of terrorism placed on a black list. They also included targeting of specific commodities, such as arms and diamonds, particularly important in view of economically motivated conflicts fought not for ideological reasons but for acquisition of natural resources. The aim of targeted sanctions was to increase the efficiency of sanctions, while at the same time decreasing their unwanted side-effects, particularly on the populations of targeted states.[42] But it is particularly in relation to measures such as the freezing of funds and other financial measures to combat individual acts of terrorism, that targeted sanctions have raised vital issues of legitimacy, in particular human rights questions such as property rights and individual due process.[43]

C. Military force

1. The use of force for human rights and humanitarian objectives

Certain of the sanctions regimes referred to above have been accompanied by resort to authorized military force, the Council calling on states acting individually, collectively, or through regional arrangements, to use 'all necessary means' for such purposes as enforcement at sea of an economic embargo decreed by the Security Council, or the removal of Iraq from Kuwait. The Council, acting

[42] Three government initiatives contributed to developing the concept of targeted financial sanctions: the Bonn-Berlin, Interlaken, and Stockholm processes. See, eg, *Targeted Financial Sanctions—A Manual for Design and Implementation: Contributions from the Interlaken Process*, The Swiss Confederation in cooperation with the United Nations Secretariat and the Watson Institute for International Studies, Brown University at www.smartsanctions.ch (last accessed 22 February 2011).

[43] Such measures and the challenges which have arisen in response to them, are more fully dealt with in the contributions of A Ciampi, E de Wet and S Zappalà to the present volume.

under Chapter VII, has also mandated peacekeeping forces to use force beyond self-defence for limited objectives. In some cases these authorizations of uses of force have had human rights related objectives, as for example to protect safe havens or 'safe areas', or humanitarian convoys for the purposes of humanitarian assistance, or to restore democracy; the Council has also established complex peacebuilding operations endowed with sweeping powers of governance, including legislative and executive, to ensure the rule of law, including human rights, in post-conflict countries.

Such authorizations hinged on Chapter VII, should not be confused with the controversial doctrine of 'humanitarian intervention' which is unilateral or multilateral military action taken outside the United Nations, the purported objective of which is to save populations from massive human rights violations at the hands of their own governments and which arguably contravenes Article 2(4) of the Charter. On the contrary, the Council's authorizations flow from its primary responsibility in the maintenance of international peace and security, regardless as to whether they have a 'humanitarian objective', ie to protect individuals within a state, or not. They are *not*, as some have alleged, 'humanitarian intervention'. Some examples of authorized military action follow.

In the case of Haiti, for example, the Council authorized the use of force under Chapter VII in order to reinstate democracy—a first—and to ensure the respect of human rights (SC Resolution 940 (1994)). Resolution 929 (1994) authorized member states cooperating with the Secretary General to use 'all necessary means to achieve . . . humanitarian objectives' in Rwanda—in fact welcoming France's offer to head a multinational force. Resolution 794 (1992) on Somalia welcomed 'the offer by a Member State . . . concerning the establishment of an operation to create such a secure environment' for humanitarian relief. Member states were also called on to act through regional organizations to take 'all necessary measures' to protect the safe areas in Bosnia (SC Resolution 836 (1993)), while the Security Council authorized under Resolution 1264 (1999), the establishment of a multinational force in East Timor to facilitate, inter alia, humanitarian assistance operations. In the case of the DRC, the Security Council authorized a multinational force in the Bunia region with a mandate to take 'all necessary means' to contribute, inter alia, to the improvement of the humanitarian situation, protection of the internally displaced persons in the camps and the civilian population (SC Resolution 1484 (2003)).

2. *Legal issues raised*

It is a truism to state that such Security Council resolutions authorizing the unilateral use of force for collective purposes have emerged out of necessity, in the absence of a military force at the Council's disposal, and on the basis of the implied powers doctrine.[44] Such authorizations, which harness unilateral action by

[44] The ICJ stated in the *Certain Expenses* case: 'It cannot be said that the Charter has left the Security Council impotent in the face of an emergency situation when agreements under Article 43 have not been concluded'. ICJ Reports (1962) 167.

effectively 'privatizing' or 'contracting out' the functions of the Security Council, have been seen in legal terms as a delegation under the Charter of the discretionary enforcement powers of the Security Council.[45] The action authorized is therefore plainly to be conducted within the overall objective of 'restoration of international peace and security' which has included, as has been seen in the Council's recent practice, enforcement of community norms. Moreover, the resolutions are based on a prior determination under Article 39 of a threat to or breach of the peace. In short, the insertion of unilateral action within Chapter VII of the Charter means that the Council continues to bear responsibility for it, although that does not exclude the responsibility of member states or regional organizations from their own or concurrent responsibility.

There was from the start, considerable controversy over such authorizations and their ambiguous legal basis, in the absence of an express provision in the Charter, apart from broad references in the resolutions to Chapter VII. Resolutions authorizing 'the use of all necessary means' imply a wide margin of discretion on the part of those called on to implement them, eg in determining when the circumstances calling for a use of force have arisen, and have been criticized as providing 'a blank cheque for excessive and indiscriminate use of force',[46] reporting procedures being quite nominal. Understandably, there has been insistence that such authorization be express.

These resolutions also serve as an authorization to take specified action which would otherwise be unlawful under international law. Even though they are non-mandatory calls to their addressees (though coercive vis-à-vis the targeted entity), they have resulted in temporarily suspending the (non-imperative) rules of customary international law as well as conventional obligations.

The Council's alleged *ex post facto* legitimization of unauthorized operations such as Resolutions 1244 (1999) on Kosovo or 1483 (2003) on Iraq have also been strongly criticized. Yet it is clear from Council debates surrounding the adoption of these resolutions that there was no intention that they be seen as an endorsement of the NATO military operation or US–UK invasion of Iraq, respectively.

3. *Responsibility to protect*

Attempts to clothe unilateral humanitarian intervention in the euphemistic jargon of a responsibility to protect have not been successful. UN reform proposals emphasize the importance of collective measures in carrying out a collective international responsibility to protect and stress their commitment to promoting and strengthening the multilateral process. The World Summit Outcome Document, for example, reaffirms in paragraph 79 'the authority of the Security Council to

[45] For a very lucid analysis of the general legal framework governing the process of delegation, see D Sarooshi, *The United Nations and the Development of Collective Security. The Delegation by the UN Security Council of its Chapter VII Powers* (1999).

[46] Malaysia in SCOR, 2963rd meeting, 76–7.

mandate coercive action to maintain and restore international peace and security'. It proclaims:

The international community, through the United Nations, also has the responsibility to use appropriate diplomatic, humanitarian and other peaceful means, in accordance with Chapters VI and VIII of the Charter of the United Nations, to help protect populations from genocide, war crimes, ethnic cleansing and crimes against humanity. In this context, we are prepared to take collective action, in a timely and decisive manner, through the Security Council, in accordance with the Charter, including Chapter VII, on a case-by case basis and in cooperation with relevant regional organizations as appropriate, should peaceful means be inadequate and national authorities are manifestly failing to protect their populations from genocide, war crimes, ethnic cleansing and crimes against humanity.[47]

The appropriateness of using military force to enforce human rights is to be seriously questioned. The unauthorized uses of force by NATO in Kosovo—bombardment of refugee convoys, use of depleted uranium, etc—and by the UK and US in Iraq leading to the devastating violence and destruction of the country since 2003, inter alia in the name of human rights, have demonstrated the often unforeseen and dramatic consequences of such measures and the anachronism that bombardment of populations and shock and awe operations represent.

The ICJ has stated that states may well have an *erga omnes* right and even an obligation to act in a matter affecting the interests of the international community. It has nevertheless considered that the means were not unlimited and rejected the United State's invocation of Nicaragua's human rights record to justify its armed intervention: 'the protection of human rights—a strictly humanitarian objective, cannot be compatible with the mining of ports, the destruction of oil installations, or again with the training, arming and equipping of the contras'.[48]

This is also why it has been stated that the Security Council in exercising its collective international responsibility to protect, is to resort to military force only in the last resort and under certain conditions. Thus the High Level Panel Report states:

207. In considering whether to authorize or endorse the use of military force, the Security Council should always address—whatever other considerations it may take into account—at least the following five basic criteria of legitimacy:

(a) *Seriousness of threat.* Is the threatened harm to State or human security of a kind, and sufficiently clear and serious, to justify *prima facie* the use of military force? In the case of internal threats, does it involve genocide and other large-scale killing, ethnic cleansing or serious violations of international humanitarian law, actual or imminently apprehended?
(b) *Proper purpose.* Is it clear that the primary purpose of the proposed military action is to halt or avert the threat in question, whatever other purposes or motives may be involved?
(c) *Last resort.* Has every non-military option for meeting the threat in question been explored, with reasonable grounds for believing that other measures will not succeed?
(d) *Proportional means.* Are the scale, duration and intensity of the proposed military action the minimum necessary to meet the threat in question?

[47] Para 139. [48] *Nicaragua Opinion*, 127, 134–5.

(e) *Balance of consequences.* Is there a reasonable chance of the military action being successful in meeting the threat in question, with the consequences of action not likely to be worse than the consequences of inaction?

It has also recommended that these guidelines be embodied in declaratory resolutions of the Security Council and General Assembly.

Moreover, such a responsibility to protect is difficult to reconcile with the Security Council's discretionary powers under Chapter VII on the basis of which the Council can choose inaction where it fails to reach consensus. The difficulty of adopting ceasefire resolutions in the cases of the Israeli bombardments of Lebanon and Gaza, or the dramatically deteriorating situation in Darfur, while the international community has remained at best on the sidelines, have revealed the problems with the doctrine of the responsibility to protect. The Secretary General's mea culpa in the cases of Rwanda and Srebrenica had underlined that the international community as a whole had to accept its share of responsibility for failing to take action to prevent the tragic course of events. Surely the 'responsibility to protect' if it is to go beyond a mere pious buzzword must mean that the Security Council has an obligation, and not mere discretion, to take some action in such circumstances—though not necessarily a military one; and that inaction in the face of violations of peremptory norms must entail the concurrent responsibility of the Security Council and the states which compose it, in particular its permanent members?

D. Measures in the context of criminal law

The Council's responses to the massive violations of human rights and humanitarian law, including ethnic cleansing, massive rape, and recruitment of child soldiers, in certain situations of armed conflicts have entailed its involvement in international criminal law which has taken different forms. Its resolutions have not only led to the institutionalization of international individual criminal responsibility, with consequent developments in procedural and substantive law, but also entailed what can only be seen as penal measures directed against individuals, both at the international and domestic levels.

1. *The impetus given to the institutionalization of international criminal law*

Although certain of the Council's resolutions had earlier referred to the liability of individuals under humanitarian law,[49] the main impetus given by the Security Council to the development of international criminal law has largely been due to the unprecedented creation of the two ad hoc international criminal tribunals for Yugoslavia (ICTY) and Rwanda (ICTR) as subsidiary organs of the Council.[50] Both were preceded by fact-finding commissions.

[49] See, eg, SC Res 670 and 674 (1990) on Iraq; and SC Res 794 and 837 (1992) on Somalia.
[50] SC Res 808, 827 (1993) and 955 (1994), respectively.

The link established between threats to international peace and security and the core crimes giving rise to individual criminal responsibility under international law was underlined by the Appeals Chamber of the ICTY, in the *Tadić* case,[51] in which it upheld the view that the legality of its creation rested on Article 41 of the UN Charter—its establishment thus constituting one measure the Security Council could itself impose under Chapter VII (as opposed to those measures it called on member states to carry out). From this perspective justice has been seen as one means of contributing to the restoration and maintenance of peace.

As the Trial Chamber of the ICTR pointed out: 'attribution of individual criminal responsibility is a fundamental expression of the need for enforcement action by the Security Council. It is indeed difficult to separate the individual from the State' in providing for sanctions. 'By establishing the two International Criminal Tribunals for the former Yugoslavia and Rwanda . . . the Security Council explicitly extended international legal obligations and criminal responsibilities directly to individuals for violations of international humanitarian law'.[52] This has been justified in view, notably, of the 'seriousness, the magnitude and the gravity of the crimes committed during the conflict'. The rules of the Tribunals also apply directly to individuals other than the accused—for example, the rules relating to the summoning of witnesses or the production of evidence.[53]

The development of mixed tribunals based on a combination of Security Council resolutions and agreement between the UN and the state concerned, has also gone in the direction of institutionalizing international criminal justice in this hybrid form. As an example, Security Council Resolution 1315 (2000) led to the creation, on the basis of an agreement between the United Nations and the government of Sierra Leone, of an independent Special Court to prosecute persons having committed serious violations of international humanitarian law as well as crimes committed under Sierra Leonean law. It has also imposed through unilateral action domestic ad hoc justice mechanisms in the context of territorial administrations—the cases of Bosnia, East Timor, and Kosovo, which combine domestic and international elements. I will not mention here the curious establishment of an international tribunal based purely on domestic law, namely the Special Tribunal for Lebanon, following on the assassination of former Prime Minister Hariri.

The outreach of Security Council mechanisms to the International Criminal Court (ICC), an independently based tribunal, also plays a role in the enforcement of human rights. There is a notable convergence of the crimes which may land

[51] ICTY, Case No IT-94-1, *The Prosecutor v Dusko Tadic a/k/a 'Dule'*, Appeals Chamber, Decision on the Defence Motion for Interlocutory Appeal on Jurisdiction, 2 October 1995; for an endorsement of this view, see ICTR, Case No ICTR 96-15-T, *The Prosecutor v Joseph Kanyabashi*, Decision on the Defence Motion on Jurisdiction, 18 June 1997.

[52] ICTR, Case No ICTR-96-15-T, *The Prosecutor v Joseph Kanyabashi*, Decision on the Defence Motion on Jurisdiction, 18 June 1997, para 35.

[53] See ICTY, Case No IT-95-14-AR 108bis, *The Prosecutor v Tihomir Blaskic*, Appeals Chamber, Judgment of 29 October 1997 on the Request of the Republic of Croatia for Review of the Decision of Trial Chamber II of 18 July 1997.

before the ICC and Security Council—genocide, crimes against humanity, war crimes and, eventually, depending on the outcome of the next review conference, aggression over which the ICC has jurisdiction; these may well be the most likely ones to be viewed by the Council as constituting threats to international peace and security in situations which come before it. The ICC Statute further engages the Security Council by embedding the Council's discretionary determinations under Article 39 within the Court's procedures, giving the Council the power to refer a situation to the Court or to defer the Court's exercise of jurisdiction (Articles 13(b) and 16 of the Statute), as well as a potential role in the determination of the crime of aggression. The enlistment of the Council in enforcing on a state its duty to cooperate with the Court in investigation and prosecution of crimes results also in the external operation of Chapter VII of the Charter.

The Council has acted on both counts of referral and deferral. Following on from the report of the International Commission of Inquiry on violations of international humanitarian law and human rights law in Darfur, and acting under Chapter VII, it referred the situation in Darfur to the ICC (SC Resolution 1593(2005)), first determining that the situation in Sudan 'continues to constitute a threat to international peace and security'.

Reference must also be made here to the notorious Resolution 1422 (2002) requesting the ICC not to proceed for a period—renewable—of 12 months, with investigations or prosecutions of officials participating in UN peacekeeping missions from states not parties to the Statute who may have committed crimes on the territory of a state party; this resolution was finally not renewed a second time in 2004, after weeks of intense debate held against the background of the tortures in Abu Ghraib.

2. *The imposition of penal measures in the context of terrorism*

SC Resolution 1373 (2001) calls on states to adopt financial measures such as the freezing of funds and financial assets against individuals suspected of the commission of ill-defined crimes considered to threaten international peace and security, and consolidated lists maintained by the Sanctions Committee pursuant to Resolution 1267 designate the targeted persons suspected of being linked with the Taliban or 'al-Qaida network' and 'other individuals, groups, undertakings and entities associated with them'. These, while presented as administrative measures, in effect function as penalties, in view of the severity of the sanction—what could amount to an indefinite freeze of assets—and the fact, inter alia, that they can constitute the basis of a criminal charge in the domestic law of states. The adoption of SC Resolution 1904 (2009), the latest step in efforts to address the challenges relating to lack of due process, and which calls for the creation of an ombudsperson to examine de-listing requests of those seeking removal from the sanctions list, still falls far short of an independent and effective review mechanism.

While Security Council counterterrorism resolutions and the challenges thereto fall outside the scope of this contribution, it is worth underlining the links that the Council draws between human rights and terrorism. For example, in Resolution

1566 (2004), the Council in 'reaffirming that terrorism in all its forms and manifestations constitutes one of the most serious threats to peace and security' considers also 'that acts of terrorism seriously impair the enjoyment of human rights' thus confirming the conclusions reached in various studies within UN human rights bodies[54] on the link between human rights and terrorism. At the same time, it reminds states:

> that they must ensure that any measures taken to combat terrorism comply with all their obligations under international law and should adopt such measures in accordance with international law, in particular international human rights, refugee, and humanitarian law.[55]

3. *Legal issues raised*

The move towards international criminal responsibility of individuals possibly provides a more acceptable alternative to that of holding entire populations accountable for the acts of their leaders. At the same time, it raises some important issues under international law.

One such issue is the relationship between peace and justice. This relationship can take the form of peace collaborating with justice (the case of Darfur). There is here a role for justice within peace; this means at the same time that justice is only viewed as instrumental for peace. But there are important implications as a result for state consent, showing that the consensual nature of the ICC Statute can nevertheless lead through its embedded mechanisms to effects on non-state parties—in this case Sudan—in addition to allowing some non-parties with clout in the Security Council to prevent the exercise of the Court's jurisdiction.[56] The rights of individuals are also affected. For such action within the Security Council, controlled as it is by the Permanent Members and on the basis of a discretionary and political decision, challenges the fundamental principle of equality of individuals before the law, allowing the nationals of some states to be indicted before the Court, while other nationals would be shielded from the administration of justice. For this relationship can also be seen as one of peace vs justice, when the two are in opposition or conflict as in SC Resolution 1422. The peace vs justice debate has been refuelled by the indictment of President Bashir of Sudan and the subsequent debate as to whether to use the Council's powers under the Court's Statute to

[54] See, eg, *Commission on Human Rights, Specific Human Rights Issues: New Priorities, in Particular Terrorism and Counter-Terrorism, Terrorism and Human Rights*. Final report of the Special Rapporteur, Kalliopi K Koufa, 11 August 2004 (E/CN.4/Sub.2/2004/47).

[55] Reiterated in SC Res 1624 (2005).

[56] The United States abstained but did not oppose the resolution because it provided safeguards protecting from investigation or prosecution the nationals and members of its armed forces as a non-state party; moreover, the resolution strangely recalls in the preamble the provisions of Art 16 with regard to deferral, rather than Art 13 on referral, and 'takes note' of the existence of agreements referred to by Art 98(2) of the Rome Statute, an oblique reference to the so-called bilateral impunity agreements which the United States concluded with a number of states to safeguard the immunity of its foreign and military personnel.

deflect the Court. It is interesting to note that some of the states who had initially been critical of Article 16 were now behind this move.

The Security Council's follow-up or rather predictable absence of follow-up to the recommendations of the Goldstone Report[57] addressed to it: (i) to promptly establish a committee of experts to monitor and assess any domestic proceedings instituted by Israel and the Hamas administration in Gaza, and (ii) to refer the situation to the ICC Prosecutor if no credible investigations have been conducted by Israel and the Hamas administration in conformity with international standards, within six months, could be characterized as neither peace nor justice.

Another issue is the relationship between law and politics, or that between judicial and political organs, which also raises the question of the relationship between state and individual responsibility. Problems arise when the political organ acts in a quasi-judicial capacity, affecting the decision-making in the judicial forum.[58] Can these remain watertight compartments?

The various judicial challenges ensuing from the lack of individual due process in the Security Council's listing process of terrorist suspects will not be revisited here, but nevertheless raise fundamental issues of the relationship between public order norms, those of peace and security on the one hand and human rights on the other.

E. Monitoring and fact-finding

The military conflicts on the African continent in the DRC, Sierra Leone, Angola, and others, sustained by the struggle for acquisition of natural resources, have generated a general pattern of gross violations of human rights and grave breaches of humanitarian law by both governments and warring factions, all leading to immense human suffering.[59] Such conflicts have underlined the ineffectiveness of traditional measures of diplomacy and peace accords, for these wars are self-perpetuating and self-financing. The targeted sanctions imposed by the Security Council have also been highly problematic in terms of monitoring and control. To embargo crucial commodities such as 'conflict diamonds', including the imposition of certification schemes, such as the Kimberley diamond certification process, has meant seeking control of the activities not only of non-state actors but also of private and business interests.

Monitoring of sanctions implementation by UN members has been assigned by the Security Council to the Secretary General as well as to the Sanctions Committees established under each sanctions regime. The appointment also of independent

[57] Report of the United Nations Fact Finding Mission on the Gaza Conflict, A/HRC/12/48, 15 September 2009.

[58] For a general discussion of these relationships see: Gowlland-Debbas, 'The Relationship between Political and Judicial Organs of International Organisations: The Role of the Security Council in the New International Criminal Court', in L Boisson de Chazournes, C Romano, and R Mackenzie (eds), *International Organisations and International Dispute Settlement: Trends and Prospects* (2002) 195–218.

[59] See, eg, the evidence submitted to the ICJ in the case of the *Democratic Republic of the Congo v Uganda* (*Case concerning Armed Activities on the Territory of the Congo (Democratic Republic of the Congo v. Uganda)*, Judgment of 19 December 2005 (available at www.icj-cij.org)) and the horrifying reports from the UN and other sources.

expert panels and monitoring groups has become a regular feature of such sanctions monitoring in order to tackle in particular the illegal trade in diamonds and arms smuggling.[60] These panels adopted a 'name and shame' approach, naming individuals and companies implicated in illegal activities. The one on Angola, for example, also identified governments (including two African sitting Heads of State and Belgium), while the one on Sierra Leone implicated the government of Liberia. The role of private industry in the conflicts over natural resources has been particularly highlighted.

4. The Effects of Security Council Enforcement Action on the Development of International Law

A. Development of fundamental norms of international law through the international criminal tribunals

It is undeniable that the cumulative actions of the Security Council under Chapter VII in condemning and instituting collective responses to situations involving breaches of fundamental norms of international law, though only the reflection of post-cold war political jostling and readjustment in the pursuit of particular interests have nevertheless served as the impetus for or had an impact on the development of fundamental norms of international criminal law—both procedural and substantive—as well as human rights and humanitarian law, through the case law of the two international tribunals, thus impacting on state as well as individual rights and obligations under international law.

Although the intention was to include in the Statutes of the ICTY and ICTR only those norms that were of customary law origin,[61] in actual fact, the Tribunals went beyond the existing law. The ICTY's pronouncements in the *Tadić* case regarding the extension to internal armed conflicts of the general rules and principles applicable to international conflicts the violations of which entail criminal responsibility,[62] the determination by the two ad hoc Tribunals that rape was a crime against humanity falling within their jurisdiction, or the development of such concepts as genocide and complicity, fairness and due process, or proportionality, served to crystallize the development of customary international law in their

[60] The first expert panel was established with regard to Angola following on from the Fowler report and its recommendations (see SC Res 1295 (2000)). Subsequent panels were established for Sierra Leone (SC Res 1306 (2000)), Liberia (SC Res 1343 (2001), 1408 (2002), and 1458 (2003)), Somalia (SC Res 1425 (2002), 1474 (2003), and 1519 (2003)). The Panel of Experts on the Illegal Exploitation of Natural Resources and Other Forms of Wealth of the Democratic Republic of Congo was established by a Security Council Presidential statement of 2 June 2000 (UN Doc. S/PRST/2000/20)).

[61] 'In assigning to the International Tribunal the task of prosecuting persons responsible for serious violations of international humanitarian law, the Security Council would not be creating or purporting to "legislate" that law. Rather the International Tribunal would have the task of applying existing international humanitarian law', Report of the Secretary General pursuant to paragraph 2 of Security Council Resolution 808 (1993), UN Doc S/25704, 3 May 1993, para 29. See also para 34.

[62] Case No IT-94-1, *The Prosecutor v. Dusko Tadić a/k/a 'Dule'*, Appeals Chamber, Decision on the Defence Motion for Interlocutory Appeal on Jurisdiction, Decision of 2 October 1995, para 137.

respective fields. The Secretary General had declared in relation to the ICTR, that the Security Council had 'elected to take a more expansive approach to the choice of the applicable law than the one underlying the statute of the Yugoslav Tribunal' and that 'Article 4 of the statute, accordingly, includes violations of Additional Protocol II, which, as a whole, has not yet been universally recognized as part of customary international law, and for the first time criminalizes common article 3 of the four Geneva Conventions'.[63] Moreover, the two criminal tribunals established by the Security Council indulged in some judicial lawmaking in being able to codify their own rules of procedure, a process which subsequently fed into the content and procedures of the Rome Statute of the ICC, although this was left to the parties themselves. The ICTY and ICTR have also had a dual role, going beyond their status as subsidiary organs and appealing to their inherent judicial powers.

B. Impact of Security Council resolutions on the development of international law

Such a legal process, along with condemnations by the Security Council of, inter alia, attacks on UN personnel in time of armed conflict (followed by the adoption by the General Assembly of the 1994 Convention on the Safety of United Nations and Associated Personnel), subsequently fed into the Rome Statute of the ICC as part of the content of core crimes.[64] The Security Council has also stated in Resolution 1325 (2000) that all parties to an armed conflict had to take into account the relevant provisions of the Rome Statute.

The Council's resolutions calling for the application of human rights in armed conflict have demonstrated the complementary use of both human rights law and humanitarian law during such conflicts and have reflected the practice of the political organs of the United Nations and the case law of international and regional judicial bodies.[65]

There has been a debate however as to the impact of Security Council resolutions on the development of customary law. The Appeals Chamber of the ICTY affirmed the relevance of Security Council resolutions to this process by stating that Security Council resolutions were 'of great relevance to the formation of *opinio juris*' in respect of criminal responsibility arising from the rules regulating internal armed conflict.[66] The Sierra Leone Special Court also gave probative value to Security

[63] Report of the Secretary General in application of paragraph 5 of resolution 955 (1994) of the Security Council, UN Doc S/1995/134, 13 February 1995, para 12.

[64] See Rome Statute of the International Criminal Court, Arts 7(1)(g) (on rape as a crime against humanity); 8(2)(biii) and (eiii) and 8(2) (bxxii) and (evi) (on attacks against UN and associated personnel and the commission of rape, respectively, as war crimes both in international and internal armed conflicts).

[65] See the series of Security Council resolutions relating to the application of human rights in occupied Iraq, such as SC Res 1483 (2003).

[66] Case No IT-94-1, *The Prosecutor v Dusko Tadić a/k/a 'Dule'*, Appeals Chamber, Decision on the Defence Motion for Interlocutory Appeal on Jurisdiction, Decision of 2 October 1995, para 133.

Council resolutions condemning the 'inhumane and abhorrent practice' of child recruitment in armed conflict.[67] In contrast, in the *Delalić* case, the ICTY Trial Chamber declared:

> the Security Council, not being a legislative body, cannot create offences. It therefore vests in the Tribunal the exercise of jurisdiction in respect of offences already recognised in international humanitarian law. The Statute does not create substantive law, but provides a forum and framework for the enforcement of existing international humanitarian law.[68]

The Council's resolutions cannot—by analogy with General Assembly resolutions—be said to reflect either *opinio juris*, or the generality of the requisite state practice. Moreover there are inherent dangers in such an approach, for Security Council practice reflects big power hegemony as seen in the way its resolutions have been used as evidence of new emerging norms on, for example, humanitarian intervention (the silence of the Security Council in the case of Kosovo) or preventive self-defence (the case of SC Resolution 1373). There are, needless to say, many risks involved in developing international law through a process that includes the ad hoc and piecemeal reactions of a political organ to particular crises, particularly in respect of the coherence of international law.

C. Security Council 'legislative' resolutions

The Security Council's resolutions were never intended to be legislative in the sense of applying outside the framework of particular cases of restoration of international peace and security, yet increasingly they are being perceived as playing a quasi-legislative role by introducing new, abstract, and general norms of international law which are open-ended and applicable to all states, as distinct from its enforcement powers on the basis of which it adopts temporary binding decisions in respect of specific crises under Chapter VII. It is also seen as imposing treaty obligations on non-parties in apparent disregard of the consensual nature of treaty obligations and some of its recent resolutions purport to act as a substitute for the many years required to negotiate a new multilateral treaty.[69]

In recent years it has gone beyond calls for the application and implementation of treaty obligations by the parties concerned, in seeming to impose existing treaty obligations on non-parties and even to legislate by imposing new norms on all states. The legitimacy of such actions has naturally been challenged. The most striking of these types of resolutions are those the Council has adopted in its

[67] Reference to SC Res 1071 (1996) and SC Res 1612 (2005); Special Court for Sierra Leone, Case no. scsl-04-14-AR72, Prosecutor v. Norman, Fofana and Kondewa, Decision on Preliminary Motion Based on Lack of Jurisdiction (Child recruitment), Appeals Chamber, Decision of 31 May 2004, para 29.

[68] Case No IT-96-21-T, *The Prosecutor v Zejnil Delalić*, Trial Chamber, Judgment of 16 November 1998, para 418.

[69] On this 'legislative' function see Abi-Saab, 'The Security Council as Legislator and as Executive in its Fights Against Terrorism and Against Proliferation of Weapons of Mass Destruction: The Question of Legitimacy', in R Wolfrum and V Röben (eds), *Legitimacy in International Law* (2008) 109; Rosand, 'Security Council Resolution 1373, the Counter-Terrorism Committee, and the Fight Against Terrorism' (2003) 97 AJIL 333.

counterterrorism action, beginning with Resolution 1373 (2001), in particular SC Resolution 1540 (2004) in which it addresses the challenge of the proliferation of weapons of mass destruction by their acquisition by non-state actors, although the existing conventions—the Chemical Weapons Convention, Nuclear Non-Proliferation Treaty, and the Biological Weapons Convention—do not clearly deal with such an issue.

But it has also done that in the field of human rights. It is evident that the Council has affected conventional human rights, humanitarian law and international criminal law core obligations through its enforcement activities.[70] Thus the mandatory Resolution 1373 (2001) which calls on states to take appropriate measures, in conformity, inter alia, with relevant human rights standards, to refuse the grant of refugee status to those who have 'planned, facilitated or participated' in terrorist acts, and declaring that 'acts, methods and practices' of terrorism are contrary to the purposes and principles of the United Nations, affects the 1951 Convention Relating to the Status of Refugees by appearing to impose an obligation on the states parties to interpret the exclusion clauses (Article 1F) by including terrorism under Article 1F thus seeming to settle an ongoing debate as to where and how it should be included.

Security Council resolutions in the field of armed conflict: on children, particularly relating to recruitment of child soldiers (SC Resolution 1612 (2005)); on women and peace and security (Resolution 1325 (2000)) and on the protection of civilians in armed conflicts, including women and children (Resolution 1296 (2000), and Resolution 1820 (2008)) have also been perceived as 'legislative' in the sense that they are general and unrelated to a particular situation, although arguably do not attempt to impose new obligations to the extent that they do not go beyond existing customary international law. However, SC Resolution 1820 (2008) which reaffirms the Council's resolve to eliminate all forms of violence against women and girls, condemning sexual violence as a tactic of war and intimidation against civilians, while not a Chapter VII resolution, makes evident the link with international peace and security and the language is strong. The Council *demands* immediate and complete halt to acts of sexual violence, and notes that:

> rape and other forms of sexual violence can constitute war crimes, crimes against humanity or a constitutive act with respect to genocide, *stresses the need for* the exclusion of sexual violence crimes from amnesty provisions in the context of conflict resolution processes, and *calls upon* Member States to comply with their obligations for prosecuting persons responsible for such acts . . .

It also complements its demands with a monitoring and sanctioning mechanism, the Council affirming its intention when establishing and renewing state-specific

[70] See, eg, Boisson de Chazournes, 'Les résolutions des organes des Nations Unies, et en particulier celles du Conseil de sécurité, en tant que source du droit international humanitaire' in L Condorelli, A-M la Rosa, and S Scherrer (eds), *Les Nations Unies et le droit international humanitaire/The United Nations and International Humanitarian Law* (1996) 149–73.

sanction regimes, to consider imposing 'targeted and graduated' measures against warring factions who committed rape and other forms of violence against women and girls.[71]

5. The Effects of Security Council Enforcement Measures on Human Rights Treaties and Constitutionally Protected Individual Rights

The resolutions of the Security Council adopted under Chapter VII, Article 41 are mandatory under Article 25. As such they must be implemented by states or incur their responsibility under international law. Paradoxically, the effective implementation of Security Council decisions, many of which, as has been seen, have a human rights protection function, have in turn set challenges to both human rights treaties and domestic law constitutional provisions, in certain cases purporting to override them. While this contribution does not address the accountability of the Security Council under human rights law, it does examine ways in which the Council's enforcement action can thus affect the obligations of states in the matter of human rights.

A. The potential power to override human rights treaties

1. The role of courts

Article 103 of the Charter, which provides that in the event of a clash between the obligations of member states under the Charter and their obligations under any other international agreement, the former prevails, has fuelled a debate arising from Security Council resolutions on the financing of terrorism, as to whether they may override the provisions of human rights treaties; more particularly, this debate has revolved around the consolidated lists of individuals and entities maintained by the Sanctions Committee pursuant to Resolution 1267 who have been subjected to the freezing of their funds and financial assets.

The lack of transparency of the procedures for adding individuals to the terrorist list maintained by the Council and the absence of due process, including the right to a fair and public hearing before an impartial review body, and the right to be informed of the reasons, 'raise serious accountability issues and possibly violate fundamental human rights norms and conventions', as the High Level Panel has stated.[72]

Regional and domestic courts, at least until the latest decision of the Court of Justice of the European Communities in the *Kadi* appeal, declined to offer remedies

[71] See Schotten and Biehler, 'The Role of the UN Security Council in Implementing International Humanitarian Law and Human Rights Law', in R Arnold and N Quénivet (eds), *International Humanitarian Law and Human Rights Law: Towards a New Merger in International Law* (2008) 309 at 325.

[72] Para 152.

for individuals from potential abuses in implementation of Security Council decisions. The unquestioning reliance of the EC Court of First Instance on Article 103 of the Charter accepting the precedence of Security Council decisions over the fundamental rights protected by the EU, its interpretation of its mandate as lacking powers of even indirect judicial review over Security Council resolutions, unless peremptory norms or *jus cogens* were concerned, and the choice the Court made in deciding between public interest norms to uphold the 'public-interest objective of fundamental importance to the international community which is to combat by all means, in accordance with the Charter of the United Nations, threats to international peace and security caused by terrorist acts' over human rights, illustrates the kinds of challenges posed by the collective security system in a rule of law context.[73] The decision by the European Court in the *Kadi* appeal,[74] while offering some form of review within the EU itself, does not really address these broader issues. Ad hoc decisions by regional courts while important for clarifying fundamental principles, are not the solution; there is a need for a global approach and for harmonization of the different rules of the international legal system.

2. An evolutionary interpretation of Article 103

A new reading of the collective security system must also entail a new look at Article 103 which should not be applied automatically by courts with no or little enquiry into the need to do so in particular situations. Unlike Article 20 of the League Covenant which called for the abrogation of existing inconsistent obligations, Article 103 is not so much a hierarchical rule reflecting the *jus cogens* character of the Charter as a conflict rule—the Vienna Convention on the Law of Treaties mentions Article 103 under its provisions relating to successive treaties not validity of treaties. Its wording reflected the fear of some delegations at the time of the framing of the Charter that Article 103 might have been construed as putting into question the validity of existing treaties. While there is no doubt—and this is confirmed by the practice—that it was intended to cover the derivative or secondary obligations of the member states, including Security Council decisions, recent attempts to widen its scope to include customary law is erroneous.[75] While the

[73] See European Court of First Instance, Case T 306/01, *Ahmed Ali Yusuf and Al Barakaat International Foundation v Council and Commission*, available at http://eur-lex.europa.eu/LexUriServ/LexUriServ.do?uri=CELEX:62001A0306:EN:HTML (last accessed 1 March 2011); Case T 315/01, *Yassin Abdullah Kadi v Council and Commission*, 21 September 2005; UK Court of Appeal, Appeal no 2005/2251, *Hilal Abdul-Razzaq Ali Al-Jedda v The Secretary of State for Defence* (2005). These cases are discussed in the contributions of A Ciampi and E de Wet to the present volume.

[74] Court of Justice of the European Communities, Joined Cases C-402P and C-415/05P, *Yassin Abdullah Kadi and Al Barakaat International Foundation v Council of the European Union and Commission of the European Communities*, 3 September 2008.

[75] The current wording which refers to 'any other international agreement' was deliberately substituted for the much more comprehensive wording of the original draft of Art 103 proposed by the Advisory Committee of Jurists: 'any other international obligations to which they are subject' (see, eg, UNCIO, Summary report of 41st meeting of the coordination committee, 13 September 1945). Moreover, the ICJ has referred to Art 103 only in relation to treaties (see, eg, *Nicaragua*, ICJ Reports (1984) 440). The meaning of 'agreement' is also clear.

Security Council can derogate from customary international law as with the operation of any normal treaty, such derogation must be express.

The purpose of Article 103 was to ensure the effectiveness of the implementation of Charter obligations and could also be used to exonerate states from responsibility under particular treaties in very particular circumstances. It reflected in part the concern at San Francisco that in view of the fact that new 'derivative' obligations might be created by Security Council decisions, treaties which were not intrinsically inconsistent with Charter obligations, such as a trade treaty, could become so in the event of a Security Council decision under Article 41. Security Council practice has revealed that this indeed is the context in which Article 103 has been referred to either expressly or by implication, eg suspension of the Chicago Convention for the purpose of severance of air communications, or explicit calls to member states to apply the sanctions notwithstanding any existing contract or international agreement.[76] For so long as the measures of the Security Council were temporary and reversible, the suspension of conflicting treaty obligations made sense, although in the *Lockerbie* case it raised other issues relating to Security Council intervention in judicial proceedings.[77] But Article 103 has to be read in the light of the evolving law of the international community; in this context one can question the application of Article 103 in situations where measures adopted by the Security Council such as blacklisting may result in indefinite suspension of individual rights. It is a very serious matter when a decision instigated by one or two permanent members of the Security Council can effectively suspend the application of international and regional human rights law.

3. *A teleological reading of Security Council resolutions*

It has been stated that:

> a conflict exists if it is possible for a party to two treaties to comply with one rule only by thereby failing to comply with another rule which has a very different objective. But any decision will involve interpretation and choice between alternative rule-formulations and meanings...

For such conflicts must be placed within the confines of a general 'system' of international law and they must be context-specific. 'A weighing of different considerations must take place... which must seek reference from... the systemic objectives of the law'. That choice should depend on 'what would be a reasonable way to apply [the rules] with minimal disturbance to the operation of the legal system'.[78]

[76] See, eg, SC Res 670 (1990) on Iraq, Note by the President of the Security Council of 10 February 1993, S/25270, and SC Res 841 (1993) on Haiti.

[77] See Gowlland-Debbas, 'The Relationship between the International Court of Justice and the Security Council in the Light of the *Lockerbie* Case' (1994) 88 AJIL 643–77.

[78] International Law Commission, Report of the Study Group, finalised by Martti Koskenniemi, A/CN.4/L.682, 13 April 2006, paras 24–5.

A teleological reading of Security Council resolutions would have to act on a presumption that the Security Council intended something not inconsistent with generally recognized principles of international law. The question must be asked: has the Security Council expressed a 'manifest intent' to override human rights treaty obligations. This is all the more so in view of the limits placed by the Purposes and Principles of the UN Charter (see Article 24(1)) on the Security Council, the human rights provisions of which have been given effect by these treaties, the Universal Declaration of Human Rights acting as the springboard.[79]

Moreover, the entrenchment of human rights in the public policy of the international community on a par with security, and the fact that human rights in the Council's practice can now be considered to be part of the security fabric, means that the tension between human rights and collective security may perhaps be only apparent.

As concerns the listing process, the emphasis given by the United Nations in its projects on an international 'rule of law', a term which has as yet to be determined, means that at least two unarguable aspects, separate but interrelated, must be respected by the Security Council in its resolutions relating to individuals: that the law must conform to certain standards of justice, including that of due process, and that there can be no power without accountability.

The General Assembly established from the start an administrative tribunal offering due process to members of its staff; other international organizations, most notably the World Bank in establishing an Inspection Panel, have also begun to read their mandates in the light of human rights and environmental standards. The Security Council can no longer remain outside such a process where it concerns the treatment of individuals suspected of terrorist or other criminal activities. The Security Council itself has ensured that the Statutes for its two international tribunals embed due process rights for individuals accused of international crimes. The 2006 amended guidelines within the Sanctions Committee for review of particular listings, the establishment of a Focal Point for De-listing based on Resolution 1730 (2006) within the UN secretariat, the appointment of an ombudsperson (SC Resolution 1904 (2009)) to participate in the de-listing procedures in connection with the Consolidated List established by SC Resolution 1333 (2000), and the possibility for states to take up the diplomatic protection of their nationals, while constituting improvements, and an acknowledgement of the need to ensure a modicum of 'fair and clear procedures', take the shape of diplomatic/political processes which cannot offer a substitute for proper judicial remedies.[80]

[79] In its 1948 Advisory Opinion on *Reservations to the Genocide Convention*, the ICJ maintained that because the Genocide Convention had been adopted (and signed) within the General Assembly, the Organization continued to have a 'legal interest' in the protection of the treaty in parallel with that of member states (*Reservations to the Genocide Convention*, Advisory Opinion, ICJ Reports (1951) 19).

[80] See the diplomatic efforts undertaken by Switzerland and Germany and *Strengthening Targeted Sanctions through Fair and Clear Procedures*, White Paper prepared by the Watson Institute Targeted Sanctions Project, Brown University, 30 March 2006. See also Fassbender, 'Study commissioned by the United Nations Office of Legal Affairs', 20 March 2006. See also Fassbender, 'Targeted Sanctions Imposed by the UN Security Council and Due Process Rights: A Study Commissioned by the UN Office of Legal Affairs and Follow-up Action by the United Nations' (2006) 3 International Organizations Law Review 437.

B. The effects of Security Council decisions on domestic law

1. *Implementation of Security Council decisions in domestic law*

It is clear that under international law a state could not invoke its domestic law as exempting it from the obligation to execute a decision of the Security Council which is mandatory under Article 25 of the Charter. However, the mechanisms by which states incorporate international law into their domestic system are largely left by international law to be regulated by municipal law. The quasi-constitutional nature of Security Council resolutions adopted in purported fulfilment of community objectives, contrasts with the place and formal ranking given to these resolutions in domestic law. Even the more recent national constitutions do not single out the decisions of the Security Council. Security Council mandatory resolutions are assimilated to non-self-executing conventional obligations and are therefore not treated in a manner distinct from other treaty obligations, which means that they may be superseded by domestic constitutions, and even in some cases, other conventional obligations where these are accorded constitutional ranking, in particular, treaties protecting fundamental human rights.

2. *Human rights issues*

But herein lies the paradox. The formal ranking in domestic law of Security Council resolutions, in turn, does not reflect the increasing intrusion of UN Security Council decisions into the domestic sphere. Moreover, the perception of Council resolutions as part of international public policy is increasingly reflected in domestic courts, especially those relating to the International Criminal Tribunals and in the context of counterterrorism.

Implementing Security Council resolutions in domestic law may therefore raise important constitutional problems, where there are conflicts between Security Council resolutions and constitutionally protected individual rights. Sanctions resolutions have required control of the activities of private parties, since they are to be applied 'notwithstanding any contract entered into or any licence granted before the date of the resolution', and even extraterritorially, which may be at variance with the constitutional or general legal order of the state concerned. Moreover, state practice indicates that, with few exceptions, individuals are not compensated for contractual losses at the domestic level.

The establishment of the two International Criminal Tribunals has, understandably, also raised constitutional problems, imposing specific obligations on member states in the field of cooperation and judicial assistance,[81] such as the production of evidence, the arrest or detention of persons and their surrender or transfer to the International Tribunals, and the recognition of judgments passed by the Tribunals, thus affecting individual liberties. This has required in some cases, adaptation of

[81] See SC Res 827 (1993), Art 4, and SC Res 955 (1994), Art 2 and Arts 29 and 28 of the Statutes of the ICTY and ICTR, respectively.

extradition law and criminal procedures, even though states have avoided constitutional problems, in particular in regard to nationals, by treating the handing over of individuals to the Tribunals as 'surrender' rather than extradition.

At the same time there has been refusal by domestic courts to control the legality of national measures which has been justified, in part, on the basis of the primacy of the UN Charter. In a decision of the District Court of the Hague of 31 August 2001 in the case of *Milošević*, rejecting a request that Milošević be released unconditionally on the grounds that the Netherlands was acting unlawfully in cooperating with the ICTY,[82] it was ruled that under the Headquarters Agreement the Netherlands had lawfully transferred its jurisdiction over the ICTY's indictees to that Tribunal, that the Statute of the ICTY gave it primacy over national courts and that UN Charter obligations prevailed over the obligations of member states.[83]

Thus implementation of Security Council resolutions shows that the relationship between the two orders of domestic and international law is dependent not only on their systemic relations but in part also, on the degree of development of international law and public policy.

6. Concluding Reflections

The collective security system has markedly evolved and from a systemic perspective, the Security Council, though a highly political organ, may now be seen as exercising certain functions of law enforcement and even purporting to act as a world 'legislature' far from the kinds of functions it was originally intended to exercise. This is a very interesting illustration of the conversion of politics into law, for a legal construction can be made out of what are in fact political and discretionary, or random exercises of police powers.

In its practice, the Council has arraigned on itself also a human rights protection function. Its resolutions have sought to qualify violations of international human rights, criminal law, and humanitarian law, invoking directly or indirectly the responsibility of states and individuals, by considering that such egregious violations constituted a threat to international peace and security. Rather than seeing a tension between human rights and maintenance of public order, human rights thus now forms a component part of the security fabric.

The paradox lies in that effective implementation of Security Council decisions has challenged in turn fundamental principles of human rights law, for its decisions

[82] *Slobodan Milošević v The State of the Netherlands* (Judgment in interlocutory injunction), 31 August 2001, President of the Hague District Court, Kort Geding 2001/258 (2001) 688.

[83] The Dutch Court also relied on *Nalitelic v Croatia* (Application No 51891/99 (Decision as to Admissibility), ECtHR, 4 May 2000) to argue that the ICTY offered sufficient procedural guarantees. See also *In the Matter of Surrender of Elizaphan Ntakirutimana*, US District Court, Southern District of Texas, No L-96-5, 17 December 1997. In the subsequent case of Milošević against the Netherlands, the ECtHR declared inadmissible the complaint brought by Milošević under several provisions of the ECtHR Statute, precisely for failure to exhaust local remedies even though it was plain that there were none that were adequate and effective. See *Slobodan Milošević v. the Netherlands* (Application No. 77631/01 (Judgment), ECtHR, 19 March 2002).

are perceived as both modifying states' human rights obligations under international law, as well as in certain cases purporting to override them. The answer does not lie solely in whether the Security Council is bound by human rights law, for challenges to Security Council resolutions have in reality been addressed to the states parties of human rights treaties. It is their responsibility under those treaties which is particularly at stake.

Finally, a fresh reading of the collective security provision in Article 1(1) of the Charter is required in the light of such concepts as human security and in view of the recent linkages between collective security and principles of justice and international law (originally only associated with peaceful settlement of disputes), as well as a careful re-thinking of the purpose of Article 103 in a very changed environment.

4

The Role for Human Rights in the Decision-making Process of the Security Council

Bardo Fassbender

'Today', Joanna Weschler wrote in 2004, 'nobody any longer seriously questions the relevance of human rights to the [Security] Council's work and the need for human rights information and analysis at every stage of the Council's action.'[1] In principle, everybody will agree with that finding. But, as happens so often, the devil is in the details. Looking at the role of human rights in the work of the Security Council of the United Nations, two sets of issues can be distinguished—'outcome-oriented' and 'procedure-oriented' issues. The first set addresses the protection and promotion of human rights as a direct goal of Security Council action. Human rights are dealt with because the Security Council conceives of them as threats to international peace and security in the meaning of the UN Charter. These human rights issues are the subject of the 'human rights agenda' of the Council in the narrow sense of the notion. Most of the literature devoted to the subject 'human rights and the Security Council' deals with this 'substantive' human rights work of the Council.[2] In contrast, the second set of issues, the 'procedure-oriented' issues, addresses questions of safeguarding human rights in the course of action directed towards other goals, that is mainly 'classical' goals of maintaining and restoring international (inter-state) peace. Here, human rights issues arise while the Council is doing (or abstaining from doing) 'something else', for instance imposing economic sanctions on a state or individuals, or authorizing the use of force against a state.

The present chapter deals with the 'procedure-oriented' aspects of human rights so understood. As literature on that subject so far is largely absent, it tries to identify a number of pertinent issues, and to build a frame of reference, making it possible to analyse how the Security Council takes into account, and is mindful of, human

[1] See Weschler, 'Human Rights', in DM Malone (ed), *The UN Security Council: From the Cold War to the 21st Century* (2004) 55.

[2] For analysis, see ibid, and the contributions of V Gowlland-Debbas and D Shraga to the present volume. The earlier work of the Council is discussed by SD Bailey in his pioneering book *The UN Security Council and Human Rights* (1994). See also Bailey, 'The Security Council', in P Alston (ed), *The United Nations and Human Rights: A Critical Appraisal* (1992) 304–36.

rights issues which 'incidentally' come up in its work. In particular, the chapter evaluates how human rights considerations and concerns can be better integrated in the decision-making processes of the Security Council.

The distinction between 'outcome-oriented' and 'procedure-oriented' aspects of human rights in the work of the Security Council is not identical with that between 'substantive human rights' (for instance the right to life, the right to liberty of person, freedom of expression, or the right of peoples to self-determination) and 'procedural human rights' (like the right to a fair and public hearing by an independent and impartial tribunal in the determination of rights and obligations, or the right to an effective remedy for acts violating fundamental rights). Both categories of rights can play a role when the Council directly intervenes in cases of violations of human rights, and also when human rights are affected by other action taken by the Council under Chapters VI and VII of the UN Charter.

In the first part of this chapter, I shall discuss the idea of an 'international rule of law' as a recent concept expressing, inter alia, certain expectations regarding the place of human rights in the work of the Security Council. The second part addresses the foundation and the extent of the human rights obligations of the Security Council in the present international legal order. In the third part, I shall describe the decision-making process of the Council with a view to the problems of transparency and legitimacy posed by that process. In the fourth part of the chapter, an effort is made to identify types of Security Council action (apart from action meant directly to promote and protect human rights) in which the problem of safeguarding human rights is acute. In the fifth part, I shall explore different options for enhancing the role for human rights in the decision-making process of the Security Council, namely an amendment of the UN Charter or the Rules of Procedure of the Security Council, a self-commitment of the Security Council by way of a resolution or a presidential statement, and institutionalized cooperation with other UN bodies, in particular the Human Rights Council and the High Commissioner for Human Rights.

1. The Security Council and the International Rule of Law

The raised expectations about the human rights performance of the Security Council which arose as a result of the criticism levelled against the sanctions practice of the Council of the 1990s, especially in the case of Iraq,[3] found a concise expression in the notion of 'the international rule of law'. That concept, it is true, is much wider than the idea that the Security Council, when performing its functions under the UN Charter, should observe and respect the rules of international law and, in particular, international human rights law. As a guiding idea or principle, the 'international rule of law' refers to every form of exercise of international authority by every international institution. It is not limited to the work of the United Nations or, more specifically, certain of its organs. However, because of

[3] See Fassbender, 'Uncertain Steps into a Post-Cold War World: The Role and Functioning of the UN Security Council after a Decade of Measures against Iraq' (2002) 13 EJIL 273 at 282 *et seq.*

the prominent role of the Security Council and the attention which its sanctions regimes attracted in the post-Cold War world, the concept appeared to be especially pertinent to the discussion about what many saw as a 'Council Unbound'.[4]

In its 2005 World Summit Outcome, the General Assembly endorsed the concept of an 'international rule of law' by 'recognizing the need for universal adherence to and implementation of the rule of law at both the national and international levels' and by reaffirming a 'commitment to the purposes and principles of the Charter and international law and to *an international order based on the rule of law* and international law, which is essential for peaceful coexistence and cooperation among States'.[5] However, the resolution did not spell out any specific consequences of that commitment for the work of the organs of the United Nations.[6]

In legal and political science literature it was tried to give the notion of an international rule of law a more concrete meaning. Having analysed how the idea of the rule of law evolved at the national level, in particular in the context of Anglo-American law on the one hand and continental European law on the other hand, Professor Simon Chesterman suggested the following 'core definition of the rule of law' with three elements summarized as 'government of laws', 'supremacy of the law', and 'equality before the law':

> First, the power of the State may not be exercised arbitrarily. This incorporates the rejection of 'rule of man', but does not require that State power be exercised for any particular purpose. It does, however, require that laws be prospective, accessible, and clear.
>
> Secondly, the law must apply also to the sovereign and instruments of the State, with an independent institution such as a judiciary to apply the law to specific cases. This implies a distinction from 'rule by law'.
>
> Thirdly, the law must apply to all persons equally, offering equal protection without prejudicial discrimination. The law should be of general application and consistent implementation; it should be capable of being obeyed. This presumes that the rule of law is more than simply 'law in the books' and that these principles also apply to 'law in action'.[7]

In a report submitted to the Security Council in 2004, the UN Secretary General propounded a similar definition, enriching it, however, with a number of additional elements, such as accountability, fairness, and participation in decision-making:

> The 'rule of law' is a concept at the very heart of the Organization's mission. It refers to a principle of governance in which all persons, institutions and entities, public and private, including the State itself, are accountable to laws that are publicly promulgated, equally enforced and independently adjudicated, and which are consistent with international human rights norms and standards. It requires, as well, measures to ensure adherence to

[4] See, eg, MJ Matheson, *Council Unbound: The Growth of UN Decision Making on Conflict and Postconflict Issues after the Cold War* (2006).

[5] GA Res 60/1, 16 September 2005, preamble, para 134 (emphasis added).

[6] But see text accompanying n 68 below.

[7] Chesterman, 'An International Rule of Law?' (2008) 56 *American Journal of Comparative Law* 331, 342 (footnote omitted). See also *The UN Security Council and the Rule of Law. The Role of the Security Council in Strengthening a Rules-based International System: Final Report and Recommendations from the Austrian Initiative, 2004–2008* (2008), distributed as UN Doc. A/63/69–S/2008/270.

the principles of supremacy of law, equality before the law, accountability to the law, fairness in the application of the law, separation of powers, participation in decision-making, legal certainty, avoidance of arbitrariness and procedural and legal transparency.[8]

Interestingly, the notion of 'rule of law' also already appears in the Universal Declaration of Human Rights. In the third paragraph of the preamble, it is mentioned in the context of the right to resistance: 'Whereas it is essential, if man is not to be compelled to have recourse, as a last resort, to rebellion against tyranny and oppression, that human rights should be protected by the rule of law'. In that phrase, the protection of human rights and fundamental freedoms, first and foremost on a national level, is understood as an element of a broader 'rule of law'.

It is the primary idea of the Universal Declaration that the primary national responsibility for the protection of human rights shall be supplemented and strengthened by an international responsibility as a sort of back-up responsibility. Similarly, the rule of law has a national and an international dimension which are interlinked. In the words of a memorandum submitted by Mexico and Liechtenstein in 2006, by which they requested the inclusion in the agenda of the General Assembly of an item entitled 'The rule of law at the national and international levels':

> The international legal order serves not only as a framework for peaceful relations and source of rights and obligations for States and other actors, but also as a source of inspiration for the development of national legal standards, in particular in the field of human rights. The strengthening of the rule of law at the international level thus has a direct impact on the rule of law at the national level.[9]

In a resolution adopted in 2007, the General Assembly reaffirmed 'its solemn commitment to an international order based on the rule of law and international law, which, together with the principles of justice, is essential for peaceful coexistence and cooperation among States'. To the two related notions of human rights and the rule of law, the General Assembly added democracy as a third notion by declaring that 'human rights, the rule of law and democracy are interlinked and mutually reinforcing and that they belong to the universal and indivisible core values and principles of the United Nations'. The Assembly also reaffirmed 'the duty of all States to refrain in their international relations from the threat or use of force in any manner inconsistent with the purposes and principles of the United Nations and to settle their international disputes by peaceful means'.[10]

Further shifting the focus of attention from the rule of law at the national level and activities of the United Nations directed at advancing the domestic effectiveness of the concept, the General Assembly, in a resolution of 2008, called upon 'the

[8] *The rule of law and transitional justice in conflict and post-conflict societies*, Report of the Secretary General, UN Doc S/2004/616, 23 August 2004, para 6.

[9] Letter dated 11 May 2006 from the Permanent Representatives of Liechtenstein and Mexico to the United Nations addressed to the Secretary-General, UN Doc A/61/142, Annex, para 2.

[10] *The rule of law at the national and international levels*, GA Res 62/70, 6 December 2007, preamble, paras 3, 4, and 6.

United Nations system to systematically address, as appropriate, aspects of the rule of law in relevant activities, recognizing the importance of the rule of law to virtually all areas of United Nations engagement'.[11] While that statement remained rather vague, the Secretary General used a more direct language when, in a report submitted in 2008, he said:

> The Organization has little credibility if it fails to apply the rule of law to itself. The United Nations is a creation of international law, established by treaty, and its activities are governed by the rules set out in its Charter. Appropriate rules of international law apply mutatis mutandis to the Organization as they do to States.[12]

In 2006 and 2010, the Security Council held open debates on '[s]trengthening international law: rule of law and maintenance of international peace and security'[13] and '[t]he promotion and strengthening of the rule of law in the maintenance of international peace and security',[14] respectively. Following the language of the General Assembly, the Council reaffirmed in 2010 'its commitment to the Charter of the United Nations and international law, and to an international order based on the rule of law and international law, which is essential for peaceful coexistence and cooperation among States in addressing common challenges, thus contributing to the maintenance of international peace and security'.[15]

The Presidential Statement of 2010 demonstrates that by now the Council has fully integrated the notion of the rule of law in its standard vocabulary, combining it easily with long-established notions and phrases. However, it is not so clear what exactly the new references to the rule of law add to what the Council has repeated many times. The Council reiterates, for instance, its commitment to the peaceful settlement of disputes, and urges states to respect the norms of international humanitarian law. It repeats its opposition to impunity for serious violations of international humanitarian law and human rights law. Surely all these issues can be brought under the caption of the rule of law. But by doing so the Council advances yet another argument for generally recognized causes rather than accepting the concept as a standard for its own decisions. Very cautiously, the Council only 'expresse[d] its commitment to ensure that all UN efforts to restore peace and security themselves respect and promote the rule of law'.[16] In the open debate of 2010, the Permanent Representative of Liechtenstein rightly criticized this overly cautious approach. He also addressed the arguments presented in favour of that approach:

[11] *The rule of law at the national and international levels,* GA Res 63/128, 11 December 2008, para 4. See also GA Res 64/116, 16 December 2009, para 4.

[12] *Strengthening and coordinating United Nations rule of law activities.* Report of the Secretary General, UN Doc A/63/226, 6 August 2008, para 27.

[13] See UNSC Verbatim Record, 22 June 2006, UN Doc S/PV.5474, and the Statement by the President of the Security Council, UN Doc S/PRST/2006/28, 22 June 2006.

[14] See UNSC Verbatim Record, 29 June 2010, UN Doc S/PV.6347 and S/PV.6457 (Resumption 1).

[15] Statement by the President of the Security Council, UN Doc S/PRST/2010/11, 29 June 2010, para 1.

[16] Ibid para 9.

We remain convinced that the best way for the Security Council to promote international law and the rule of law is to lead by example. We challenge the view—and, to some extent, the conventional wisdom—that regards the Council as a purely political body. Its authority is based on the world's supreme international treaty, the United Nations Charter. The Council is legally bound by the applicable rules of the Charter and of international law. Those rules leave the Council much room to take decisions based on political, legal and other considerations—but that room is not without limits. It is both a legal necessity and a wise policy choice for the Council to respect and promote international law and the rule of law.[17]

Ambassador Wenaweser reminded the Council that it must 'remain vigilant in ensuring that its work remains within the legal bounds and spirit of its constitution, that is, the Charter'.[18]

2. Human Rights Obligations of the Security Council

Today, public opinion takes it for granted that the Security Council is 'bound by human rights', and no government of a UN member state will argue against that view as a matter of principle.[19] It appears to be a counterintuitive proposition to say that a principal organ of an organization which has made the promotion of human rights one of its major goals itself is free to disregard human rights. However, when the UN Charter was drafted, human rights were at the international level still moral postulates and political principles only. Given the state of development of international human rights in 1945, it would have been difficult for the founders of the United Nations to make, through respective Charter provisions, human rights directly binding on the Organization as a whole or particular organs. But in any case the founding states did not find it necessary to establish such obligations. As mentioned above, they apparently never entertained the thought that action taken by the United Nations could violate the human rights of individuals.

When, much later, the two international covenants on human rights were adopted in 1966, the United Nations was not included as a party. The covenants—as well as all other human rights treaties created under the auspices of the UN—were drafted only with a view to the performance of states, not of international organizations. For instance, in Article 2(1) of the International Covenant on Civil and Political Rights (ICCPR) it is stated that '[e]ach State Party to the present Covenant undertakes to respect and to ensure to all individuals within its territory and subject to its jurisdiction the rights recognized in the present Covenant'. Even today the United Nations could not become a party to the treaties and conventions in question because they are only open to accession by states (see, eg, Article 48 ICCPR).

[17] UNSC Verbatim Record (provisional), 29 June 2010, UN Doc S/PV.6347 (Resumption 1) 6.
[18] Ibid 7.
[19] This section draws on Fassbender, 'Sources of Human Rights Obligations Binding the UN Security Council', in PHF Bekker, R Dolzer, and M Waibel (eds), *Making Transnational Law Work in the Global Economy: Essays in Honour of Detlev Vagts* (2010) 71.

It does not follow from the fact alone that UN member states, or even an overwhelming majority of member states, ratified certain human rights instruments that an according obligation of the Organization has come into existence.[20] The concept of international person, or subjects of international law, is based on a distinction between particular subjects and their particular rights, duties, or powers.[21] As the International Court of Justice (ICJ) held, '[t]he subjects of law in any legal system are not necessarily identical in their nature or in the extent of their rights, and their nature depends upon the needs of the community'.[22] Accordingly, the rights and duties of intergovernmental organizations, as autonomous subjects of international law, on the one hand, and of their member states, on the other hand, must be distinguished.[23] However, this traditional picture has been modified by a development in the law of the European Community/European Union. The EC (EU) has recognized both human rights treaty obligations of member states as well as 'constitutional traditions common to the Member States' as sources of Community law from which direct obligations of the EC (EU) itself arise.[24] By analogy, there is an increasingly broader basis for referring to the constitutional traditions and values common to the member states of the United Nations, which include commitments to fundamental rights and freedoms, as a source of UN law.[25]

As regards customary international law and general principles of law as possible sources of human rights obligations of the UN and the Security Council, there is today broad agreement among governments and international lawyers that many of the rules enunciated in the Universal Declaration of Human Rights have crystallized as customary international law—in particular the right to life, the prohibition of torture (as the reverse side of a right to physical integrity), the protection of personal freedom, and the prohibition of discrimination on racial grounds.[26]

It has been argued that the respective customary obligations are also binding on international organizations, as subjects of international law, to the extent that the organizations engage in activities which are likely to affect the mentioned rights of individuals.[27] However, as was mentioned before, international human rights law

[20] But see Reinisch, 'Securing the Accountability of International Organizations' (2001) 7 *Global Governance* 131–49, 137 *et seq* and 141–3, arguing that the UN is bound 'transitively' by international human rights standards as a result and to that extent that its members are bound ('functional treaty succession by international organizations to the position of their member states').

[21] See R Jennings and A Watts (eds), *Oppenheim's International Law* (1992, 9th edn), vol I, pt 1, 119 *et seq*; HG Schermers and NM Blokker, *International Institutional Law* (1995, 3rd edn) 976 *et seq*.

[22] *Reparation for Injuries Suffered in the Service of the United Nations (Advisory Opinion)*, ICJ Reports (1949) 178.

[23] See, in general, Blokker, 'International Organizations and Their Members' (2004) 1 *International Organizations Law Review* 139, 152 *et seq*.

[24] See Art 6(3) of the Treaty on European Union of 7 February 1992, as amended by the Treaty of Lisbon of 13 December 2007; Official Journal of the EU C 83, 30 March 2010.

[25] For discussion, see Fassbender (n 19 above) 75 *et seq*.

[26] See C Tomuschat, *Human Rights: Between Idealism and Realism* (2008, 2nd edn) 37–8, with further references.

[27] See Reinisch, 'Governance Without Accountability?' (2001) 44 *German Yearbook of International Law* 270, 281 *et seq*.

was primarily designed to protect human beings against their own state. In general, it was not considered necessary to secure protection against acts of 'governmental' power with a direct impact on individuals issued by organs of international organizations, as there virtually were not any such acts. Accordingly, there was little room for a development of rules of customary international law about the obligation of international organizations to comply with particular human rights standards.

To the extent that certain human rights standards are concurrently recognized in the domestic (constitutional) law of a great number of states of all regions of the world, they have become rules of international law in the form of general principles of law in the meaning of Article 38(1)(c) of the ICJ Statute. Although the standards in question describe obligations of governments vis-à-vis their citizens (and foreigners under their jurisdiction) in the sphere of domestic law, the general principles of international law which have arisen on the basis of those widely recognized standards are also applicable to international organizations as subjects of international law when those organizations exercise 'governmental' authority over individuals.[28]

To return to the general intuition speaking in favour of human rights obligations of the UN, it may be said that the development of international human rights law since 1945, to which the work of the United Nations has decisively contributed, has given grounds for legitimate expectations that the UN itself, when its action has a direct impact on the rights and freedoms of an individual, will observe human rights and fundamental freedoms.[29] As Judge Simma remarked, 'wherever the future of its human rights work may lead to, the further realization of the promise of the United Nations Charter to promote and encourage respect for human rights for all will be one of the decisive tests of the legitimacy of the world organization'.[30] The United Nations would contradict itself if, on the one hand, it constantly admonished its member states to respect human rights and, on the other hand, it refused to respect the same rights when relevant to its own action.

Notwithstanding the growing legal importance, for the United Nations, of human rights treaty law on the one hand and constitutional values and traditions common to UN member states on the other hand, the principal source of human rights obligations of the United Nations is the UN Charter as the constitution of the United Nations.[31] The same conclusion was already arrived at by Sir Hersch Lauterpacht when he wrote as early as in 1950: 'The provisions of the Charter on the subject [of human rights] impose legal obligations not only upon the Members of the United Nations. They imply a comprehensive legal obligation

[28] See D Sarooshi, *International Organizations and Their Exercise of Sovereign Powers* (2005) 16. For the applicability of general principles of law in the law of international organizations, see generally Schermers and Blokker (n 21 above) 984 *et seq.*

[29] See also Reinisch, 'Developing Human Rights and Humanitarian Law Accountability of the Security Council for the Imposition of Economic Sanctions' (2001) 95 *American Journal of International Law* 851, 869.

[30] See Simma, 'Human Rights', in C Tomuschat (ed), *The United Nations at Age Fifty: A Legal Perspective* (1995) 263 at 280.

[31] For a summary of my work describing the UN Charter as a constitution, see B Fassbender, *The United Nations Charter as the Constitution of the International Community* (2009).

upon the United Nations as a whole.'[32] The degree of legal obligation, Sir Hersch Lauterpacht wrote, is particularly high with regard to a subject matter which is a constant and fundamental theme of the Charter.[33] The United Nations is an organization based on the concept of the rule of law. The organs of the UN are bound to comply with the rules of the UN Charter, which has a dual constitutional function—it is both the constitution of the United Nations as an organization and the constitution of the international community 'as a whole'.[34]

In consequence of two developments—the coming into existence of a firmly recognized body of human rights in international law, promoted by the UN, and the expansion of functions of the UN into new areas resulting in acts with a direct impact on the rights of individuals—the references of the UN Charter to human rights have developed into rules embodying direct human rights obligations of the organs of the United Nations. Today, the Charter obliges the organs of the United Nations, when exercising the functions assigned to them, to respect human rights and fundamental freedoms of individuals to the greatest possible extent.[35] The United Nations cannot attain its purpose of achieving 'international co-operation . . . in promoting and encouraging respect for human rights and fundamental freedoms for all' (Article 1(3) of the UN Charter) if it disregards these rights and freedoms when exercising jurisdiction over individuals. This author agrees with Professor I Brownlie who said:

> Even if the political organs [of the UN] have a wide margin of appreciation in determining that they have competence by virtue of Chapter VI or Chapter VII, and further, in making dispositions to maintain or restore international peace and security, it does not follow that the selection of the modalities of implementation is unconstrained by legality. *Indeed when the rights of individuals are involved, the application of human rights standards is a legal necessity.* Human rights now form part of the concept of the international public order.[36]

In the absence of a specification of such rights and freedoms in the Charter itself, the Universal Declaration of Human Rights and the ICCPR serve, first and foremost, as relevant standards. Both instruments may well be counted among the 'constitutional by-laws' of the international community[37] because they complement, and implement objectives of, the UN Charter.

In the practice of the UN, human rights obligations have been expressly recognized by the Organization in two important areas. With regard to UN peacekeeping operations, the UN Secretary General in 1999 promulgated 'fundamental principles and rules of international humanitarian law applicable to United

[32] H Lauterpacht, *International Law and Human Rights* (1950) 159. See also ibid 221 and Thallinger, 'Sense and Sensibility of the Human Rights Obligations of the United Nations Security Council' (2007) 67 *Zeitschrift für öffentliches Recht und Völkerrecht* 1015, 1023 *et seq.*

[33] Lauterpacht, ibid 159.

[34] See Fassbender (n 31 above) 116.

[35] For a discussion of this topic, with special emphasis on the Security Council, see Reinisch (n 29 above) 853 *et seq.*

[36] Brownlie, 'The Decisions of Political Organs of the United Nations and the Rule of Law', in R St J Macdonald (ed), *Essays in Honour of Wang Tieya* (1993) 91 at 102 (emphasis added).

[37] For an explanation of this notion, see Fassbender (n 31 above) 122 *et seq.*

Nations forces conducting operations under United Nations command and control'.[38] In East Timor and Kosovo, respectively, the UN Transitional Administration in East Timor (UNTAET) and the UN Interim Administration in Kosovo (UNMIK) proclaimed the 'applicability' of human rights standards by stipulating that 'in exercising their functions, all persons undertaking public duties or holding public office [in the respective territories] shall observe internationally recognized human rights standards'.[39]

3. The Decision-making Process of the Security Council: Problems of Transparency and Legitimacy

It is not possible to evaluate the place of human rights in the decision-making process of the Security Council without looking more closely at that process itself. What do we mean by 'decision-making process'? In a narrow sense, the term denotes the procedure of the Council leading to one of the decisions provided for in the UN Charter, especially decisions of a 'binding nature' under Chapter VII of the Charter. More broadly understood, the term means all official deliberations of the Council which pursue a purpose within the mandate of the Security Council. An even broader use of the term would also include the informal discussions of the Council.

Where do we find information about the Council's decision-making? For the official meetings of the Council, we can turn to the Provisional Rules of Procedure adopted by the Security Council in its first meeting in 1946 and amended a few times since.[40] The Provisional Rules deal with issues like how meetings are called, how the agenda for a meeting is drawn up and adopted, in which way the presidency of the Council is held in turn by the members, or what languages

[38] See 'Observance by United Nations forces of international humanitarian law', Secretary General's Bulletin, UN Doc ST/SGB/1999/13, 6 August 1999, reprinted in (1999) 38 *International Legal Materials* 1656. Cf Shraga, 'UN Peacekeeping Operations: Applicability of International Humanitarian Law and Responsibility for Operations-Related Damage' (2000) 94 *American Journal of International Law* 406; K Wellens, *Remedies against International Organisations* (2002) 162–6; and Thallinger (n 32 above) 1024–6. For an overview of the previous debate concerning the applicability of international humanitarian law to UN operations, see Shraga, 'The United Nations as an Actor Bound by International Humanitarian Law', in L Condorelli, A-M La Rosa, and S Scherrer (eds), *Les Nations Unies et le droit international humanitaire—The United Nations and International Humanitarian Law* (1996) 317.

[39] See UNTAET, Reg No 1999/1, 'On the Authority of the Transitional Administration in East Timor', Doc UNTAET/REG/1999/1, 27 November 1999; UNMIK, Reg No 1999/1, 'On the Authority of the Interim Administration in Kosovo', Doc UNMIK/REG/1999/1, 25 July 1999. Cf Mégret and Hoffmann, 'The UN as a Human Rights Violator? Some Reflections on the United Nations Changing Human Rights Responsibilities' (2003) 25 *Human Rights Quarterly* 314, 333 *et seq.* For analysis of a particular human rights problem in UN-administered Kosovo, see Abraham, 'The Sins of the Savior: Holding the United Nations Accountable to International Human Rights Standards for Executive Order Detentions in its Mission in Kosovo' (2003) 52 *American University Law Review* 1291.

[40] The Rules as amended in 1982 were issued as UN Doc S/96/Rev.7. For text, see www.un.org/Docs/sc/scrules.htm (last accessed 1 March 2011]).

may be used in speeches before the Council. But all these rules, including those about the 'conduct of business' (Chapter VI of the Provisional Rules), only address formalities; there is nothing in the Rules about issues of substance. Those issues are exclusively being dealt with in the UN Charter. In addition, 'much of the practice of the Security Council is based on custom'.[41] This observation is in line with the finding that in the procedure of the Council 'informal and incremental change is more likely to be effective, and has been more effective, than change through the Rules of Procedure or the formal establishment of new machinery'.[42]

It was not long after the Security Council had overcome its Cold War paralysis, that Professor Michael Reisman observed that 'as the Council has become more effective and powerful, it has become more secretive'.[43]

> Like a parliamentary matryoshka (doll), it now contains ever-smaller 'mini-Councils', each meeting behind closed doors without keeping records, and each taking decisions secretly. Before the plenary Council meets in 'consultation'... the P-5 have met in 'consultation'... and before they meet, the P-3, composed of the United States, the United Kingdom and France, have met in 'consultation' in one of their missions in New York... After the fifteen members of the Council have consulted and reached their decisions, they adjourn to the Council's chamber, where they go through the formal motions of voting and announcing their decision. Decisions that appear to go further than at any time in the history of the United Nations are now ultimately being taken, it seems, by a small group of states separately meeting in secret.[44]

It must, however, be mentioned that it is not only the P-3 or P-5 who meet in private outside of formal Council meetings. For instance, there are meetings of the non-aligned members of the Council who belong to the Movement of Non-Aligned Countries (NAM). Another, less coherent group is that of the 'non-non-aligned', that is the non-permanent members of the Council not belonging to NAM. To mention another format, France and the United Kingdom are consulting with non-permanent members being member states of the European Union.[45]

Similar to Professor Reisman, the French Permanent Representative to the UN, Ambassador Mérimée, explained in 1994 that 'informal consultations have become the Council's characteristic working method, while public meetings, originally the norm, are increasingly rare and increasingly devoid of content'.[46] That way, the rule

[41] SD Bailey and S Daws, *The Procedure of the Security Council* (1998, 3rd edn) 17.

[42] MC Wood, 'Security Council Working Methods: Recent Developments' (1996) 45 *International and Comparative Law Quarterly* 150, 161.

[43] Reisman, 'The Constitutional Crisis in the United Nations' (1993) 87 *American Journal of International Law* 83, 85.

[44] Ibid 85 *et seq.*

[45] For an analysis of groups of states in the UN system and their development in the various phases of UN history, see Morphet, 'States Groups at the United Nations and Growth of Member States at the United Nations', in P Taylor and AJR Groom (eds), *The United Nations at the Millennium: The Principal Organs* (2000) 224 *et seq.* The role of the 'Groups of Friends of the Secretary-General' is analysed by Prantl and Krasno, 'Informal Groups of Member States', in JE Krasno (ed), *The United Nations: Confronting the Challenges of a Global Society* (2004) 311–57 at 335 *et seq.*

[46] See UNSC Verbatim Record, 16 December 1994, UN Doc S/PV.3483, at 2 (quoted in Wood (n 42 above) 155). See also Aust, 'The Role of Human Rights in Limiting the Enforcement Powers of the Security Council: A Practitioner's View', in E de Wet and A Nollkaemper (eds), *Review of the*

pronounced in the Rules of Procedure ('Unless it decides otherwise, the Security Council shall meet in public', Rule 48) has become the exception as far as the substantial discussions of the Council are concerned.

Informal 'consultations of the whole' are private meetings of all 15 Council members, presided over by the Council president. 'The main differences with Council meetings, public or private, are that no official records of consultations of the whole are kept, and that non-members of the Council cannot attend... Consultations of the whole are not "meetings" of the Council under the terms of the Charter or the Rules of Procedure.'[47] They are not held in the Council Chamber but in the 'Consultations Room', a special room near it.

But is the secretiveness of the Council such a bad thing? Behind the critique of the Council's working methods is the ideal of a political decision-making process as an open and transparent discussion in which every participant can put forward his or her point of view and arguments can be appraised by all participants. Obviously, this ideal situation of open and reasoned deliberation is inherently related to ('deliberative') democracy[48] as a form of government determined, inter alia, by the axiom of equality of all citizens. Carried over to the Security Council, this means that ideally every member state of the United Nations (or, beyond that, every 'stakeholder' affected by the decisions of the Council) shall be equally informed about the workings of the Council and shall have an equal voice in the discussions about issues on the agenda of the Council. It is true that, different from the General Assembly, the Security Council is a body of limited membership. But according to Article 24(1) of the UN Charter, the members of the United Nations 'confer on the Security Council primary responsibility for the maintenance of international peace and security, and agree that in carrying out its duties under this responsibility the Security Council acts on their behalf'. This system of delegated powers presupposes that the general membership is kept informed about the work carried out in its name by the Council (and not only the final results of that work) so that it can determine whether that work is really done in the interest of all members. In reality, the course of events and discussions resulting in a certain decision of the Council, made without discussion in a brief formal meeting, very often is unknown or unclear. The lack of transparency leads to a decrease in procedural legitimacy of the decisions made by the Council.

That the secretiveness of the Council poses a problem in terms of the transparency, legitimacy, and accountability of the Security Council was acknowledged by the governments of UN member states when they recommended, in the 2005 World Summit Outcome, 'that the Security Council continue to adopt its working methods so as to increase the involvement of States not members of the Council in

Security Council by Member States (2003) 31 *et seq*, and J Dedring, *The United Nations Security Council in the 1990s: Resurgence and Renewal* (2008) 3 *et seq*.

[47] Bailey and Daws (n 41 above) 61.

[48] For analysis of that theory and the possibility and prospects of its transfer to the international level, see Johnstone, 'Legislation and Adjudication in the UN Security Council: Bringing Down the Deliberative Deficit' (2008) 102 *American Journal of International Law* 275, 277–83.

its work, as appropriate, enhance its accountability to the membership and increase the transparency of its work'.[49]

The improvement of working methods in that direction has indeed been a part of the larger project of Security Council reform since the early 1990s; it is an integral part of the mandate of the Open-ended Working Group on issues of Security Council reform established by the General Assembly in 1993.[50] Also in 1993, the Security Council established an Informal Working Group on Documentation and Other Procedural Questions (IWG) to enhance and streamline ways and means whereby the Security Council addresses issues related to its documentation and other procedural questions.[51] In 2006, the Security Council approved a note by the President of the Security Council[52] with a view to enhancing the efficiency and transparency of the Council's work, as well as its interaction and dialogue with non-Council members. A year later, the Security Council approved another note by its President[53] which contained several additional agreed measures. In a note approved by the Council in 2008[54] the provisions concerning the summary statement of matters of which the Security Council is seized (seizure statement) were consolidated and revised. In July 2010, the Security Council approved a note by its President[55] which incorporates and further develops the previous notes, by superseding those notes.

According to this latest note (paragraph 3), the members of the Security Council agree, inter alia, 'that the President of the Council or his or her designate should provide substantive and detailed briefings to Member States in a timely manner. Such briefings should take place shortly after informal consultations of the whole.' Further, the Council members encourage the President of the Council to hold an informal briefing on the programme of work open to all member states, after its adoption by the Council (paragraph 4). Chairs of the subsidiary bodies of the Council or their designates are invited to give, on a regular basis, informal briefings, when appropriate, on their activities to interested member states (paragraph 5). The Council members intend to request the Secretariat to give ad hoc briefings at informal consultations on a daily basis, if necessary, when a situation justifies such briefings (paragraph 6). They invite the Secretariat to continue its practice of circulating the briefing texts (paragraph 7). In its section IV, the note of July 2010 includes a number of detailed rules about the procedure of informal consultations. As regards the formal meetings of the Council, the note says that '[i]n order to increase the transparency of its work, the Security Council reaffirms its

[49] GA Res 60/1, 16 September 2005, para 154.

[50] GA Res 48/26, 3 December 1993. See B Fassbender, *UN Security Council Reform and the Right of Veto: A Constitutional Perspective* (1998) 226 *et seq*.

[51] For more information, see the official website of the Security Council at www.un.org/sc/wgdocs (last accessed 1 March 2011).

[52] UN Doc S/2006/507, 19 July 2006. See also the debate of the Security Council on the implementation of that note: UNSC Verbatim Record, 27 August 2008, UN Docs S/PV.5968 and S/PV.5968 (Resumption 1).

[53] UN Doc S/2007/749, 19 December 2007.

[54] UN Doc S/2008/847, 31 December 2008.

[55] UN Doc S/2010/507, 27 July 2010.

commitment to increase recourse to open meetings, particularly at the early stage in its consideration of a matter' (paragraph 28). Improvements of the annual report of the Security Council submitted to the General Assembly are addressed in section XII of the note. The note addresses the drafting of resolutions of the Council in the following terms (paragraphs 42–44):

42. The members of the Security Council reaffirm that all members of the Security Council should be allowed to participate fully in the preparation of, inter alia, the resolutions, presidential statements and press statements of the Council. The members of the Security Council also reaffirm that the drafting of all documents such as resolutions and presidential statements as well as press statements should be carried out in a manner that will allow adequate participation of all members of the Council.
43. The members of the Security Council intend to continue to informally consult with the broader United Nations membership, in particular interested Member States, including countries directly involved or specifically affected, neighbouring States and countries with particular contributions to make, as well as with regional organizations and Groups of Friends, when drafting, inter alia, resolutions, presidential statements and press statements, as appropriate.
44. The members of the Security Council agree to consider making draft resolutions and presidential statements as well as other draft documents available as appropriate to non-members of the Council as soon as such documents are introduced within informal consultations of the whole, or earlier, if so authorized by the authors of the draft document.

Paragraph 43 reflects the wish of the troop-contributing countries and those that make large financial contributions to peace missions to be involved in the preparation and modification of mandates for such missions.

While these efforts of the Council to improve its working methods with a view of enhancing the transparency and legitimacy of its decisions are commendable, their practical effects should not be overrated. There are certain, almost 'natural' limits to the openness of the work of the Council which follow from the nature of the Council. The Security Council as established by the UN Charter is a political body made up of diplomats who—in spite of President Woodrow Wilson's demands of 1918 that 'the processes of peace... shall be absolutely open und that they shall involve and permit henceforth no secret understandings of any kind' and that 'diplomacy shall proceed always frankly and in the public view'[56]—engage in secret discussions and understandings when they consider this as necessary or useful. This will always be the case in emergency situations when international peace and security is threatened. Accordingly, secretiveness—of the permanent members in their relationship with the non-permanent members, and of the Council members vis-à-vis the general membership of the UN—will prevail in all cases in which the non-permanent members or the general membership, respectively, will be most eager to receive accurate and timely information. In other words, the transparency provided for in the Presidential Notes discussed above is limited to the 'ordinary', day-to-day business of the Council. The 'mini-Councils' phenomenon described

[56] See President Wilson's 'Fourteen Points' speech, delivered to Congress on 8 January 1918, reprinted in HS Commager (ed), *Documents of American History* (1973, 9th edn), vol II, 137 *et seq*.

by Professor Reisman[57] results from the special position accorded to five permanent members of the Council with the veto power (Article 27(3) UN Charter), and the wish and practice of the three Western permanent members to coordinate their views before meeting with Russia and China.

4. Types of Security Council Action in which the Problem of Safeguarding Human Rights is Acute

If we try to identify principal types of Security Council action (apart from action meant directly to promote and protect human rights)[58] in which the problem of safeguarding human rights (both substantive and procedural rights) is acute, we may draw up the following tentative list:

(1) action regarding the maintenance of international peace and security in general (including UN peacekeeping operations and the use of armed force 'authorized' by the Security Council);
(2) 'targeted sanctions' directed at individuals;
(3) legislative acts;
(4) (quasi-) judicial acts;
(5) international territorial administration.

Within the scope of the present book chapter, only some of the issues arising in those five categories of Council action can be briefly mentioned.

As regards *action for the purpose of maintaining and restoring international peace and security in general*, the Council acknowledged that comprehensive economic sanctions can detrimentally affect the human rights of the general population of a country on which such sanctions are imposed, and especially the rights of members of the most vulnerable groups of the population (women, children, the elderly).[59] In the case of the sanctions against Iraq upheld after the liberation of Kuwait, such humanitarian concerns were the reason for establishing the 'Oil for Food' programme in 1995. In Resolution 986, the Security Council declared to be 'concerned by the serious nutritional and health situation of the Iraqi population, and by the risk of a further deterioration in this situation', and to be 'convinced of the need... to provide for the humanitarian needs of the Iraqi people until the fulfilment by Iraq of the relevant Security Council resolutions'.[60] The Council decided that the income raised by the sale of Iraqi oil should be used 'to finance the export to Iraq... of medicine, health

[57] See text accompanying n 44 above.

[58] For that distinction, see the introductory section of the present chapter.

[59] For an overview, see T Meron, *The Humanization of International Law* (2006) 497–509 and Cortright, Lopez, and Gerber-Stellingwerf, 'Sanctions', in TG Weiss and S Daws (eds), *The Oxford Handbook on the United Nations* (2007) 349 at 357 *et seq*. For a critique of the Iraq sanctions because of their impact on human rights, see, eg, de Wet, 'Human Rights Limitations to Economic Enforcement Measures Under Article 41 of the United Nations Charter and the Iraqi Sanctions Regime' (2001) 14 *Leiden Journal of International Law* 277.

[60] UN SC Res 986, 14 April 1995, preamble paras 2 and 3. See also UN SC Res 687, 3 April 1991, para 20.

supplies, foodstuffs, and materials and supplies for essential civilian needs'.[61] Human rights may also be negatively affected as a result of an 'authorization' of a use of military force by individual member states (including the occupation and administration of territory) because in such cases the degree of control exercised by the Council over what is happening 'on the ground' is relatively small.[62]

Further, the Security Council recognized the special vulnerability of children and women in its 'non-country specific resolutions' with respect to *children affected by armed conflict* and *women and peace and security*. The Council not only admonished the states parties to armed conflict to respect and ensure the human rights of children and women, but also committed itself by deciding 'to continue the inclusion of specific provisions for the protection of children in the mandates of United Nations peacekeeping operations', and by calling upon 'all parties concerned to ensure that the protection, rights and well-being of children affected by armed conflict are specifically integrated into all peace processes, peace agreements and post-conflict recovery and reconstruction planning and programmes'.[63] In its 2008 resolution on 'women and peace and security', the Council affirmed its intention, 'when establishing and renewing state-specific sanctions regimes, to take into consideration the appropriateness of targeted and graduated measures against parties to situations of armed conflict who commit rape and other forms of sexual violence against women and girls in situations of armed conflict'.[64]

In the case of *targeted sanctions of the Security Council directed against individuals*, procedural human rights as well as substantive rights are at stake.[65] Of the various sanctions regimes, the one established against individuals and entities belonging to, or associated with, al-Qaida and/or the Taliban[66] has gained particular importance because of the relatively high number of individuals and entities listed. This sanctions regime also differs from the others in that, after the Taliban were removed from power in Afghanistan, there is no special link between the targeted individuals and entities and a specific country. Among the procedural rights, especially the due process of law rights are affected when individuals are placed on a list of targeted persons and entities, or seek to be removed from such a list.[67] Accordingly, UN

[61] UN SC Res 986, 14 April 1995, para 8(a).

[62] See Aznar-Gómez, 'A Decade of Human Rights Protection by the UN Security Council: A Sketch of Deregulation?' (2002) 13 *European Journal of International Law* 223, 235 *et seq*.

[63] SC Res 1612, 26 July 2005, paras 12 and 14.

[64] SC Res 1820, 19 June 2008, para 5.

[65] See the contributions by A Ciampi, E de Wet, and S Zappalà to the present volume.

[66] SC Res 1267, 15 October 1999 and following resolutions, including SC Res 1904, 17 December 2009. For an overview of the work and procedure of the 1267 Committee of the Security Council, see Rosand, 'The Security Council's Efforts to Monitor the Implementation of Al Qaida/Taliban Sanctions' (2004) 98 AJIL 745. For a critical discussion of the negative repercussions of the Committee's work for human rights, see Foot, 'The United Nations, Counter Terrorism, and Human Rights: Institutional Adaptation and Embedded Ideas' (2007) 29 *Human Rights Quarterly* 489.

[67] I have dealt with that issue in great detail in a study commissioned in 2005 by the Under-Secretary-General for Legal Affairs and Legal Counsel of the United Nations. A final version of the study was submitted by its author on 20 March 2006, and made public by the Office of Legal Affairs in July 2006. See Fassbender, 'Targeted Sanctions Imposed by the UN Security Council and Due Process Rights: A Study Commissioned by the UN Office of Legal Affairs and Follow-up Action by the United Nations' (2006) 3 *International Organizations Law Review* 437.

member states in the 2005 World Summit Outcome called upon the Security Council 'to ensure that fair and clear procedures exist for placing individuals and entities on sanctions lists and for removing them'.[68] Of substantive human rights, the right to property, the right to liberty, and freedom of movement are especially concerned by targeted sanctions.

The Security Council has recognized that threats to international peace and security caused by terrorist acts must be combatted 'in accordance with the Charter of the United Nations and international law, including *applicable international human rights, refugee and humanitarian law*'.[69] Following the precedent of humanitarian exemptions established in the case of the sanctions against Iraq,[70] the Council provided for such exemptions also in the framework of targeted sanctions.[71] When proposing names to the 1267 Committee for inclusion on the 'Consolidated List', member states shall provide a detailed statement of case, and that statement shall be releasable, upon request, except for the parts a member state identifies to the Committee as being confidential.[72] The Committee shall make accessible on its website, at the same time a name is added to the Consolidated List, a narrative summary of reasons for listing for the corresponding entry or entries.[73] By Resolution 1904 (2009), the Council established an Office of the Ombudsperson to 'receive requests from individuals and entities seeking to be removed from the Consolidated List'; the Ombudsperson shall perform her tasks in an independent and impartial manner.[74] Although the Office of the Ombudsperson does not function in a court-like manner and does not have the competence to grant a de-listing request, but is only authorized to 'lay out for the Committee the principal arguments concerning the delisting request',[75] the appointment of the Ombudsperson for the first time has brought into play an independent actor in the de-listing procedure whose findings and arguments the 1267 Committee must take into due consideration.[76] As the Legal Adviser of the Mexican Ministry of Foreign Affairs, Ambassador Joel Hernández,

68 GA Res 60/1, 16 September 2005, para 109.

69 See, eg, SC Res 1904, 17 December 2009, preamble para 3, emphasis added.

70 See text accompanying n 60 above.

71 For the 1267 sanctions regime, see SC Res 1452, 20 December 2002, paras 1 and 2; SC Res 1735, 22 December 2006, paras 15 *et seq*; SC Res 1904, 17 December 2009, para 7.

72 SC Res 1904, 17 December 2009, para 11.

73 Ibid para 14.

74 Ibid paras 20 and 21.

75 Ibid Annex II para 7(c).

76 In my study of 2006 (n 67 above), I affirmed a right of a listed person or entity 'to an effective remedy against an individual measure before an impartial institution or body previously established' (para 12). I further wrote (para 12.9): 'As regards the form and modalities of an effective remedy, the Security Council enjoys a considerable measure of discretion. Among the options available to the Council are the establishment of

- an independent international court or tribunal;
- an ombudsman office, as it exists in a number of States and in the European Union as an alternative remedial mechanism;
- an inspection panel following the model of the World Bank Inspection Panel;
- a commission of inquiry; or
- a committee of experts serving in their personal capacity, as it exists, for instance, in accordance with Article 28 of the International Covenant on Civil and Political Rights.'

recently said, 'the creation of the Ombudsperson represents, arguably, a paradigm shift in the Security Council'.[77]

In 2001, the Security Council started establishing a *'legislative' practice*. That expression is meant to say that the Council does not take measures against a particular state in a particular situation but engages in a general norm-setting, requiring states to comply with certain commands or prohibitions for an indefinite period of time or in an unspecified number of future cases.[78] The first major example was Resolution 1373 (2001),[79] by which the Council made the rules of the International Convention for the Suppression of the Financing of Terrorism,[80] which at the time had not yet entered into force due to an insufficient number of ratifications, binding on member states. Resolution 1373 was followed by Resolution 1540 (2004) which aims at curtailing the proliferation of nuclear, chemical, and biological weapons, especially to non-state-actors.[81] As a matter of principle, legislative action of the Security Council is also prone to affecting human rights.

Certain measures of the Security Council provided for in Chapter VI of the UN Charter have a *quasi-judicial character* in that they correspond to measures which on a domestic plane are generally taken by courts in a judicial procedure. For instance, according to Article 34 of the Charter the Security Council may investigate any dispute or situation which might lead to international friction or give rise to a dispute. Article 36 of the Charter authorizes the Council to recommend, at any stage of a dispute, 'appropriate procedures or methods of adjustment', including a judicial settlement by the ICJ. At the request of all parties to a particular dispute, the Council may also make itself recommendations with a view to a settlement of the dispute (Article 38 UN Charter).

The Security Council also engages in a quasi-judicial activity when, in the framework of one of the targeted sanctions regimes, it decides about a de-listing request submitted by a targeted individual (through the focal point procedure[82] or the Ombudsperson procedure[83]) or a government acting on his or her behalf.[84] Lastly, the establishment of ad hoc international criminal tribunals[85] comes under the heading of a judicial activity of the Council in a wider sense.

[77] See 'Taking Stock: The UN Security Council and the Rule of Law', Remarks by Ambassador J Hernández, New York, 28 October 2010, 7, available at http://ar.unrol.org (last accessed 1 March 2011).

[78] See, in particular, Talmon, 'The Security Council as World Legislature' (2005) 99 AJIL 175; Bianchi, 'Assessing the Effectiveness of the UN Security Council's Anti-terrorism Measures: The Quest for Legitimacy and Cohesion' (2007) 17 EJIL 881; and Johnstone (n 48 above) 283–94.

[79] SC Res 1373, 28 September 2001.

[80] Adopted by GA Res 54/109, 9 December 1999. The Convention entered into force on 10 April 2002.

[81] SC Res 1540, 28 April 2004.

[82] SC Res 1730, 19 December 2006.

[83] SC Res 1904, 17 December 2009.

[84] See Johnstone (n 48 above) 294–9.

[85] See SC Res 827, 25 May 1993 (former Yugoslavia); SC Res 955, 8 November 1994 (Rwanda); SC Res 1757, 30 May 2007 (Lebanon). As to the latter, see Fassbender, 'Reflections on the International Legality of the Special Tribunal for Lebanon' (2007) 5 *Journal of International Criminal Justice* 1091.

As a last type of Security Council action in which the problem of safeguarding human rights is acute, *international territorial administration by the United Nations* can be mentioned. Whenever the Council decides to establish an interim, or transitional, administration for a specific territory—as it did in the cases of Kosovo[86] and East Timor[87]—it encounters the question of how to protect the human rights of the respective population against an encroachment by the local UN administration, or an administration acting with the authorization of the United Nations.

5. Enhancing the Role for Human Rights in the Decision-making Process of the Security Council

As explained above,[88] the UN Charter requires the Security Council, as indeed all organs of the United Nations, to observe 'human rights and fundamental freedoms' (Article 1(3) UN Charter) as defined, in particular, in the Universal Declaration of Human Rights and the two International Covenants on Human Rights of 1966, when taking action which has a direct impact on the rights of individuals. Occasionally it has been remarked that the Security Council is a political organ, and not a court. This is certainly true, but this qualification does not exempt the Council from its human rights obligations which arise from the UN Charter. The governments of member states are also political organs but no one would deny that they are nevertheless obliged to respect the international human rights commitments accepted by their states. In the same way as governments, the members of the Security Council can seek legal advice.

However, the general principle that the Security Council is bound by human rights must be translated into concrete terms, that is applied to the circumstances of a particular case. In each case, it must first be established which, and whose, human rights exactly could be negatively affected by an act or measure contemplated by the Council. Next, it is necessary to find out whether consideration of the various human rights at stake, and of the different groups of people being entitled to those rights, suggests one and the same course of action to be taken by the Council, or whether that consideration leads to contradictory approaches. In the latter case, the Council needs to decide whether, under the specific circumstances, the protection of one particular human right is more important than that of another right. In other words, the Council must balance one human right against another, and possibly also the interests of one particular group of people against those of another group, an exercise national and regional human rights courts are familiar with.

[86] SC Res 1244, 10 June 1999.

[87] SC Res 1272, 25 October 1999. According to para 1 of the resolution, the Security Council decided 'to establish . . . a United Nations Transitional Administration in East Timor (UNTAET), which will be endowed with overall responsibility for the administration of East Timor and will be empowered to exercise all legislative and executive authority, including the administration of justice'.

[88] See section 2 above.

The Council must also weigh its human rights commitments up against its Charter responsibility to maintain and restore international peace and security. That responsibility, with the express authority to use armed force to give effect to its decisions (Article 42 UN Charter), entails, for instance, that the Council may refrain from observing the right to life or the right to physical integrity. The Council may also, for example, discriminate against persons on the grounds of their nationality when it imposes economic sanctions on a particular country and its citizens. When imposing sanctions on individuals in accordance with Chapter VII of the UN Charter, the Security Council must strive for discharging its principal duty to maintain or restore international peace and security while, at the same time, respecting the human rights and fundamental freedoms of targeted individuals to the greatest possible extent. There is a duty of the Council duly to balance the general and particular interests which are at stake. Every measure having a negative impact on human rights and freedoms of a particular group or category of persons must be necessary and proportionate to the aim the measure is meant to achieve.

While every single case to be dealt with by the Security Council is different, one may still try to distinguish certain types of action and to develop corresponding differentiated standards regarding the role of human rights in the decision-making process of the Council. Based on the established idea of the three branches of government, the following modes of Council action can be identified:

(1) 'executive' action aiming at the maintenance or restoration of international peace and security in a specific situation;
(2) 'legislative' action for the purpose of maintaining international peace and security in a general way; and
(3) 'judicial' and 'quasi-judicial' action.

Another distinction can be based on different degrees of urgency of Security Council action. Generally, 'executive' action in a particular case will be of the most urgent character, for instance action in case of an imminent threat to the peace, action in case of an imminent humanitarian catastrophe, or action in form of a reaction to a breach of the peace or act of aggression.[89] Provisional measures taken in accordance with Article 40 of the UN Charter 'in order to prevent an aggravation' of a situation threatening world peace will also generally be of an urgent nature. If rapid action is necessary, one cannot expect the Council to be as circumspect and attentive to possible adverse human rights consequences as, for example, in the case of legislative acts the drafting of which usually takes many months.

What could be done in practical terms in order to enhance the role for human rights in the decision-making process of the Security Council? Of the various possible avenues, four shall be mentioned here:

(1) an amendment of the UN Charter;
(2) an amendment of the Rules of Procedure of the Security Council;

[89] See Art 39 UN Charter.

(3) a self-commitment of the Security Council by way of a resolution or a presidential statement;
(4) institutionalized cooperation with other UN bodies, in particular the Human Rights Council and the High Commissioner for Human Rights.

In constitutional perspective, a formal amendment of the UN Charter to the effect that the Security Council must consider human rights in a principled way whenever it takes decisions which could impair such rights would be highly desirable. However, given the well-known difficulties of mustering the majorities necessary for amending the Charter,[90] it is extremely improbable that member states will agree on such an amendment. In addition, any clause addressing such a mandatory consideration of human rights is likely to be drafted in general and vague terms only—in which case its effectiveness would be rather limited.

As regards the *second option*, Chapter VI of the Provisional Rules of Procedure of the Security Council, dealing with the 'conduct of business' of the Council, is a place where rules about a principled inclusion of human rights considerations in the decision-making of the Council could be inserted. However, as mentioned above[91] the existing Rules are of a purely formal character; they are not concerned with issues of substance. Further, the members of the Security Council, in particular the permanent members, have been traditionally reluctant to commit themselves to rigid rules of procedure. Since 1946, there have been only six minor amendments of the Provisional Rules of Procedure, the most recent of which (adding Arabic to the Council's working languages) was adopted in 1982.[92]

With regard to the *third option*, the Security Council already used the method of agreeing on presidential statements for the purpose of improving its working methods.[93] It could well rely on the same instrument for specifying how it intends to integrate human rights considerations in its decision-making process. A resolution expressing a respective self-commitment would have a similar practical effect but be of a higher symbolic meaning. As the Swiss Ambassador to the UN stated in 2009, 'contrary to decisions on the enlargement [of the Security Council], improvements in the area of working methods are most likely not subject to Charter amendment and can be pursued in an ongoing process of constant evolution, consistent application and implementation'.[94] A self-commitment by way of a presidential statement or a resolution goes well with that idea of an evolutionary improvement of the procedure of the Council. Either form (the presidential statement more so than the resolution) allows for adjustment and adaptation in accordance with changed circumstances or an increased readiness of Council members to systematically integrate human rights in their deliberations. A presidential statement (which can be replaced rather easily and informally by a new

[90] See Arts 108 and 109 UN Charter.
[91] See text accompanying n 40 above.
[92] See Bailey and Daws (n 41 above) 13 *et seq*.
[93] See text accompanying n 52 *et seq* above.
[94] Statement by Ambassador P Maurer in the Intergovernmental negotiations of the UNGA on the reform of the Security Council, 7 April 2009, 2 (on file with author).

statement) would probably be much more specific about how to take account of human rights in the decision-making process of the Security Council than any formal amendment of the UN Charter or the Provisional Rules of Procedure.

A possible *fourth option* is to introduce forms of institutionalized cooperation with other UN bodies, in particular the Human Rights Council and the High Commissioner for Human Rights. There are elements of the practice of the Council in recent years on which one could build such a cooperation. In August 1992, the Security Council invited for the first time a special rapporteur of the Commission on Human Rights, Mr Max Van der Stoel, to address the Council. In September 1999, the Council for the first time extended an invitation to the High Commissioner for Human Rights, Ms Mary Robinson, to speak to the Council in an open debate on the protection of civilians in armed conflict.[95] In 2002, the Council invited the High Commissioner for Human Rights to brief the members of the Council in consultations of the whole on the situation in the Democratic Republic of Congo. In the same year, the High Commissioner briefed the Counter Terrorism Committee of the Security Council (CTC)[96] on the human rights implications of the international action against terrorism. In 2006, the Executive Directorate of the CTC (CTED) was authorized to 'liaise with the Office of the High Commissioner for Human Rights and, as appropriate, with other human rights organizations in matters related to counter-terrorism'.[97] Special rapporteurs appointed by the Commission on Human Rights regularly submitted reports to the Security Council. The Council is also taking advantage of information on human rights issues provided by non-governmental organizations.

The Human Rights Council (HRC) created in 2006, in replacement of the Commission on Human Rights, as a subsidiary organ of the General Assembly ranks foremost as a possible institutional partner of the Security Council when it comes to the protection and promotion of human rights.[98] In the founding resolution of the HRC, the General Assembly emphasized the pertinence of human rights for the work entrusted by the UN Charter to the Security Council when it acknowledged that 'peace and security, development and human rights are the pillars of the United Nations system and the foundations for collective security and well-being', and recognized that 'development, peace and security and human rights are interlinked and mutually reinforcing'.[99] The Security Council, it is true,

[95] Further briefings took place in April 2001, and twice each in 2002, 2003, 2004, and 2005. See 'Security Council Report': Update Report on Briefings by the High Commissioner for Human Rights to the Security Council and the Peacebuilding Commission, 29 May 2007, 2 *et seq*, available at www.securitycouncilreport.org (last accessed 2 March 2011). See also Weschler (n 1 above) 64 *et seq*.

[96] Committee established pursuant to Resolution 1373 (2001) concerning counter-terrorism.

[97] See 'Conclusions for policy guidance regarding human rights and the CTC', CTC Policy Guidance PG.2, 25 May 2006 (on file with author). For context, see Flynn, 'The Security Council's Counter-Terrorism Committee and Human Rights' (2007) 7 *Human Rights Law Review* 371, 382 *et seq*.

[98] See Fassbender, 'Architectural Clarity or Creative Ambiguity? The Place of the Human Rights Council in the Institutional Structure of the United Nations', in U Fastenrath, R Geiger, D-E Khan, A Paulus, S von Schorlemar, and C Vedder (eds.), *From Bilateralism to Community Interest: Essays in Honour of Judge Bruno Simma* (2011) 443.

[99] GA Res 60/251, 15 March 2006, preamble, para 6.

sees and treats the HRC not as an organ standing by itself but as a part of the structure of the General Assembly. With its notorious high sense of self-confidence, the Security Council usually deals formally only with other principal organs of the United Nations.[100] The HRC cannot rely on a provision analogous to Article 65 of the UN Charter according to which the ECOSOC 'may furnish information to the Security Council and shall assist the Security Council *upon its request*'.[101] However, in accordance with Rule 39 of its Provisional Rules of Procedure the Security Council 'may invite members of the Secretariat *or other persons*, whom it considers competent for the purpose, to supply it with information or to give other assistance in examining matters within its competence'.[102] Because of 'the need for human rights information and analysis at every stage of the [Security] Council's action',[103] which today is indeed no longer questioned by any UN member state, the Security Council may, and indeed should, involve in its work the HRC, rapporteurs appointed by it, or UN officials supporting the HRC, in particular the High Commissioner for Human Rights. As regards the future role of the HRC in its relation to the Security Council, a provision of the founding resolution of the Peacebuilding Commission could give some guidance. Here the General Assembly and the Security Council decided that in situations on the agenda of the Security Council with which it is actively seized 'the main purpose of the Commission will be to provide advice to the Council at its request'.[104]

6. Concluding Remarks

There can be no doubt about the outstanding importance of human rights in the contemporary international legal order, and about the necessity of a Security Council adhering to those rights. Any disregard of human rights by the Council today inevitably produces a 'legitimacy deficit' which impairs member states' compliance with the decisions taken by the Council.[105] There is no general contradiction between the protection of human rights and effective action by the Security Council. It would be wrong to create the impression that such action is generally prone to human rights violations. To the contrary, human rights of men, women, and children in situations of war, internal conflict, and threats to the peace

[100] But see the exceptions mentioned by Bailey and Daws (n 41 above) 297: 'Certain subsidiary organs established by the Assembly have played a part in the work of the [Security] Council, either because they have been placed by the Assembly in a special relation to the Council or because the Council has made use of the services of a subsidiary organ or invited its officers to participate in debates. Some of these subsidiary organs are still active (Relief and Works Agency for Palestine Refugees in the Near East, the Committee on the Peaceful Uses of Outer Space, the Committee on the Exercise of the Inalienable Rights of the Palestinian People).'

[101] Emphasis added. For an account of the rather sparse interaction of the Security Council and ECOSOC in the area of human rights, see Bailey and Daws (n 41 above) 301 *et seq*.

[102] Emphasis added.

[103] See text accompanying n 1 above.

[104] GA Res 60/180 and SC Res 1645, 20 December 2005, para 16.

[105] See D Shraga's contribution to the present volume, section 7.

are much more jeopardized by a passive than by an active Security Council. The world still requires an exercise of more, not less authority on a global level, and international lawyers should encourage this development rather than warn against it by wrongly presenting the Security Council to the world public as a new leviathan.[106] 'The problem is not so much that the Security Council is a threat to human rights, but of getting it to authorize action to protect human rights.'[107]

[106] See Fassbender, 'Quis judicabit? The Security Council, Its Powers and Its Legal Control' (2000) 11 EJIL 219, 220.

[107] See Aust (n 46 above) 33.

5

Security Council Targeted Sanctions and Human Rights

Annalisa Ciampi

1. Introduction

This study addresses the problems raised in a human rights perspective by United Nations (UN) financial sanctions countering terrorism. After setting out the general legal framework for the imposition of targeted sanctions, the analysis will develop along the following lines. First, I shall tackle the issue at the universal level and inquire into what kind of protection the UN system provides to individuals and entities targeted by UN sanctions. In relation thereto, an attempt will be made to qualify existing remedies, which can only be resorted to after the restrictive measures have been taken, while contrasting them with the total absence of *ex ante* remedies. In this context, we will discuss in particular whether the protection afforded to the affected individual or entity by the state of nationality (or residence) can be characterized as an exercise of diplomatic protection vis-à-vis the Organization.

I shall then consider the legal challenges brought to the regime at the regional and member state level with a view to verifying whether the lack of judicial guarantees at the universal level (where sanctions are imposed) is (or can be) effectively remedied, in whole or in part, at the regional and/or national level (where sanctions are implemented). In this regard, we shall see which objective grounds make protection afforded at these levels ineffective and/or less favourable than that provided for when individual rights are similarly affected outside the scope of a UN sanctions regime.

The third and distinct line of analysis considers a dimension that—to distinguish it from the previous ones—can be described as 'external' to the mechanisms for the imposition and implementation of targeted sanctions. This includes international human rights monitoring bodies such as the UN Committee of Human Rights (HRC) and the European Court of Human Rights (ECtHR). In relation thereto, we shall inquire into whether these bodies are capable of protecting the rights of targeted individuals and entities when national as well as (other) international institutions have failed to do so.

The last part of the chapter sums up the results of this multi-level analysis and discusses possible scenarios for reform. The International Criminal Court (ICC) and the International Independent Investigation Commission (hereinafter the 'Commission'), established by the Security Council to investigate the terrorist bombing that killed the former Prime Minister of Lebanon, show that international bodies can occasionally, albeit imperfectly, contribute to the legitimacy of the Security Council's action. It is foreseen that none of the proposals currently under consideration for improving the *review* of situations of individuals and entities targeted by UN sanctions will achieve its expected result, unless the Security Council overcomes the political considerations that actually prevent existing *listing* mechanisms from being brought into line with basic human rights procedural guarantees.

2. General Legal Framework

A. 'Humanitarianism' and the law of international cooperation

The issue of the Security Council's targeted sanctions and human rights cannot be properly addressed without taking into account the broader general legal framework regarding the current state of international law and international relations. This appears to be characterized by at least two general features: the influence of human rights in all areas of the law and the unprecedented development of international organizations, both regional and universal.

Changes brought about by the human rights movement cannot be exhaustively numbered here. By way of example, suffice it to mention the criminalization of violations of international humanitarian law; the tendency of the law of state responsibility to shift from bilateralism to community interests; a growing convergence between the principle of diplomatic protection of nationals and human rights law, because states exercising diplomatic protection prefer to ground their action in basic human rights than in the international minimum standard; the number of human rights treaties that are among the most important treaties of our time; the developments in the doctrine of the subjects of international law, which now includes non-state actors, and the proliferation of international courts that may be seized by individuals and other private actors. I shall refer to this overall phenomenon as 'humanitarianism' or 'humanization of international law'.[1]

The emergence of international organizations as international subjects has meant that international law has passed from the phase when it was primarily a law of coexistence of states to a new law of cooperation relating to economic, social, cultural, scientific, and technological collaboration. The international law of coexistence has been increasingly superseded by the new international law of

[1] Both expressions are taken from Meron, 'International Law in the Age of Human Rights. General Course on Public International Law' (2003) 301 *Recueil des Cours de l'Académie de La Haye* 9. For a revised and updated version, see T Meron, *The Humanization of International Law* (2006). That the protection of human rights by means of international law is today one the principal goals of the international legal order, was reaffirmed by the 2005 World Summit Outcome resolution adopted by the UN General Assembly via GA Res 60/1, 24 October 2005, paras 119–20 and 138–40.

cooperation and the range of the fields for international cooperation is continually expanding.

At least to some extent, the two phenomena have proceeded 'hand-in-hand'. While the origin of international organizations can be traced back to the 19th century, the human rights movement is a more recent—post-Second World War—development. There is no doubt, however, that the creation of the UN has given a decisive impetus to both. As is well known, the UN Charter includes among the purposes of the Organization: '[t]o achieve international co-operation in solving international problems of an economic, social, cultural, or humanitarian character, and in promoting and encouraging respect for human rights and for fundamental freedoms for all without distinction as to race, sex, language, or religion' (Article 2 (3) of the UN Charter).[2] Moreover, all multilateral human rights treaties have been negotiated in the framework of international organizations: universal—the UN and its specialized agencies—and regional such as the Council of Europe, the Organization of American States, and the African Union. Organs to promote and protect human rights have been established under the authority flowing from human rights clauses of the UN Charter as well as on the basis of the relevant instruments at the regional level.

On the other hand, the trend to humanize the law has affected in particular the UN. If the whole system of international law can be read in a key of human rights promotion and advancement, so can the law of the UN.

In light thereof, it would seem only natural that the Security Council, as the organ that the UN Charter entrusts with the primary responsibility for the maintenance of international peace and security (Article 24), would consider itself constrained by the same international standards. Few statements could be more distant from the truth.[3]

One need not call into question the centrality given to human rights in the work of the UN or that human rights have increasingly been taken into account by the Security Council, such as in peacekeeping operations, to consider that the existing mechanisms for listing and de-listing individuals and entities targeted by UN sanctions still fall short of meeting basic human rights standards.

In order to tackle the issue of human rights protection of individuals and entities included in UN sanctions lists, it is useful to recall the origin of this relatively recent phenomenon as well as to identify the human rights affected by targeted sanctions regimes.

[2] See also Art 55 of the UN Charter: 'With a view to the creation of conditions of stability and well-being which are necessary for peaceful and friendly relations among nations based on respect for the principle of equal rights and self-determination of peoples, the United Nations shall promote... universal respect for, and observance of, human rights and fundamental freedoms for all without distinction as to race, sex, language, or religion.'

[3] On the Security Council's ambivalence as to the promotion of human rights by others and the application of legal constraints to its own initiatives, see, eg, Chesterman, '"I'll Take Manhattan": The International Rule of Law and the United Nations Security Council' (2009) 1 *Hague Journal on the Rule of Law* 67, available at http://journals.cambridge.org/action/displayJournal?jid=ROL (last accessed 10 February 2011).

B. Targeted sanctions rationale and applicable human rights standards

Targeted sanctions are today an important tool in the maintenance and restoration of international peace and security. Although not a totally new phenomenon,[4] it is only in recent practice that they have become the ordinary measure not involving the use of armed force resorted to by the Security Council in the discharge of its 'primary' responsibility for the maintenance of international peace and security.

In principle, Security Council sanctions have been targeted against specific individuals and entities with the purpose of avoiding, or at least reducing, the humanitarian concerns arising under general sanctions regimes. The latter, by definition, affect the life of innocent people (ie the population at large of the target state(s)). The humanitarian consequences of the embargo on trade with Iraq through the 1990s, coupled with its lack of effectiveness with respect to the achievement of its stated aims, are exemplary of the hurdles encountered by general sanctions. Targeted sanctions are intended to limit the collateral impact of economic sanctions such as general embargoes and the like, while at the same time ensuring that effect be given to Security Council decisions.[5]

Another factor contributing to this shift from general to targeted sanctions regimes is the nature of current threats to international peace and security. Challenges such as international terrorism and the proliferation of nuclear weapons exceed the reach of the nation state and require that measures be taken against individuals not necessarily associated with states or state actors.

This does not mean that the practice followed by the Security Council of targeting sanctions against individuals and entities has been confined to the fight against international terrorism (or the proliferation of weapons of mass destruction). In relation to the Democratic Republic of Congo (DRC), for example, sanctions have been imposed on persons acting in violation of the arms embargo established by Resolution 1493 (2003).[6] Resolution 1591 (2005) concerning Sudan has set restrictive measures against those 'who impede the peace process, constitute a threat to stability in Darfur and the region, commit violations of international humanitarian or human rights law or other atrocities, violate the measures implemented by Member States . . . or are responsible for offensive military over-flights'. Targeted

[4] The first sanctions *decided* by the Security Council were directed against the leadership of Southern Rhodesia, at the time a British colony, not a sovereign state. See SC Res 232, 16 December 1966. See also SC Res 1127, 28 August 1997, concerning Angola, which imposed sanctions against 'all senior officials of UNITA [Uniao Nacional para a Indipendencia Total de Angola] and . . . adult members of their immediate family', and SC Res 1137, 12 November 1997, targeting 'all Iraqi officials and members of the Iraqi armed forces who were responsible for or participated in the instances of non-compliance'.

[5] See, eg, SC Res 1730, 19 December 2006, stressing that the Security Council '*[c]ontinu[es]* in its resolve to ensure that sanctions are carefully targeted in support of clear objectives and implemented in ways that balance effectiveness against possible adverse consequences' (preamble, 4th para).

[6] On SC Res 1596 (2005) see n 107 below and the corresponding text.

sanctions in order to contrast the proliferation of arms of nuclear weapons were decided in relation to North Korea and Iran.[7]

For the reasons that we shall see, however, the regime established to fight international terrorism pursuant to Resolution 1267 (1999), adopted on 15 October 1999 (modified and strengthened by subsequent resolutions, including Resolutions 1333 (2000), 1390 (2002), 1455 (2003), 1526 (2004), 1617 (2005), 1735 (2006), and 1822 (2008)), sets the benchmark of questions raised, in general, by the Security Council's targeted sanctions.

There are 11 regimes of targeted sanctions currently in place.[8] For each regime, a sanctions committee has been established. Sanctions committees are subsidiary organs of the Security Council, of which they reflect the composition. Unlike the Security Council, however, the committees make decisions by *consensus* of its members. Only if consensus cannot be reached on a particular issue, and after further consultations, may the matter be submitted to the Security Council. This means that *any* committee's member (not only the permanent five, but also the ten rotating states which happen to hold a seat in the Security Council and hence in the sanctions committees) has a power of veto in the committees' deliberations. As will be shown, the *consensus* rule has a major impact on the characterization of the current procedures for listing and de-listing individuals and entities.

Targeted sanctions typically include so-called financial sanctions and travel (or visa) bans, sometimes accompanied by an arms embargo. For the purpose of this study, I shall focus on financial sanctions as the restrictive measures that are most problematic in a human rights perspective.

Financial sanctions consist in the freezing of 'the funds, other financial assets and economic resources . . . that are owned or controlled by the persons or entities designated'.[9] No generally accepted definition, however, exists for these measures. According to the resolutions of the Security Council (and other relevant UN documents, such as the guidelines adopted by the various sanctions committees) financial sanctions, like travel bans and arms embargoes, 'are preventive in nature and are not reliant upon criminal standards set out under national law'.[10]

[7] See SC Res 1718 (2006) and 1737 (2006)—the latter followed by SC Res 1747 (2007) and 1803 (2008)—concerning North Korea and Iran, respectively.

[8] For an overview see the UN Security Council Sanctions Committees website at www.un.org/sc/committees/index.shtml (last accessed 10 February 2011).

[9] The quotation is taken from SC Res 1737, 23 December 2006, para 8(d), but the formulation is practically identical in all resolutions imposing financial sanctions. According to the French text, states are required to 'geler les fonds, avoirs financiers et ressources économiques' (ibid).

[10] See, eg, SC Res 1735, 22 December 2006, concerning measures against al-Qaida, the Taliban and their associates, preamble, 10th para. And most recently, SC Res 1822, 30 June 2008, '*[r]eiterating* that the measures referred to in paragraph 1 of this resolution, are preventative in nature and are not reliant upon criminal standards set out under national law' (preamble, 13th para). In accordance thereof, the Guidelines adopted by the 1267 Committee state: 'A criminal charge or conviction is not necessary for inclusion on the List as the sanctions are intended to be preventive in nature'. Security Council Committee Established Pursuant to Resolution 1267 (1999) Concerning Al-Qaida and the Taliban and Associated Individuals and Entities, Guidelines of the Committee for the Conduct of its Work (adopted on 7 November 2002, as amended on 10 April 2003, 21 December 2005, 29 November 2006, 12 February 2007, and 9 December 2008, available at www.un.org/sc/committees/1267/pdf/1267_guidelines.pdf, section 6(c) (last accessed 10 February 2011)).

The freezing of assets is generally established for a limited period of time (usually 12 months). Therefore, they cease to have effect from the date of the elapse thereof but can be extended by a new Security Council resolution. Where no timeframe is defined, the Security Council reserves the power to terminate the restrictive measures once it determines that the obligations set out in the resolution have been fulfilled (or that the relevant threat has ceased to exist). On this basis, the sanctions regime established pursuant to Resolution 1267 (1999) on 15 October 1999 has been in force for more than ten years.[11]

Independently from their formal qualification,[12] and whether they are annually renewed or imposed for an indefinite period of time, it is beyond doubt that a person's right to the free disposition of his or her funds and economic resources, if not permanently limited, is significantly affected by financial sanctions.[13] Apart from affecting the right to property (or the peaceful enjoyment thereof), financial sanctions also impinge upon one's right to exercise an economic activity or profession.[14] Moreover, the inclusion of a name on a list of individuals or entities targeted by UN sanctions amounts to an interference with the person's right to respect for his or her private and family life. Indeed, one's reputation and image are affected as a mere consequence of the listing, independently from the actual implementation of the restrictive measures in question.

The rights to property, to exercise an economic activity and to privacy are not absolute. They may be subject to limitations justified by objectives of general interests and in accordance with the requirements of necessity and proportionality. Any such restriction, however, implies a procedural guarantee, without which no interference can be deemed justified, irrespective of the motives pursued by the restrictive measures.

[11] In certain, albeit exceptional, cases, restrictive measures are also formally permanent. See SC Res 1483, 22 May 2003, concerning the situation between Iraq and Kuwait, which provides that 'all Member states in which there are . . . funds . . . shall freeze without delay those funds or other financial assets or economic resources and, unless these funds or other financial assets or economic resources are themselves the subject of a prior judicial, administrative, or arbitral lien or judgement, immediately shall cause their transfer to the Development Fund for Iraq'.

[12] For the view that assets-freeze amounts to a sanction 'belonging to the criminal sphere', see, eg, De Wet, 'The Role of Human Rights in Limiting the Enforcement Power of the Security Council: A Principled View', in E de Wet and A Nollkaemper (eds), *Review of the Security Council by Member States* (2003) 7 at 15.

[13] In the case of SC Res 1483 (2003) (n 11 above), the transfer to the special Development Fund for Iraq obviously implies that the targeted individuals and entities are permanently deprived of the use of, if not also the title to, their property.

[14] Financial sanctions could even result in the impairment of a person's right to life, when in consequence thereof a person is deprived of the means to provide for basic expenses, such as foodstuffs or medical treatment. In order to avoid this risk, however, all sanctions regimes provide for exemptions to the assets-freeze measures. For the conditions and procedures applicable to the exemptions to the assets-freeze measure imposed by the Security Council on the individuals and entities on the 1267 Consolidated List see www.un.org/sc/committees/1267/fact_sheet_assets_freeze.shtml (last accessed 10 February 2011).

Finally and most importantly, 'targeted sanctions', unlike traditional sanctions imposed on the basis of objective criteria of general and abstract application,[15] are individual measures imposed upon certain natural or legal persons, for example, because of their 'association' with a terrorist organization or their involvement in the commission of a terrorist act or the violations of international human rights and humanitarian law. I shall revert to the grounds for the imposition of financial sanctions countering terrorism.[16] For present purposes, it suffices to note that the non-normative, but concrete and individual, nature of the measures at stake implies the need to comply with the basic requirements of due process.

Individuals and entities enjoy the substantive rights (including procedural rights) mentioned above and the fundamental guarantees of due process under all multilateral human rights treaties, both universal and regional. Virtually all member states of the UN have ratified the International Covenant on Civil and Political Rights. Our analysis will therefore proceed on the basis of the assumption that these rights ought to be respected, whether the Security Council is itself bound to comply with international human rights standards or not.

On the one hand, states are not freed from their obligations arising under human rights treaties to which they are a party because they have transferred a part of their sovereign power to an international organization, such as the UN, endowed with the authority to issue binding decisions. On the other hand, one cannot accept that *any* decision of the Security Council trumps a state's human rights obligations under Article 103 of the UN Charter.[17] Article 103 has, in fact, to be read in the context of the other provisions of the Charter.

As recalled above, the promotion and protection of human rights and fundamental freedoms is included among the purposes of the UN. Arguably, the objective of maintaining international peace and security takes precedence over all other purposes of the Organization. It is submitted, however, that any such priority is not unqualified. Should security concerns trump human rights by all means and in all circumstances, the latter would be deprived of most, if not all, of their normative as well as practical value. What is to be implied from Article 103 is instead that peace and security concerns *do* supersede human rights provided that these concerns are met in conformity with the general principles of necessity and proportionality.[18]

This conclusion finds confirmation in the reaffirmation by the Security Council of the need 'to combat by all means, in accordance with the Charter of the United

[15] See, eg, SC Res 820, 27 April 2003, on the situation in Bosnia and Herzegovina, imposing sanctions on 'any person or undertaking in or operating from' the former Yugoslavia (Serbia and Montenegro).

[16] See section 3A1 below.

[17] As is well known, under Art 103 of the UN Charter: 'In the event of a conflict between the obligations of the Members of the United Nations under the present Charter and their obligations under any other international agreement, their obligations under the present Charter shall prevail.'

[18] For a full development of this argument, see A Ciampi, *Sanzioni del Consiglio di sicurezza e diritti umani* (2007) 135–73, esp at 156.

Nations and international law, including applicable international human rights, refugee, and humanitarian law, threats to international peace and security' and 'to continue to ensure that fair and clear procedures exist for placing individuals and entities on the Consolidated List and for removing them as well as for granting humanitarian exemptions'.[19]

From the point of view of the parties affected, it does not necessarily matter whether the obligation to comply with human rights standards is an obligation that actually accrues to states only and/or the Security Council itself. What is extremely relevant in a human rights perspective is that fair and clear procedures exist and are applicable to all individuals and entities affected by UN targeted sanctions regimes. This is indispensable in order to ensure the certainty of the law, but is all the more essential for the purposes of the equality of treatment of individuals and entities in similar situations. The principle of equality probably does not yet apply across national frontiers (with the notable exception of the judicial space of the European Union (EU)). Irrespective of whether the principle of equality applies worldwide, however, measures imposed at the UN level require that they be imposed, maintained, and reviewed pursuant to uniform procedures.

3. The 1267 Committee

A. Listing and de-listing procedures

As mentioned in the Introduction, the present study is focused on the financial sanctions administered by the so-called 1267 Committee, also known as 'the Al-Qaida and Taliban Sanctions Committee' (hereinafter also the 'Committee'), established by Security Council Resolution 1267 (1999). Since most of the other UN targeted sanctions committees have relied on the 1267 Committee's precedents, the tasks and procedures of this Committee are representative of the practice of other sanctions committees.

The Committee initially operated in the absence of any guidelines, and procedures totally lacked transparency. With a number of resolutions—in particular: Resolutions 1617 (2005), 1730 (2006), 1735 (2006), 1822 (2008), and 1904 (2009)—the Security Council has provided for a review of listing decisions, a de-listing procedure, and a possibility of addressing a de-listing request to a newly established 'Office of the Ombudsperson'.[20] In implementation thereof, the Committee, like all other

[19] SC Res 1822, 30 June 2008, preamble, paras 3 and 23.

[20] For an examination of developments brought about by SC Res 1730 and 1735 (2006), see Arcari, 'Sviluppi in tema di tutela dei diritti di individui iscritti nelle liste dei comitati delle sanzioni del Consiglio di sicurezza' (2007) 90 *Rivista di diritto internazionale* 657; Bothe, 'Security Council's Targeted Sanctions against Presumed Terrorists: The Need to Comply with Human Rights Standards' (2008) 6 *Journal of International Criminal Justice* 541; Reich, 'Due Process and Sanctions Targeted Against Individuals Pursuant to Resolution 1267 (1999)' (2008) 33 *Yale Journal of International Law*, available at http://papers.ssrn.com/sol3/papers.cfm?abstract_id=1268163 (last accessed 10 February 2011).

sanctions committees, has adopted, and subsequently amended, guidelines for the conduct of their work.[21]

In addition to procedures for the inclusion of new names on the list administered by the 1267 Committee (the 'Consolidated List') and the removal of entries therefrom, the Guidelines regulate the updating of existing information on, and review of, the Consolidated List, the mechanisms for authorizing exemptions to the restrictive measures as well as the Committee's reporting and outreach activities. In line with its ultimate objective, which is to address the human rights issues raised by Security Council targeted sanctions regimes, however, the analysis will concentrate on the listing and de-listing procedures.[22]

In relation thereto, the fundamental distinction to be drawn is that between protection afforded *ex ante*, ie before a person's name is actually included in the Consolidated List, and the remedies available once the measures have been imposed on (if not already implemented against) the targeted individual or entity. We shall refer to protection *via* these latter remedies as *ex post* protection.

As will be shown, while being placed on the list is relatively easy, getting off is much more difficult.[23] For, while protection *ex ante*—in particular, the right to be informed and to be heard before interference with a person's rights actually occurs—is practically non-existent, protection *ex post* does not yet offer the affected individual or entity an appropriate remedy for effectively challenging—within a reasonable time from their adoption—the restrictive measures imposed against him or her.

1. The absence of any ex ante protection

Minimum substantive standards require a clear definition of the grounds for the imposition of sanctions and the applicable evidentiary requirements. Despite recent improvements, however, procedures remain excessively vague under both counts.

Listing requests are submitted by states. Member states are encouraged to submit to the Committee for inclusion on the Consolidated List 'names of individuals, groups, undertakings and entities participating, by any means, in the financing or support of acts or activities of Al-Qaida, Usama bin Laden and the Taliban, and other individuals, groups, undertakings and entities *associated with them*'[24]. A description of acts or activities indicating that an individual, group, undertaking, or entity is 'associated with' al-Qaida, Usama bin Laden or the Taliban was introduced by Resolution 1617 (2005) and reaffirmed in Resolution 1822

[21] Guidelines of the Committee for the Conduct of its Work (adopted on 7 November 2002, as amended on 10 April 2003, 21 December 2005, 29 November 2006, 12 February 2007, 9 December 2008, 22 July 2010, and 26 January 2011; hereinafter the 'Guidelines'), available at www.un.org/sc/committees/1267/pdf/1267_guidelines.pdf (last accessed 10 February 2011). The Guidelines are reprinted in the Annex to the present volume.

[22] 'Listing' and 'De-listing' are dealt with under sections 6 and 7, respectively, of the Guidelines. If not indicated otherwise, all quotations in the next two paragraphs are taken therefrom.

[23] For the view that persons in the UN terrorist list 'stand even less chance of escaping this fate than they do of being released from Guantánamo Bay', see 'UN Law. Coming Up Trumps', *The Economist* (2 February 2009) 59.

[24] SC Res 1822 (2008), para 9 (emphasis added).

(2008). Such acts or activities 'include: (*a*) participating in the financing, planning, facilitating, preparing, or perpetrating of acts or activities by, in conjunction with, under the name of, on behalf of, or in support of; (*b*) supplying, selling or transferring arms and related material to; (*c*) recruiting for; or (*d*) otherwise supporting acts or activities of: Al-Qaida, Usama bin Laden or the Taliban, or any cell, affiliate, splinter group or derivative thereof'.

This is not an exhaustive list. Moreover, the ground of 'otherwise supporting acts or activities of' al-Qaida, Usama bin Laden, or the Taliban is as vague as the 'associated with' standard that it purports to clarify.

Proposals for listing should be submitted using the cover sheet available on the Committee's website and shall include as much relevant and specific information as possible. States 'shall provide a detailed statement of case'. This, in turn, 'should' provide: '(1) specific findings demonstrating the association or activities alleged; (2) the nature of the supporting evidence (e.g., intelligence, law enforcement, judicial, media, admissions by subject, etc.) and (3) supporting evidence or documents'.

The use of recommendatory, rather than mandatory, language is a clear indication that, although highly desirable, this information is not required for the purposes of listing.

A criminal charge or conviction is not necessary for inclusion on the Consolidated List, because, as mentioned above, the sanctions are intended to be preventive, not criminal, in nature. But there are not minimum evidentiary requirements either (in the Guidelines or relevant Security Council resolutions). States can withold from the general public (including the interested party) even the supporting evidence or documents that *can* be supplied, by simply identifying those parts of the statement of the case that may be released upon request to interested states. Only the part of the statement of the case that may be publicly released will be used by the Committee for development of the 'narrative summary of reasons for listing' to be made available on the Committee's website. This usually consists of a statement of two to three paragraphs providing the information necessary for the positive identification of the individual or entity concerned and the association or activities alleged. No specific finding or evidence demonstrating it, however, has to be made available. In fact, none of the 'narrative summaries' so far accessible on the Committee's website provide any indication whatsoever of the evidence or documents supporting the allegations.[25]

Once a request for listing has been submitted, the proposed name is added to the Consolidated List if no objection is raised by a member of the Committee (within five working days following circulation of the proposal or a shorter period, in urgent situations).[26] If, after consultations, consensus cannot be reached, the matter may be submitted to the Security Council. The nature of the listing procedure, however, especially in the absence of any specific requirements about

[25] The 1267 Committee's Narrative Summaries of Reasons for Listing are available at www.un.org/sc/committees/1267/narrative.shtml (last accessed 10 February 2011).

[26] This is in accordance with the consensus rule which applies to all of the Sanctions Committees' decision making.

the grounds and supporting evidence which justify the request, makes it unlikely for a state to object to a proposal for listing.

The whole process is therefore unsuitable for debate by the Committee of the grounds that justify the proposed listing and/or the sufficient nature of the evidence gathered for the purposes of supporting the allegations.

Within three working days *after* a name has been added to the Consolidated List, the country in which the individual or entity is located and, in the case of individuals, the country of which the person is a national, are notified with the portion of the statement of the case that can be publicly released and a description of the effects of a designation, the Committee's procedures for considering de-listing requests as well as the provisions for available exemptions. The country or countries so notified are required to take all possible measures to notify and inform in timely manner the listed party.

Not only therefore are the substantive standards deficient, but from a procedural point of view as well, no *ex ante* protection of any sort is provided for the newly listed individuals and entities. They will be informed of the measures imposed on them and the consequences arising therefrom only after the inclusion of their name on the Consolidated List (and possibly even after their funds, other financial assets, and economic resources have been frozen).

These features impinge upon the fairness of the listing procedure. But they also—at least to some extent, irremediably—affect the possibility of effective, both administrative and judicial, review.

2. *Ex post remedies*

A petitioner (individual(s), groups, undertakings, and/or entities on the Consolidated List) may submit a petition to request review of the case by explaining why he or she does not (or no longer) meet(s) the criteria for listing. A standard form available on the Committee's website can be used for this purpose.

Before the Security Council adopted Resolution 1904 on 17 December 2009, requests for de-listing could be submitted either directly to the Focal Point established pursuant to Security Council Resolution 1730 (2006) (hereinafter, the 'Focal Point'),[27] or through the permanent mission of his or her state of residence or nationality to the UN. A state could, however, decide that, as a rule, its nationals or residents should address their de-listing requests directly to the Focal Point.[28]

The Focal Point did not deal with the merits of the petitions. It performed the twofold function of a clearing house and a consultations facilitator. In the first place, the Focal Point verified that a request was new (or, if repeated, that it contained some additional information) and informed the petitioner of the general procedure for processing it. It then forwarded the request to the designating state(s)

[27] Focal Point for De-listing established pursuant to SC Res 1730 (2006) at www.un.org/sc/committees/dfp.shtml (last accessed 10 February 2011).

[28] The state will do so by a declaration addressed to the Chairman which will be published on the Committee's website. To date, only France has submitted such declaration.

as well as to the state(s) of nationality and residence, and facilitated consultations between them.

In paragraph 20 of Resolution 1904 (2009), the Security Council decided that 'when considering delisting requests, the [1267] Committee shall be assisted by an Office of the Ombudsperson, to be established for an initial period of 18 months from the date of adoption of this resolution'. The Council further decided (in paragraph 21) that 'after the appointment of the Ombudsperson, the Office of the Ombudsperson shall receive requests from individuals and entities seeking to be removed from the Consolidated List . . . and that, after the appointment of the Ombudsperson, the Focal Point mechanism established in resolution 1730 (2006) shall no longer receive such requests'. However, the resolution goes on to say that the Focal Point would continue to receive requests from individuals and entities seeking to be removed from other sanctions lists. The Committee shall also continue to consider de-listing requests of member states.

The de-listing procedure to be observed by the Office of the Ombudsperson and the Committee is now described in detail in Annex II of Resolution 1904 (2009). The annex provides for three distinct phases after a de-listing request has been received, namely: (1) information gathering by the Ombudsperson (two months); (2) dialogue of the Ombudsperson with the petitioner (two months); and (3) Committee discussion and decision (two months).

At the end of the second phase, the Ombudsperson, with the help of the Monitoring Team, shall draft and circulate to the Committee a 'Comprehensive Report' that will:

> (a) [s]ummarize and, as appropriate, specify the sources of, all information available to the Ombudsperson that is relevant to the delisting request . . . (b) [d]escribe the Ombudsperson's activities with respect to this delisting request . . . (c) [b]ased on an analysis of all the information available to the Ombudsperson and the Ombudsperson's observations, lay out for the Committee the principal arguments concerning the delisting request (Annex II, paragraph 7).

Finally, '[a]fter the Committee has had thirty days to review the comprehensive report, the chair of the Committee shall place the delisting request on the Committee's agenda for consideration' (paragraph 8).

The maximum that the petitioner could obtain from the Focal Point was that his or her request be put on the Committee's agenda. In contrast, the new procedure leads to a report on the individual case submitted to the 1267 Committee by the Ombudsperson, including a recommendation whether the de-listing request should be approved or not. Although this clearly amounts to an improvement of the petitioner's position, the procedures for processing de-listing requests still appear far from satisfactory in at least three different ways.

As far as the *initiative* for the procedure is concerned, the individual is not provided with a right of direct access to the Committee. The Committee will only deal with a de-listing request upon a state's recommendation or upon action taken by the Ombudsperson (comprehensive report).

With regard to the *outcome*, the removal of the petitioner's name from the Consolidated List will, as under the previous procedure, only be obtained by consensus. Paragraph 10 of Annex II expressly states that '[a]fter the Committee consideration, the Committee shall decide whether to approve the delisting request *through its normal decision-making procedures*'.[29] This means that any state member of the Committee at the time the request is being processed can prevent the de-listing. No explanation, let alone a qualified one, is necessary for a state to object. In most instances, the state opposing the request will be the designating state, but an objection could very well be raised by any Committee's member.[30] Should the case be referred to the Security Council, it would still be subject to the voting procedure of this latter organ and therefore to the veto power of its permanent members. However, under the new procedure, the Committee shall convey to the Ombudsperson, if it decides to reject the de-listing request, its decision 'including, as appropriate, explanatory comments, any further relevant information about the Committee's decision, and an updated narrative summary of reasons for listing' (Annex II, paragraph 12). This can be regarded as a cautious admission of the Council that a substantial explanation of a negative decision is desirable.

Finally, and most importantly, at no point is the petitioner entitled to be heard in person during either the 'dialogue' phase or the 'Committee discussion and decision' phase. Moreover, neither the 'dialogue' nor the discussion in the Committee necessarily imply that the petitioner's claim will be examined on the merits in relation to the grounds and supporting evidence at the origin of the listing. Since the designating state can withhold the relevant information even from the Committee, the review of one's case implies the risk that the decision on de-listing be driven by political, rather than by legal, considerations. Here still lies, it is submitted, one of the major problems, in a human rights perspective, of the whole process.

B. The limits of an ex post political remedy

No doubt can be raised as to the political nature of the de-listing procedure.

The true initiation of the process in principle depends on the discretion of the state(s) of nationality and the designating state(s), as well as of any one member of the Committee, if the request is submitted through the Ombudsperson. The body entrusted with the power to decide whether a name ought to be removed from the Consolidated List is purely political because of its composition and voting procedure: the Committee is an organ made up of representatives of the same states that sit in the Security Council, which make decisions by consensus; this implies the veto power of any one of its members, whose position will be mainly determined by

[29] Emphasis added.

[30] The *Sayadi and Vinck* case, which is examined in section 5A below, provides an example of one such instance.

political considerations. There is no remedy before a court of law (or any other organ) if the Committee rejects a petition for de-listing.[31]

Even if the petitioner were given direct access to the Committee, the composition and deliberation process of the latter would prevent one from considering that the total lack of protection afforded *ex ante* is compensated in whole or in part *ex post*.

In light thereof, no real relief may be expected from the possibility of construing an obligation—rather than a mere right—of the state of nationality (or residence) to espouse the petitioner's request for de-listing for the purpose of including his or her case on the Committee's agenda. Indeed, several elements point in this direction. Preliminary to their identification, however, is the qualification of the action of the national state (or, eventually, of another state), when it recommends removal of a name from the Consolidated List.

1. The problem of qualifying the action of the state espousing the petitioner's request for de-listing

Where the state of nationality takes up the petitioner's case, it seems natural to qualify its action as an exercise of diplomatic protection. For this purpose, however, it is necessary to identify both the internationally wrongful act for which reparation is sought and the true addressee of such exercise.[32]

That the inclusion of a person's name in the Consolidated List, because of a total lack of (*ex ante*) protection of the listed parties, is per se unlawful, whatever the grounds and supporting evidence, would—at least, at present—be hardly sustainable. Should one hold so, the Consolidated List as a whole would be unlawful and any listed individual or entity would be entitled to the removal of his or her name therefrom, in accordance with the general principle that reparation should, as far as possible, eradicate all consequences of the internationally wrongful act. No practice, however, supports such a radical view.

[31] As is well known, the UN Charter does not provide for a general system of judicial review of the acts of the Organization (including Security Council binding resolutions and acts taken in implementation thereof by its subsidiary organs). Judicial review by the ICJ cannot be excluded, in accordance with the general rules governing the Court's exercise of jurisdiction. The ICJ's contentious jurisdiction, however, is limited to interstate proceedings, while its advisory jurisdiction is only open to other UN organs and to specialized agencies. In no case can procedures be taken at the initiative of, or include the participation of, private parties.

[32] See Art 1 of the Draft Articles on Diplomatic Protection adopted by the International Law Commission (ILC) in 2006, which describes diplomatic protection as the invocation of the responsibility of a state that has committed an internationally wrongful act in respect of a national of another state, by the state of which that person is a national, with a view to implementing responsibility: 'For the purposes of the present draft articles, diplomatic protection consists of the invocation by a state, through diplomatic action or other means of peaceful settlement, of the responsibility of another state for an injury caused by an internationally wrongful act of that state to a natural or legal person that is a national of the former state with a view to the implementation of such responsibility.' UN Doc A/61/10. See also the ILC Commentary on Art 1 for the view that diplomatic protection 'is a procedure for securing the responsibility of the state for injury to the national flowing from an internationally wrongful act' (ibid).

It is more reasonable to consider that de-listing requests ought to be granted only when the person does not meet, or no longer meets, the criteria for listing. By requiring the petitioner to explain 'why he/she *no longer* meets the criteria',[33] the Committee's Guidelines unequivocally point in this direction. It is not even conceived therein that listing may be unfounded, let alone unlawful, from its origin.

If maintaining the petitioner's name on the Consolidated List when there are no (longer) substantive grounds to support it is an internationally wrongful act, who is responsible for that act?

Names are added to, as well as removed from, the Consolidated List by the Committee, which is a subsidiary organ of the Security Council. The Committee's acts are therefore directly attributable to the Security Council and hence to the UN.

Traditionally, a claim brought in the exercise of diplomatic protection is an inter-state claim, but no principle prevents one from applying the same concept in the context of a claim between a state and an international organization. One can thus consider that diplomatic protection can be exercised in relation to an international wrongful act of an international organization, with a view to the implementation of the responsibility of the latter.[34]

What remains problematic, however, is the possibility for the organization in question to provide for the reparation sought. As recalled above, any decision (including decisions on de-listing requests) is subject to the consensus rule and consensus may very well be lacking due to the objection of one (or more) member state(s).[35]

The possibility of invoking the responsibility of a state (eventually in addition to the responsibility of the UN) for the *implementation* of the measures which follow from the inclusion of a person's name in the Consolidated List would be of little use. Even if successful, such an exercise would never result in the removal of the entry from the Consolidated List, as this can only be done by the Committee itself. The best possible outcome for the individual would be the annulment of the national measures implementing the UN sanctions against him or her. This would remove some, but not all, of the effects of the listing. The restrictive measures imposed by the Security Council would remain not only internationally binding but also applicable in all member states but the state whose responsibility is invoked. Moreover, as highlighted above,[36] there are fundamental rights, such as the right to privacy, which would continue to be

[33] Section 7(d); emphasis added.

[34] The works of the ILC in relation to the Draft Articles on the Responsibility of International Organizations do imply the possibility of applying by analogy the concept of diplomatic protection to the invocation of the international responsibility of an international organization by a state (or another international organization).

[35] Should consensus not be achieved in the Committee, the matter is referred to the Security Council, where deliberations require nine favourable votes, with the non-negative vote of the permanent five.

[36] See section 2B.

impeded because of the listing, independently from the implementation of the restrictive measures attached thereto.[37]

The protection of the petitioners' rights would, instead, be advanced if a state could be held accountable for *objecting* to a de-listing request where there are no (longer) grounds that justify the listing. The cessation of this allegedly internationally wrongful act would automatically result in the removal of the person's name from the Consolidated List. But how to define when an objection is unfounded for lack of objective grounds or evidence to support the allegations against the listed party? As pointed out above, the limited information available to the Committee makes any such inquiry speculative rather than practical.

As to the traditional requirements of diplomatic protection (nationality and exhaustion of local remedies), they do not raise particular problems. Exhaustion of the local remedies rule is complied with to the extent that no remedy is available to the listed parties except for the de-listing procedure provided for under the Committee's Guidelines.[38]

When the petitioner's request is espoused by a state other than the state of nationality (or residence), that state acts outside the scope of diplomatic protection. It still takes, however, a remedial action to secure protection of that person and to obtain reparation for the internationally wrongful act inflicted. The rights for which protection is sought are obviously human rights that any state is entitled to protect.

The Committee's Guidelines already recognize that the protection of the listed individuals and entities ought not to depend entirely upon, or be left to, the state of nationality. Moreover, when a petition is submitted through the Office of the Ombudsperson, the procedure leads to a decision of the Committee based on the comprehensive report submitted by the Ombudsperson. Accordingly, the case will be placed on the Committee's agenda.

2. *The possibility of construing an obligation to act of limited usefulness*

A state is free in principle to decide whether to exercise diplomatic protection in favour of a national. It is under no duty or obligation to do so.[39]

International practice, however, does not rule out the possibility to construe an obligation, under certain circumstances, at least to take into account the views of

[37] A further, more radical objection to the possibility of holding a state accountable in relation to the implementation of targeted sanctions is that, in the absence of an international mechanism, this would be left to the national authorities of the member states. The problems arising therefrom are discussed in section 4 below.

[38] On the exceptions to the local remedies rule in the context of diplomatic protection, see Art 15 of the Draft Articles on Diplomatic Protection (n 32 above), providing inter alia that: '[l]ocal remedies do not need to be exhausted where: (a) There are no reasonably available local remedies to provide effective redress, or the local remedies provide no reasonable possibility of such redress'. Moreover, one could even argue that the local remedies rule is not applicable to the present case, as UN member states have validly derogated therefrom on the basis of the Committee's Guidelines, which, in turn, implemented the relevant Security Council resolutions adopted under Chapter VII of the Charter.

[39] See Art 2 of the Draft Articles on Diplomatic Protection (n 32 above): 'A state has the right to exercise diplomatic protection in accordance with the present draft articles.'

the individual seeking protection for his or her rights.[40] A trend towards the formation of a rule for this purpose is already emerging.[41] Moreover, the internal law of a state may oblige a state to extend diplomatic protection to a national, even if international law imposes no such obligation. The constitutions of many states recognize the right of the individual to receive diplomatic protection for injuries suffered abroad, which must carry with it the corresponding duty of the state to exercise protection. A number of national court decisions indicate that although a state has a discretion whether to exercise diplomatic protection or not, there is an obligation on that state, subject to judicial review, to do something to assist its nationals, which may include an obligation to give due consideration to the possibility of exercising diplomatic protection.[42]

The case most in point in the matters of UN sanctions is the judgment of the Brussels Court of First Instance (4th section) of 11 February 2005 in the case *Nabil Sayadi and Patricia Vinck v. Belgium.*[43]

The Court condemned the Belgian state 'à demander sous le bénéfice de l'urgence au Comité des sanctions des Nations Unies de radier les noms des demandeurs de la liste et d'en communiquer la preuve aux demandeurs, à peine d'une astreinte de 250 euros par jour de retard, à compter de l'expiration du délai de 30 jours à partir de la signification du présent jugement.' We will revert to the follow-up of this case that Sayadi and Vinck ultimately brought before the HRC.[44] Suffice it to mention that only four years after this judgment has the Belgian government been able to obtain the removal of their names from the Consolidated List.[45]

The Court of First Instance of the European Communities (CFI) in the *Ayadi* case,[46] in relation to the de-listing procedure before the 1267 Committee, also held that particular obligations are imposed on the member states of the Community

[40] 'The discretionary nature of the state's right to exercise diplomatic protection is affirmed by draft article 2 of the present draft articles and has been asserted by the International Court of Justice and national courts, as shown in the commentary to draft article 2. Despite this there is growing support for the view that there is some obligation, however imperfect, on states, either under international law or national law, to protect their nationals abroad when they are subjected to significant human rights violations.' See ILC Commentary (n 32 above).

[41] See Art 19 of the Draft Articles on Diplomatic Protection: 'A state entitled to exercise diplomatic protection according to the present draft articles, should: (a) Give due consideration to the possibility of exercising diplomatic protection, especially when a significant injury has occurred; (b) Take into account, wherever feasible, the views of injured persons with regard to resort to diplomatic protection and the reparation to be sought; and (c) Transfer to the injured person any compensation obtained for the injury from the responsible state subject to any reasonable deductions.'

[42] For an overview of such cases, see ILC Commentary *sub* draft Art 2.

[43] *Tribunal de Première Instance de Bruxelles (quatrième section)*, Judgment of 11 February 2005, *Nabil Sayadi and Patricia Vinck v Belgium* (unreported).

[44] See section 5A below.

[45] The irony of the case is that Sayadi and Vinck were included on the Consolidated List upon the designation of Belgium and on this account the HRC has held it accountable for a twofold violation of the UN Covenant of Human Rights.

[46] Case T-253/02, *Chafiq Ayadi v Council of the European Union*, CFI Judgment of 12 July 2006, [2006] ECR II-2139.

when a request for removal from the list is addressed to them (Recital 144 of judgment).

In the CFI's view, '[t]he Member states must thus ensure, so far as is possible, that interested persons are put in a position to put their point of view before the competent national authorities when they present a request for their case to be reviewed . . . in such a way as to take due account of the difficulties that the persons concerned may encounter in ensuring the effective protection of their rights, having regard to the specific context and nature of the measures affecting them' (Recital 147 of judgment).[47] Moreover, 'having regard to the fact . . . that individuals are not entitled to be heard in person by the Sanctions Committee, with the result that they are dependent, essentially, on the diplomatic protection afforded by states to their nationals, the Member states are required to act promptly to ensure that such persons' cases are presented without delay and fairly and impartially to the Committee, with a view to their re-examination, if that appears to be justified in the light of the relevant information supplied' (Recital 149 of judgment). Finally, 'it is open to the persons concerned to bring an action for judicial review . . . against any wrongful refusal by the competent national authority to submit their cases to the Sanctions Committee for re-examination and, more generally, against any infringement by that national authority of the right of the persons involved to request the review of their case' (Recital 150 of judgment).[48]

Only the above-mentioned ruling of the *Tribunal de Première Instance de Bruxelles*, which the CFI expressly referred to, so far supports these statements. Moreover, the CFI's ruling still awaits confirmation by the Court of Justice of the European Communities (ECJ), before which an appeal is pending.[49]

At the UN level, the Sanctions Monitoring Team, a committee of experts established by the Security Council pursuant to Resolution 1564 (2004) with the task of assisting the 1267 Committee in the exercise of its functions, suggested as early as 2005 that:

> the Committee could require in its guidelines that states forward petitions for de-listing to the Committee . . . The Team believes that, after the requisite consultations between the

[47] 'Thus, the Member states would not be justified in refusing to initiate the review procedure provided for by the Guidelines solely because the persons concerned could not provide precise and relevant information in support of their request, owing to their having been unable to ascertain the precise reasons for which they were included in the list in question or the evidence supporting those reasons, on account of the confidential nature of those reasons or that evidence' (Rec 148 of judgment).

[48] 'It follows that, in an action in which it is alleged that the competent national authorities have infringed the right of the persons involved to request review of their cases in order to be removed from the list at issue, it is for the national court to apply, in principle, national law while taking care to ensure the full effectiveness of Community law, which may lead it to refrain from applying, if need be, a national rule preventing that result . . . such as a rule excluding from judicial review a refusal of national authorities to take action with a view to guaranteeing the diplomatic protection of their nationals.' It thus invited the applicant to avail himself of the opportunities for judicial remedy offered by Irish domestic law to challenge the Irish authorities' failure to cooperate in good faith with him, by whom its request to be removed from the list at issue was pending (Rec 152–3 of judgment).

[49] See Case C-403/06 P, *Chafiq Ayadi v Council of the European Union*, Appeal brought on 27 September 2006 by Chafiq Ayadi against the judgment of the Court of First Instance (Second Chamber) delivered on 12 July 2006 in Case T-253/02, OJ 2006 C 294/32.

state of residence and/or citizenship and the original designating state, in accordance with the guidelines, the state of residence and/or citizenship could be required to submit the de-listing petition to the Committee along with an approval, objection or neutral position. In this manner, the Committee would be the body to make the final decision, and listed individuals and entities would receive additional procedural protection.[50]

This suggestion has had no follow-up in the practice of the Sanctions Committee. It is doubtful, however, that the 1267 Committee (as any other sanctions committee) would have the power to impose upon the member states an obligation which finds no basis in a resolution of the Security Council adopted under Chapter VII of the UN Charter. And it is very unlikely that the Security Council will ever resort to its binding (or even recommendatory) powers to impose (or advance the formation of) an obligation of such a sort. Signs in this direction have therefore to be found outside the Committee's practice.

Whether the existence of a duty to exercise 'diplomatic protection' is affirmed on the basis of general international law, national law or human rights norms pertaining to a special conventional regime such as the EU, this would not significantly advance the protection afforded to the listed parties under existing procedures.

Until minimum substantive standards and minimum evidentiary requirements as to the grounds and the supporting evidence which justify the listing are introduced, not only the listing phase, but also the processing of de-listing requests risk nevertheless remaining at the mercy of any one state. In the case of de-listing, this risk is even greater because, as noted above, the consensus rule applying within the Committee results in the power of any of its members to veto a de-listing request.

Here lies one of the major obstacles to the improvement of current procedures for listing and de-listing individuals and entities targeted by UN sanctions. As we shall see, these very same reasons make any possibility of effective judicial review by a court or tribunal, both national or international, theoretical at the very best, rather than real and effective.

4. Legal Challenges to the Regime at the Regional and Member State Level

The features of the UN system according to which names are added to and removed from the Consolidated List and for removing them lie at the origin of some of the major restrictions to the protection afforded to the listed individuals and entities at the national and regional levels. They make it very difficult, if not impossible, for any national or international court to provide an effective judicial review.

[50] *Second Report of the Analytical Support and Sanctions Monitoring Team Established Pursuant to Resolution 1526 (2004)*, UN Doc S/2005/83, 15 February 2005, para 56; *Third Report of the Analytical Support and Sanctions Monitoring Team Established Pursuant to Resolution 1526 (2004)*, UN Doc S/2005/572, 9 September 2005, para 55.

The possibility of *directly* challenging the acts of the Committee before a national or international court will be generally precluded under the principle of immunity of international organization and/or the general rules governing international adjudication and the effects of treaties.

National proceedings directly challenging Security Council decisions and/or the acts taken by the competent sanctions committee in implementation thereof, will be generally barred under the principle of immunity of international organizations. As a rule, national courts lack jurisdiction to entertain actions against the UN.[51]

The jurisdiction of an international court and tribunal is determined by its constituent instrument. No international court will therefore have jurisdiction over the acts of the Organization, unless the latter is a party thereof (or has otherwise consented to the court's exercise of jurisdiction).

The only option available to affected individuals and entities is to challenge the measures of *implementation* of UN targeted sanctions. [52] This possibility cannot be ruled out altogether. It is, however, subject to several limitations.

The first general limit restriction to a challenge brought by a listed party against the measures of implementation of UN sanctions insofar as they apply to him or her, relates to the effects that flow from the very fact of one individual or entity having his or her name included in a list of targeted sanctions. A successful challenge against the measures of implementation of an assets freeze (or a travel or visa ban) could result in the annulment (and possibly reparation) of the measure itself. In other words, it cannot remove the petitioner's name from the list but only set aside the measure(s) taken in implementation thereof. The compromising of one's right to privacy, honour, and reputation which directly flows from the listing cannot be remedied nor brought to an end.

Another general issue, connected to the first, is the responsibility accruing to the state under international law for the failure to implement the UN sanctions in relation to the individual or entity having successfully challenged the national measures before its courts. Even if the consequences thereof ought not to be exaggerated, the risk of a fragmentation of Security Council resolutions along the borders of national (or supranational, in the case of the EU) jurisdictions is real.

Other obstacles—apparently no easier to overcome—stand in the way of a person seeking to protect his or her rights by bringing a challenge before a court of law. I shall discuss this scenario, by dealing separately with the situations of individuals and entities 'targeted' by UN financial sanctions in a member state of

[51] For an analysis of the relevant rules of German law, see Fassbender, 'Art. 19 Abs. 4 GG als Garantie innerstaatlichen Rechtsschutzes gegen Individualsanktionen des UN-Sicherheitsrates [Article 19 para 4 of the German Constitution as a Guarantee of Legal Protection Against Targeted Sanctions of the UN Security Council Before German Courts]' (2007) 132 *Archiv des öffentlichen Rechts* 257–86.

[52] There is also the possibility for an individual to bring an action against the state of nationality (or residence) to have it espouse his or her request for de-listing for the purposes of recommending it to the competent sanctions committee. However, because of the political nature of the sanctions committees' mechanism for processing de-listing requests, a state's recommendation for de-listing is a mere pre-condition which is necessary for placing the case on the competent committee's agenda: its acceptance remains subject to the consensus rule which applies to all committee's deliberations. See section 3B2 above.

the EU, because of the specificities of the problems arising in relation thereto with respect to listed parties affected by Security Council sanctions outside the EU.

A. UN sanctions before the Community courts

In EU member states, the implementation of UN financial sanctions generally takes place through Community measures.

As is well known, a system for implementing sanctions falling within the Community competence has existed since the 1990s, before being expressly provided for in the Treaties (with the Amsterdam Treaty). It applies in relation to the implementation of UN sanctions regimes, but also when the EU adopts 'autonomous sanctions', ie measures vis-à-vis individuals and entities, independently from a decision of the Security Council.

The mechanism is based on a combination of EU and Community competences. It is premised on the adoption of a common position (or a joint action) by the Council acting within the second pillar (Common Foreign and Security Policy) of the EU. This is followed by the 'necessary urgent measures' taken at the Community level, in accordance with Articles 60 and 301 of the EC Treaty.[53] These provisions empower the Council of the EU to take measures acting 'by a qualified majority on a proposal from the Commission', as regards third states.[54] Measures targeted against individuals and entities can be adopted under Articles 60 and 301, together with Article 308 of the EC Treaty (Article 352 of the Treaty on the Functioning of the EU).[55] This implies that the Council will act unanimously on a proposal from the Commission and after consulting the European Parliament.

The Community's competence to adopt or implement targeted sanctions has been the object of various challenges before the Community. This competence appears, however, to be sufficiently settled after the ruling handed down by the ECJ on 3 September 2008, in *Kadi*.[56] With the same judgment the Court reversed the solutions given in the CFI's ruling of 21 September 2005[57] on a number of legal issues which cannot be exhaustively dealt with here.[58] The General Court of the

[53] With the entry into force of the Treaty of Lisbon on 1 December 2009, the respective treaty provisions became Arts 75 and 215 of the Treaty on the Functioning of the European Union.

[54] Art 301 is worded as follows: 'Where it is provided, in a common position or in a joint action adopted according to the provisions of the Treaty on European Union relating to the common foreign and security policy, for an action by the Community to interrupt or to reduce, in part or completely, economic relations with one or more third countries, the Council shall take the necessary urgent measures. The Council shall act by a qualified majority on a proposal from the Commission.' Under Art 60, para 1: 'If, in the cases envisaged in Article 301, action by the Community is deemed necessary, the Council may, in accordance with the procedure provided for in Article 301, take the necessary urgent measures on the movement of capital and on payments as regards the third countries concerned.'

[55] As is well known, this article entitles the Community (Union) to act to attain one of the objectives of the Community, when the Treaty has not provided the necessary powers.

[56] C-402/05 P *Kadi v Council/Commission*, Judgment of 3 September 2008, [2008] ECR I-6351.

[57] T-315/01 *Kadi v Council/Commission*, Judgment of 21 September 2005, [2005] ECR II-3649.

[58] Dealing with the whole range of legal issues at stake in the *Kadi* rulings would exceed the scope of this chapter. For a thorough examination thereof, see Poli and Tzanou, 'The Kadi Rulings: A Survey

European Union (as the CFI is called following the entry into force of the Treaty of Lisbon) in principle followed the judgment of the ECJ in a new decision of 30 September 2010.[59]

For the purposes of our analysis I shall focus on the ECJ's statement that Community measures of implementation of UN-targeted sanctions are subject to the principle of full judicial review for the purposes of protection of fundamental human rights.

Ruling on the relationship between EU law and international law,[60] the ECJ held that the EU, not being a member of the UN, is not bound by Security Council resolutions. In the Court's view, Article 307 of the EC Treaty cannot be interpreted as allowing member states to derogate from their obligations under the Treaties for purposes of complying with their obligations under the Charter. Community measures of implementation of UN sanctions, therefore, fall under the principle of full judicial review of Community acts. Hence, there is the possibility of assessing their conformity with the principles of respect of human rights and fundamental freedoms, which form part of the very foundation of the European legal order.

On the merits, the ECJ decided to annul Regulation (EC) No 881/2002, insofar as it concerned Kadi and the Al Barakaat International Foundation, as their 'rights of the defence, in particular the right to be heard, and the right to effective judicial review of those rights, were patently not respected' (Recital 334 of judgment).

So far as concerns the rights of the defence, in particular the right to be heard, with regard to restrictive measures such as those imposed by the contested regulation, the ECJ conceded that 'the Community authorities cannot be required to communicate those grounds *before* the name of a person or entity is entered in that list for the first time': 'such prior communication would be liable to jeopardise the effectiveness of the freezing of funds and resources imposed by that regulation. In order to attain the objective pursued by that regulation, such measures must, by their very nature, take advantage of a surprise effect and . . . apply with immediate effect' (Recitals 338–40; emphasis added). However, the Court noted that neither the contested regulation nor Common Position 2002/402 to which the former refers provides for a procedure for communicating the evidence that justifies the inclusion of the names of the persons concerned in Annex I to that regulation and for hearing those persons, either at the time of that inclusion or *later*. The Court also noted that the Council *at no time* informed the appellants of the evidence brought against them for including their names in Annex I to the contested regulation and, consequently, the imposition of the restrictive measures laid down by the latter:

of the Literature', *Yearbook of European Law* (forthcoming) and in M Cremona and S Poli (eds), *Challenging the EU Counter-terrorism Measures through the Courts*, EUI Working Papers (2009).

[59] T-85/09, *Kadi v Commission/Council*, Judgment of 30 September 2010. Mr Kadi had sought annulment of a new regulation adopted by the Commission on 28 November 2008 maintaining the freeze of Mr Kadi's funds. The General Court decided that the regulation was adopted in breach of Mr Kadi's rights of defence, his right to effective judicial review, and his right to property. Consequently, the Court annulled the regulation insofar as it concerns Mr Kadi.

[60] See paras 290–325.

> Because the Council neither communicated to the appellants the evidence used against them to justify the restrictive measures imposed on them nor afforded them the right to be informed of that evidence within a reasonable period after those measures were enacted, the appellants were not in a position to make their point of view in that respect known to advantage. Therefore, the appellants' rights of defence, in particular the right to be heard, were not respected. In addition, given the failure to inform them of the evidence adduced against them . . . the appellants were also unable to defend their rights with regard to that evidence in satisfactory conditions before the Community judicature, with the result that it must be held that their right to an effective legal remedy has also been infringed (Recitals 348–9).

Finally, because that infringement was not remedied in the course of the proceedings, the Court found that it was 'not able to undertake the review of the lawfulness of the contested regulation in so far as it concerns the appellants, with the result that it must be held that, for that reason too, the fundamental right to an effective legal remedy which they enjoy has not, in the circumstances, been observed' (Recital 351).

With regard to the breach of the right to respect for property entailed by the freezing measures, the Court stated that the restrictive measures imposed by the contested regulation constitute restrictions of the right to property which might, in principle, be justified. However, 'the applicable procedures must also afford the person concerned a reasonable opportunity of putting his case to the competent authorities . . . which constitutes a procedural requirement inherent in Article 1 of Protocol No 1 to the ECHR' (Recital 368). Because the contested regulation, insofar as it concerned the applicant, was adopted without furnishing any guarantee enabling him to put his case to the competent authorities, 'in the circumstances of the case, the imposition of the restrictive measures laid down by the contested regulation in respect of Mr Kadi, by including him in the list contained in Annex I to that regulation, constitutes an unjustified restriction of his right to property' (Recital 370).

In accordance thereof, the ECJ annulled the regulation implementing the Security Council's asset-freezing resolutions insofar as it concerned the applicant, on the ground that they violated the rights to a fair procedure and to property protection.

B. UN sanctions and national courts

Remedies are rare at the national level and only exceptionally resorted to. Very few, if any, are successful.

According to the ninth report of the Monitoring Team to the 1267 Committee,[61] the number of legal challenges involving individuals and entities on the Consolidated List concerning al-Qaida, the Taliban, and their associates at the

[61] *Ninth Report of the Analytical Support and Sanctions Monitoring Team Established Pursuant to Resolution 1526 (2004) and Extended by Resolution 1822 (2008)*, UN Doc S/2009/245, 28 February 2009. *Annex I, Litigation relating to individuals and entities on the Consolidated List*, para 1.

beginning of 2009, stands at 30.[62] Four actions brought before national courts are reported to have been dismissed in Pakistan, Switzerland, Turkey, and the United States, while a very limited number of proceedings remain pending (in Pakistan, the United Kingdom, and the United States).[63]

A study on UN sanctions and human rights recently conducted within the Committee of Experts of Public International law of the Council of Europe (CAHDI) also shows that few decisions exist at the national level on the matter, even in states where the principle of judicial review extends to UN resolutions and/or domestic measures adopted in execution thereof.[64]

Emblematic of the attitude of national courts faced with the issue of the legality of restrictive measures adopted in the implementation of UN sanctions is the ruling by the Federal Tribunal in Lausanne—the highest court in Switzerland—upholding the sanctions measures against Youssef Mustapha Nada Ebada.[65] Following the reasoning of the CFI's judgment of 21 September 2005 in *Kadi*,[66] the Federal Tribunal stated that the Swiss sanctions were not 'autonomous', but the result of the 'binding effect' of the decisions of the UN Security Council taken under Chapter VII of the UN Charter and that the binding effect of UN SC decisions could only be limited by a norm of *jus cogens*. Regarding Nada's claim that UN sanctions were adopted in breach of *jus cogens* (referring to basic human rights), the Tribunal said that 'fundamental rights (such as property rights, the right to a fair trial and the right to an effective judicial protection) are not absolute' and held that the procedural guarantees considered by the plaintiff as ineffective in the case of UN sanctions (right to a fair trial and right to an effective remedy) did not constitute 'core provisions of international human rights conventions'. The very same arguments were used by the same court to

[62] This number, however, includes cases brought before the ECJ and the CFI, the ECtHR and the HRC.

[63] National proceedings initiated by individuals and entities listed by the 1267 Committee concerning al-Qaida, the Taliban, and associated individuals and entities, are periodically reported to the Committee in annexes to the Monitoring Team's annual reports. In 2004, the report included 13 cases initiated before a national court by targeted individuals and entities (see *Second Report of the Analytical Support and Sanctions Monitoring Team Appointed Pursuant to Resolution 1526 (2004) Concerning Al-Qaida and the Taliban and Associated Individuals and Entities*, UN Doc S/2005/83, 15 December 2004, para 50). In 2005, it counted only ten pending cases (one in the Netherlands, two in Pakistan, two in Switzerland, one in Turkey, and four in the United States). See *Fifth Report of the Analytical Support and Sanctions Monitoring Team Established Pursuant to Resolution 1526 (2004) and Extended by Resolution 1617 (2005)*, 20 September 2006 (UN Doc. S/2006/750, *Annex III, Litigation by or relating to individuals on the Consolidated List*).

[64] The database 'Implementation of UN sanctions and respect for human rights', containing the replies—given by approximately two-thirds of the member states of the Council of Europe—to a questionnaire focusing on national practice concerning the relationship between UN targeted sanctions and human rights, is accessible on the CAHDI website at www.coe.int/t/dlapil/cahdi/default_en.asp (last accessed 10 February 2011).

[65] Case 1A.45/2007, Bundesgericht (Federal Tribunal of Lausanne), decision of 14 November 2007, 133 Entscheidungen des Schweizerischen Bundesgerichts II-450, also available on the website of the Federal Tribunal at www.bger.ch/index/jurisdiction/jurisdiction-inherit-template/jurisdiction-recht/jurisdiction-recht-urteile2000.htm (last accessed 10 February 2011).

[66] See n 57 above.

reject a challenge brought by Ali Ghaleb Himmat to the imposition of sanctions against him. That suit was dismissed on 22 April 2008.[67]

One cannot entirely rule out the spillover effects of the judgment of the ECJ overturning the CFI in *Kadi* over the jurisprudence of national (and international) courts. Whether this will prompt the Swiss Federal Tribunal to revise its position in respect of Swiss measures of implementation of Security Council resolutions remains to be seen.

What seems certain, instead, is that the ECJ *Kadi* ruling will, in principle, prevent individuals and entities targeted by UN sanctions in the EU from challenging the Community measures of implementation thereof before national courts of member states.

As is well known, national review of Community acts is precluded in principle under the Community law doctrines of supremacy and direct effect. The Constitutional Courts of some member states, including Germany and Italy, have developed the so-called 'counter-limits' doctrine.[68] They retain their power of judicial review, should the EU legal order fail to ensure adequate protection of human rights and fundamental freedoms, as provided for in their national constitutions. The very assertive position of the ECJ with respect to human rights allegedly violated by the implementation of UN sanctions should leave little scope for the national courts to invoke the application of this constitutional doctrine.

In the best possible scenario, however, a national court (possibly of a non-EU member state), which accepts subjecting the legality of national measures of implementation of UN sanctions to a meaningful review, will encounter problems similar to those outlined above in relation to the possibility of effective judicial review before the Luxembourg courts.

In most cases, national courts will be prevented from examining the reasons which justify the listing of the party concerned (apart from the scant information that can be gleaned from the narrative summary of the reasons for listing available on the Committee's website). A request for more information directly addressed to the Sanctions Committee would hardly achieve its purposes for it is highly unlikely that the specific allegations together with the supporting evidence and documentation will have been (or be) supplied to the Committee itself. Only before the national courts of the designating state is a listed party likely to effectively challenge the grounds at the origin of imposition of the restricted measures on him or her. Once again, the riddle is always that the Committee itself does not possess the information that it is expected to share.

Other reasons stand in the way of considering the protection of human rights at the national level as a suitable solution to the problem of the compatibility of UN sanctions with human rights.

[67] Case 1A.48/2007, Federal Tribunal of Lausanne, decision of 22 April 2008.

[68] See *Solange I*, Bundesverfassungsgericht (BVerfG), decision of 29 May 1976, 37 BVerfGE 271; *Solange II*, decision of 22 October 1986, 73 BVerfGE 339; and *Maastricht*, decision of 12 October 1993, 89 BVerfGE 155, (1994) 33 ILM 395. In Italy, the counter-limits doctrine was first developed in *Frontini* (Case 183/73, *GC* [1973] 2401) and subsequently reaffirmed in *Granital* (Case 170/84, *GC* [1984] 1098) and *Fragd* (Case 232/89, *GC* [1989] 1001).

As mentioned at the beginning of this section, not all member states of the UN have introduced—or provide under the general rules of their legal system—the possibility of an effective challenge of national measures that implement Security Council resolutions in relation to fundamental human rights and the procedural requirements thereof. The availability of such a remedy appears to be the exception, rather than the rule. This circumstance alone prevents any uniformity of solutions at member state level.

As highlighted in section 2B, although the principle of equality does not probably (yet) apply across national frontiers (with the notable exception of the EU judicial space), fundamental reasons of fairness and justice require that, should national judicial review be considered an adequate substitute for fair procedures at the UN level, this guarantee should be satisfied worldwide. The simple fact that the existence and the kind of available remedies greatly vary in different states infringes the fundamental guarantee that similar situations receive equal treatment unless a different treatment can be objectively and reasonably justified.

5. International Human Rights Monitoring Bodies

Fundamentally, the same obstacles make it unlikely that rights and freedoms of individuals and entities targeted by UN sanctions receive adequate protection through the international monitoring mechanisms set up under existing human rights treaties. At the universal level, we shall consider the HRC, a body created by the International Covenant on Civil and Political Rights. We will then deal with the relevant case law of the ECtHR, operating at regional level under the European Convention of Human Rights (ECHR).

A. Human Rights Committee

On 29 December 2008, the HRC delivered its opinion ('views') with respect to the communication filed against Belgium by Nabil Sayadi and Patricia Vinck, both Belgian nationals and residents.[69]

For the purpose of understanding the findings of the HRC, it is necessary to recall the background to the case.

Sayadi's and Vinck's names were included on the Consolidated List by the 1267 Committee in January 2003, upon the designation of Belgium. According to the information provided for by Belgium on the basis of criminal investigations started on 3 September 2002, Sayadi and Vinck were, respectively, the director and secretary of *Fondation Secours International*, reportedly the European branch of

[69] Views of the Human Rights Committee under Art 5, para 4 of the Optional Protocol to the International Covenant on Civil and Political Rights of 22 October 2008 concerning Communication No 1472/2006, *Nabil Sayadi and Patricia Vinck v Belgium* (CCPR/C/94/D/1472/2006, 29 December 2008, Annual Report of the Human Rights Committee, UN DOC a/64/40, Vol II (2009), Annex VII, section BB (pp 242–274)).

the Global Relief Foundation, an American association that has been on the Consolidated List since 22 October 2002.[70] In consequence thereof, they were subject to a travel ban as well as to the freezing of all their financial assets. They were not given access to the 'relevant information' justifying their listing.

On 11 February 2005, a Belgian civil court ordered the Belgian state to initiate the procedure to have their names removed from the Consolidated List.[71] In pursuance thereof, Belgium requested the Committee to de-list the authors. The criminal investigation was dismissed on 19 December 2005.

Sayadi and Vinck have thus faced a very peculiar situation. They were listed on the basis of the information provided for by their national state, which was later unable to obtain the removal of their name from the Consolidated List because of the objection of some Committee members: notably, the United States.

Notwithstanding a further request by the Belgian state, Sayadi's and Vinck's names were still on the Consolidated List at the time the HRC delivered its views.

They filed their initial submission on 14 March 2006 against Belgium and a number of other states. On 10 May 2006, however, the HRC made public its decision to register the complaint exclusively against Belgium.[72] This decision deserves some comment.

The HRC considered the communication manifestly inadmissible insofar as it was directed against states that have not accepted that the HRC receive and rule on communications from individuals who claim to be victims of a violation of any of the rights set forth in the Covenant on Civil and Political Rights (not being a party to the Optional Protocol thereto). This is the case, for example, of the United States. As to the states which had ratified the Optional Protocol, the HRC held the communication's admissibility to be subject to the requirement of exhaustion of local remedies in each of these states, a condition that it deemed prima facie satisfied only in relation to Belgium.[73] But how could Sayadi and Vinck be expected to avail themselves of remedies in states with which they had no connection whatsoever?

Since the 1267 Committee included their names on the Consolidated List (January 2003), Sayadi and Vinck had been subject to a travel ban and deprived of all their economic resources, which prevented them from leaving the state where they were found at the time of the listing, ie Belgium, and therefore from challenging the restrictive measures imposed on them in any state but Belgium. Arguably, the applicants' case should have been considered as falling under one of

[70] The authors' names were also placed on the lists appended to the European Union Council Regulation (27 January 2003) and a Belgian ministerial order (31 January 2003) (see paras 2.2 and 2.3 of the views of the HRC).

[71] See n 43 above and the corresponding text.

[72] See *Dossier de presse. Création du comité de vigilance. en matière de lutte contre le terrorisme: le Comité T*, 26 June 2006, at www.liguedh.be/les-dossiers-de-presse/143-dossier-de-presse-creation-du-comite-t (last accessed 5 June 2011).

[73] In accordance with Art 5(2)(b) of the Optional Protocol, the HRC shall not consider any communication from an individual unless it has ascertained that: 'The individual has exhausted all available domestic remedies. This shall not be the rule where the application of the remedies is unreasonably prolonged.'

the exceptions to the local remedies rule, in particular, because they were 'manifestly precluded from pursuing local remedies' and/or they had 'no relevant connection' with the state alleged to be responsible.[74]

Should this application of the domestic remedies rule be confirmed by the HRC in subsequent cases, it would unduly restrict—it is submitted—the scope of complaints which may be brought to the attention of the HRC by individuals and entities on the Consolidated List. *Admissibility* would be declared only insofar as communications are directed against the state where they happen to be found when sanctions are imposed against them, which in most cases will be their state of domicile or residence. This would significantly limit also the usefulness of such complaints, when—as is often the case—the inclusion of a person's name on the Consolidated List or its removal therefrom depend upon the initiative and/or the consent of a state different from the country where he/she is actually able to legally challenge the imposition of the sanctions against him or her. This is clearly shown by the outcome of the communication of Sayadi and Vinck insofar as it was directed against Belgium.

The majority of the HRC took the view that Belgium had violated Articles 12 and 17 of the Covenant on the right of liberty of movement and to protection from attack on honour and reputation, respectively.[75]

In relation to Article 12, the Committee noted that '[t]he proposal for the listing, made by the state party on 19 November 2002, came only a few weeks after the opening of the investigation on 3 September 2002. According to the authors, this listing appears to have been premature and unjustified'. It also noted 'that the authors' names were transmitted to the Sanctions Committee even before the authors could be heard'. It thus found that 'even though the state party is not competent to remove the authors' names from the United Nations and European lists, it is responsible for the presence of the authors' names on those lists and for the resulting travel ban' (paragraph 10.7 of the views).

Similarly, as to the alleged breach of Article 17, the HRC recalled 'that it was the state party that communicated all the personal information concerning the authors

[74] See, eg, Art 15 ('Exceptions to the local remedies rule') of the Draft Articles on Diplomatic Protection (n 32 above): 'Local remedies do not need to be exhausted where: (a) There are no reasonably available local remedies to provide effective redress, or the local remedies provide no reasonable possibility of such redress; (b) There is undue delay in the remedial process which is attributable to the state alleged to be responsible; (c) There was no relevant connection between the injured person and the state alleged to be responsible at the date of injury; (d) The injured person is manifestly precluded from pursuing local remedies; or (e) The state alleged to be responsible has waived the requirement that local remedies be exhausted.'

[75] Sayadi and Vinck claimed the violation of a number of rights under the Covenant, namely: the right to an effective remedy; the right to liberty of movement; the right to leave a country, including one's own; the right to a fair trial; the principle of equality of arms; the presumption of innocence; a reasonable timeframe for proceedings; right to enforcement of remedies; the principle of legality of penalties; protection from arbitrary or unlawful interference with one's privacy; the right to freedom of thought, conscience, and religion; the right to freedom of association; the principle of non-discrimination. The HRC declared inadmissible the claims under Arts 18, 22, 26, and 27, as 'the authors had not sufficiently substantiated their complaints for the purposes of admissibility'. It further held that other provisions of the Covenant—namely, Arts 2(3), 14(1), (2), and (3), and 15—invoked by the applicants, had not been violated.

to the Sanctions Committee in the first place. The state party . . . did so on 19 November 2002, without waiting for the outcome of the criminal investigation initiated at the request of the Public Prosecutor's Office'. It restated 'that, in the present case, even though the state party is not competent to remove the authors' names from the United Nations and European lists, it is responsible for the presence of the authors' names on those lists. The Committee concludes that the facts, taken together, disclose that, as a result of the actions of the state party, there has been an unlawful attack on the authors' honour and reputation. Consequently, the Committee concludes that there has been a violation of article 17 of the Covenant' (paragraph 10.13).

Both findings on the *merits* of violations of Articles 12 and 17 are based on the role of the respondent state in the listing of the complainants. The 1267 Committee published Sayadi's and Vinck's names and identifying information in the context of sanctions against al-Qaida and the Taliban at the request of, and based on information provided for by, the Belgian authorities. Belgium's responsibility followed from the fact that its proposal for listing was submitted after only three months of criminal investigations and before sufficient information was gathered with a view to determining that restrictive measures were actually necessary to protect national security or public order. This position restricts the scope of review by the HRC of the legality of state action with respect to communications from individuals seeking to have their names removed from the Consolidated List of the 1267 Committee.

Since the HRC found that the Covenant had been violated exclusively in relation to the Belgian proposal for listing, had their name not been included on the Consolidated List at the request and on the basis of the information of the Belgian authorities, it seems logical to conclude that Belgium would have been cleared of *all* violations alleged by the applicants.

A natural corollary of the far too restrictive approach taken by the HRC in relation to both admissibility and the merits of the complainants' submissions is the conclusion that:

> Although the state party is itself not competent to remove the authors' names from the Sanctions Committee's list, the Committee is nevertheless of the view that the state party has the duty to do all it can to have their names removed from the list as soon as possible, to provide the authors with some form of compensation and to make public the requests for removal. The state party is also obliged to ensure that similar violations do not occur in the future. (paragraph 12 of the views)[76]

As the HRC itself acknowledges,[77] however, Belgium initiated a de-listing procedure twice, both times unsuccessfully. One finds it hard therefore even to conceive what further action could be put into place by the Belgian authorities in order to provide the complainants with an effective remedy, as would be required in

[76] The HRC also expressed its wish 'to receive from the state party, within 180 days, information about the measures taken to give effect to the present Views' (para 13).

[77] Para 8.3 of the views.

principle under Article 2(3)(a) of the International Covenant on Civil and Political Rights, in a situation where Belgium is at the same time the state of nationality and the designating state, while the United States vetoed the removal of the two names from the Consolidated List.

B. European Court of Human Rights

The attempts by individuals and entities affected by UN sanctions to obtain redress of the alleged violations of their rights before the ECtHR were even less successful.

In *Bosphorus*, an airline charter company incorporated in Turkey alleged that the impounding of its leased aircraft by Ireland had breached its rights under Article 1 of Protocol No 1. The Irish authorities had acted pursuant to Regulation (EEC) No 990/93, which in turn implemented Security Council Resolution 820 (1993) concerning measures against the former Yugoslavia. In a judgment of 30 June 2005,[78] the ECtHR found that no violation of the Convention had been committed by the respondent state.

According to the ECtHR, a state party's measure implementing EC regulations, which in turn implements Security Council resolutions, falls under Article 1 of the ECHR and therefore within the jurisdiction *ratione materiae* and *ratione personae* of the Court. This principle is, however, to be reconciled with the 'important general interest' of compliance with legal obligations flowing from a state party's membership of an international organization such as the EC. In the Court's view, 'state action taken in compliance with such legal obligations is justified as long as the relevant organisation is considered to protect fundamental rights, as regards both the substantive guarantees offered and the mechanisms controlling their observance, in a manner which can be considered at least equivalent to that for which the Convention provides' (Recital 155 of judgment). 'If such equivalent protection is considered to be provided by the organisation, the presumption will be that a state has not departed from the requirements of the Convention when it does no more than implement legal obligations flowing from its membership of the organisation. However, any such presumption can be rebutted if, in the circumstances of a particular case, it is considered that the protection of Convention rights was manifestly deficient. In such cases, the interest of international cooperation would be outweighed by the Convention's role as a 'constitutional instrument of European public order' in the field of human rights' (Recital 156). The Court

[78] *Bosphorus Hava Yollari Turizm ve Ticaret Anonim Şirketi v Ireland*, ECtHR (Grand Chamber), Judgment of 30 June 2005, *Reports of Judgments and Decisions*, 2005, Vol VI. Among the many commentaries, see Conforti, 'Le principe de l'équivalence et le contrôle sur les actes communautaires dans la jurisprudence de la Cour européenne des droits de l'homme', in S Breitenmoser, B Ehrenzeller, M Sassòli, W Stoffel, and B Wagner Pfeifer (eds), *Human rights, Democracy and the Rule of Law. Liber amicorum Luzius Wildhaber* (2007) 173; Costello, 'The Bosphorus Ruling of the European Court of Human Rights: Fundamental Rights and Blurred Boundaries in Europe' (2006) *Human Rights Law Review* 87; Gaja, 'The Review by the European Court of Human Rights of Member States' Acts Implementing European Union Law: "Solange" Yet Again?', in PM Dupuy et al (eds), *Common Values in International Law. Essay in Honour of Christian Tomuschat* (2006) 517; Hoffmeister, 'ECtHR Review of National Measures Enforcing EC Regulation Implementing UN Security Council Decision' (2006) AJIL 442.

found that that the EC provided for a system for the protection of human rights 'equivalent', in principle, to that provided in the European Convention and that in the specific case there had been no 'manifest deficiency' thereof.

In *Bosphorus* the Court dealt with a restrictive measure imposed on the applicant as part of a general sanctions regime. One can see no reason why the Court would depart from these principles in a case which put into question compliance with Community measures adopted in implementation of UN-targeted sanctions.

On the one hand, targeted sanctions, by definition, rule out any discretion not only as to the kind of restrictive measures to be applied but also in relation to the individuals and entities imposed upon. Their names are placed on the lists appended to the EC regulation, in accordance with the relevant determinations of the Security Council and the competent sanctions committee. The 'general interest' to ensure compliance with legal obligations flowing from a state's membership of the EC is even more significant in relation to targeted sanctions than with respect to general regimes. The same solution should therefore be applied a fortiori. On the other hand, the ECtHR found that the EC offered 'equivalent protection' at a time when it was still unclear whether the Luxembourg courts would be prepared to annul Community measures adopted in the implementation of UN sanctions, for the purposes of upholding the fundamental human rights of the listed individuals and entities. ECJ judgments had shown an inclination of that Court to uphold the validity of Community measures on the ground that they contributed to the fulfilment of the overall objective pursued by the Security Council with the sanctions complained of: namely, the achievement of peace and security. This notwithstanding the recognition that the contested measures significantly interfered with the fundamental human rights of the persons concerned.[79] In this perspective, the ECJ *Kadi* ruling of 3 September 2008 reinforces the view of the ECtHR that the EC does now protect fundamental rights in a manner at least 'comparable' to that for which the Convention provides.

What is uncertain, instead, is whether the ECtHR will be ready to take up the protection of human rights in relation to UN targeted sanctions in proceedings brought against a state party to the Convention that is not a member of the EU. Conditions are obviously not ripe for a finding that the UN system protects human rights in any manner comparable to the European Convention.[80] In this case,

[79] The ECJ, in Case C-84/95, *Bosphorus v Minister for Transport, Energy and Communications and others*, Judgment of 30 July 1996, [1996] ECR I-3978, in response to a reference for a preliminary ruling by the Irish Supreme Court, had considered restrictions on the exercise of the right of property and freedom to pursue an economic activity to be justified in the general interest: 'the importance of the aims pursued by the regulation at issue is such as to justify negative consequences, even of a substantial nature, for some operators . . . As compared with an objective of general interest so fundamental for the international community, which consists in putting an end to the state of war in the region and to the massive violations of human rights and humanitarian international law in the Republic of Bosnia-Herzegovina, the impounding of the aircraft in question, which is owned by an undertaking based in or operating from the Federal Republic of Yugoslavia, cannot be regarded as inappropriate or disproportionate' (Recs 23 and 26 of judgment).

[80] The question as to whether under the current system of sanctions the individuals or entities concerned have an acceptable opportunity to be heard through a mechanism of administrative review

therefore, there should be no place for the doctrine of 'equivalent protection'. Moreover, in the joined cases *Behrami* and *Saramati*,[81] concerning proceedings respectively instituted against France and against France and Norway (the latter a state not party to the EU), the Court took the view that the impugned actions and omissions, which had taken place in the context of an operation authorized by the Security Council under Chapter VII of the UN Charter, were attributable to the UN and not to the respondent states.[82] However, the Court expressly distinguished the circumstances of the cases with which it was concerned from those in the *Bosphorus* case. In *Bosphorus* it had declared itself competent in relation to the seizure of the applicant's leased aircraft carried out by the respondent state authorities, on the state's territory, and pursuant to a decision by one of its ministers, despite the fact that the source of the impugned seizure was an EC Council Regulation implementing a UN Security Council resolution. 'In the present cases, the impugned acts and omissions of KFOR and UNMIL cannot be attributed to the respondent states and, moreover, did not take place on the territory of those states or by virtue of a decision of their authorities. The present cases are therefore clearly distinguishable from the *Bosphorus* case in terms both of the responsibility of the respondent states under Article 1 and of the Court's competence *ratione personae*' (Recital 151 of judgment). The invocation of the rule on the (lack of) attribution as construed by ECtHR in *Behrami* and *Saramati* should therefore be ruled out in a *Bosphorus*-like situation.

The Court will deal with the issue of human rights protection in relation to the implementation of UN sanctions in a non-EU member state with the application filed by Nada against Switzerland. Following rejection of his challenge to the imposition of sanctions against him by the Swiss Federal Court,[83] Nada claimed before the ECtHR, inter alia, a violation of his right to a fair trial under Article 6 of the ECHR.

Under the current procedures for listing and de-listing individuals and entities at the UN level, however, introducing adequate human rights guarantees at the implementation phase, while ensuring full compliance with the decisions of the Security Council and the determinations of the relevant sanctions committee taken thereunder, will prove an almost impossible task. Should the Court uphold the violation(s) of the Convention, therefore, the Swiss state would most likely find itself in the awkward situation of choosing between compliance with the judgment of the Court, thereby violating its obligations under the UN Charter,

forming part of the United Nations legal system, was tackled and answered in the negative by the ECJ in *Kadi* (see Recs 320–5 of judgment).

[81] Joined Applications No 71412/01 and 78166/01, *Behrami & Behrami v France* and *Saramati v Norway and France*, ECtHR (Grand Chamber), Decision of 2 May 2007, available in the ECHR's HUDOC database at www.echr.coe.int/ECHR/EN/Header/Case-Law/Decisions+and+judgments/HUDOC+database (last accessed 5 June 2011). For comments, see Bodeau-Livinec, Buzzini, Villalpando, 'ECtHR Judgment on Applicability of European Convention on Human Rights to Acts undertaken Pursuant to UN Chapter VII Operation in Kosovo' (2008) AJIL 323; Larsen, 'Attribution of Conduct in Peace Operations: The "Ultimate Authority and Control" Test' (2008) 19 EJIL 509.

[82] Therefore, they fell outside the jurisdiction *ratione personae* of the Court.

[83] See n 65 above.

or maintaining the restrictive measures imposed upon Nada (until his name is removed from the Consolidated List).

6. Results of the Multi-level Analysis and Prospects for Reform

A. The rhetoric of 'clear and fair procedures'

Procedures for listing and de-listing individuals and entities targeted by UN sanctions, especially in the context of the fight against international terrorism (and the financing thereof), have been extensively criticized. Doubts have been formulated in academic writings,[84] papers of non-governmental organizations,[85] and, as we shall see, court decisions.[86]

In the World Summit Outcome Document, adopted on 24 October 2005, the Heads of state and government of the member states of the UN 'call[ed] upon the Security Council with the support of the Secretary General to ensure that fair and clear procedures exist for placing individuals and entities on sanctions lists and for removing them, as well as for granting humanitarian exceptions'.[87] This was reflected in a statement issued on 22 June 2006 by the President of the Security Council, according to which: 'The Council is committed to ensuring that fair and clear procedures exist for placing individuals and entities on sanctions lists and for removing them, as well as for granting humanitarian exemptions. The Council reiterates its request to the 1267 Committee to continue its work on the Committee's guidelines, including on listing and de-listing procedures'.[88]

Notwithstanding the express commitment of the Security Council to establish fair and clear procedures for placing individuals and entities on sanctions lists and for removing them (as well as for granting humanitarian exemptions), however, no proper balance has yet been established between the principle of respect for fundamental rights and individual liberties and the need to ensure the effectiveness of sanctions for the purposes of international security.

[84] See in particular the following three reports brought to the attention of the Security Council and the General Assembly: I Cameron, *The European Convention on Human Rights, Due Process and UN Security Council Counter-Terrorism Sanctions*, Council of Europe Restricted Document, February 2006; Fassbender, *Targeted Sanctions and Due Process. The responsibility of the UN Security Council to ensure that fair and clear procedures are made available to individuals and entities targeted with sanctions under Chapter VII of the UN Charter*, Study commissioned by the United Nations Office of Legal Affairs, 20 March 2006 (published with an introduction and additional documents in: (2006) 3 *International Organizations Law Review* (*IOLR*) 437); and *Strengthening Targeted Sanctions through Fair and Clear Procedures*, White Paper prepared by the Watson Institute Targeted Sanctions Project, Brown University, 30 March 2006 (Annex to the letter dated 19 May 2006 from the Permanent Representatives of Germany, Sweden and Switzerland to the United Nations addressed to the President of the Security Council, UN Doc. A/60/887–S/2006/331).

[85] See, eg, Human Rights Watch, *U.N.: Sanctions Rules Must Protect Due Process*, 4 March 2002, available at http://hrw.org/english/docs/2002/03/04/global5839.htm (last accessed 10 February 2011).

[86] See also above, in particular, sections 4 and 5.

[87] UN Doc A/RES/60/1, 24 October 2005.

[88] UN Doc S/PRST/2006/28, 22 June 2006.

A Special Rapporteur on the promotion and protection of human rights and fundamental freedoms while countering terrorism was set up by the Commission on Human Rights (now the HRC), with the primary task of making recommendations and giving advice to states on the protection and promotion of human rights while countering terrorism, and gathering information about possible violations of human rights, for instance, through country visits.[89]

The Parliamentary Assembly of the Council of Europe (PACE) criticized the current practice in no uncertain terms, at its January session of 2008.[90] Backing an independent report, the PACE considered that the procedures used by the UN Security Council and the EU to blacklist individuals and groups suspected of having connections with terrorism violate basic rights: 'the procedural and substantive standards currently applied by the UNSC and by the Council of the European Union, despite some recent improvements, in no way fulfil the minimum standards . . . and violate the fundamental principles of human rights and the rule of law'.[91] The PACE invited the UN, the EU, and the member states of the Council of Europe to ensure the necessary improvements to procedures governing targeted sanctions regimes at the level of the UN and the EU and, so long as these shortcomings persist, to establish appropriate procedures for implementing sanctions at the national level. It insisted that they must be reviewed 'to preserve the credibility of the international fight against terrorism'.[92]

General Assembly Resolution 63/185, adopted on 3 March 2009, on 'Protection of human rights and fundamental freedoms while countering terrorism',[93] specifically '*[r]ecognize[d]* the need to continue ensuring that fair and clear procedures under the United Nations terrorism-related sanctions regime are strengthened in

[89] The task of the Special Rapporteur was established by the Commission on Human Rights Resolution 'Protection of human rights and fundamental freedoms while countering terrorism 2005/80' (available at www.ohchr.org). The Special Rapporteur must also promote best practices, report regularly to the Commission on Human Rights (now the Human Rights Council) and the UN General Assembly, and act in close cooperation with other human rights mechanisms. These reports are available at www2.ohchr.org/english/issues/terrorism/rapporteur/reports.htm (last accessed 10 February 2011).

[90] See PACE Res 1597 (2008) and Recommendation 1824 (2008), both adopted 23 January 2008 and based on the Report (Doc 11454) of the Committee on Legal Affairs and Human Rights (Rapporteur D Marty, Switzerland) entitled 'United Nations Security Council and European Union blacklists', Doc 11454, available at http://assembly.coe.int/Main.asp?link=/Documents/WorkingDocs/Doc07/EDOC11454.htm (last accessed 10 February 2011). The Council of the EU addressed the issue in its document 'Basic Principles on the Use of Restrictive Measures (Sanctions)', 7 June 2004, Doc 10198/1/04 PESC 450 REV1; see also Council Guidelines on implementation and evaluation of restrictive measures (sanctions) in the framework of the EU Common Foreign and Security Policy, 2 December 2005, Doc 15114/05 PESC 1084 Fin 475.

[91] PACE Res 1597 (2008) para 6. See also PACE Recommendation 1824 (2008), which invited to the same effect the Committee of Ministers to take up the issue of targeted sanctions.

[92] The position of the PACE was echoed by the statements of Council of Europe Human Rights Commissioner: 'Serious human rights violations during anti-terror campaign must be corrected—and never repeated', 4 February 2008, at www.coe.int/t/commissioner/Viewpoints/080204_en.asp (last accessed 10 February 2011)) and 'Arbitrary procedures for terrorist black-listing must change', 1 December 2008, at www.neurope.eu/articles/90850.php (last accessed 10 February 2011). In the words of the Human Rights Commissioner, '"Blacklisting" is indeed a striking illustration of how human rights principles have been ignored in the fight against terrorism.'

[93] GA Res 63/185, 3 March 2009.

order to enhance their efficiency and transparency, and welcomes and encourages the Security Council's continued enhancement of efforts in support of these objectives, while emphasizing the importance of these sanctions in countering terrorism' and '*[u]rge[d]* states, while ensuring full compliance with their international obligations, to include adequate human rights guarantees in their national procedures for the listing of individuals and entities with a view to combating terrorism' (paragraphs 19 and 20; emphasis in the original).[94] For the reasons outlined above, however, the prospect of an increase in the challenges before national courts would not necessarily result in effective protection of the fundamental human rights of targeted individual and entities.[95]

B. Suitable models and workable solutions

1. *The EU model for the implementation of 'autonomous sanctions'*

A more suitable model for the imposition of UN targeted sanctions is provided by the EU mechanism elaborated with reference to sanctions adopted within the framework of Security Council Resolution 1373 (2001), adopted on 28 September 2001. This is a particular case of autonomous sanctions, ie sanctions decided, at least in part, independently from a UN Security Council resolution.

With Resolution 1373 (2001), paragraph 1(c), the Security Council decided that:

> all states shall: Freeze without delay funds and other financial assets or economic resources of persons who commit, or attempt to commit, terrorist acts or participate in or facilitate the commission of terrorist acts; of entities owned or controlled directly or indirectly by such persons; and of persons and entities acting on behalf of, or at the direction of such persons and entities, including funds derived or generated from property owned or controlled directly or indirectly by such persons and associated persons and entities.

It did not establish, however, a sanctions committee for the purpose of targeting individuals and entities. The task of identifying those 'who commit, or attempt to commit, terrorist acts or participate in or facilitate the commission of terrorist acts' was left to the discretion of the member states.

[94] With the same document, the General Assembly '*[r]eaffirm[ed]* that states must ensure that any measure taken to combat terrorism complies with their obligations under international law, in particular international human rights, refugee and humanitarian law'; '*[e]xpresse[d] serious concern* at the occurrence of violations of human rights and fundamental freedoms in the context of countering terrorism' and '*[u]rge[d]* states, while countering terrorism, to ensure due process guarantees, consistent with all relevant provisions of the Universal Declaration of Human Rights, and their obligations under the International Covenant on Civil and Political Rights, the Geneva Conventions of 1949 and the Additional Protocols thereto, of 1977, and the 1951 Convention relating to the Status of Refugees and the 1967 Protocol thereto in their respective fields of applicability' (paras 1, 3, and 12; emphasis in the original).

[95] Although not as explicitly as GA Res 185/63, SC Res 1922 (2008) seems, if not to advocate for, at least to consider that challenges at the national level may be compatible with the UN sanctions regime. See para 27 of SC Res 1822 (2008), where the Security Council '*[r]eiterates* the importance of all states identifying, and if necessary introducing, adequate procedures to implement fully all aspects of the measures' (emphasis in the original).

Pursuant to Council Common Position of 27 December 2001 on the application of specific measures to combat terrorism (2001/931/CFSP),[96] Article 1(4), the list 'shall be drawn up on the basis of precise information or material in the relevant file which indicates that a decision has been taken by a competent authority... For the purposes of this paragraph "competent authority" shall mean a judicial authority, or, where judicial authorities have no competence in the area covered by this paragraph, an equivalent competent authority in that area'.[97] In implementation thereof, Regulation (EC) No 2580/2001 on specific restrictive measures directed against certain persons and entities with a view to combating terrorism,[98] provided that the Council, acting by unanimity, shall establish, review, and amend the list of persons, groups and entities to which this Regulation applies, in accordance with the Common Position 2001/931/CFSP.[99] Both acts have been amended over time with a view to updating the list.[100]

This model is transposable, in principle, at the universal level. If minimum substantive and evidentiary standards are workable at the EU level, they should also be applicable by all UN member states. Notwithstanding the requirements provided for in Article 1(4) of Common Position 2001/931/CFSP, however, the restrictive measures imposed thereunder have given rise to a number of legal challenges.

The Organisation des Modjahedines du peuple d'Iran (OMPI), for example, has already brought three actions for annulment against Regulation (EC) No 2580/2001. Each time, the CFI annulled the impugned regulation insofar as it concerned the OMPI and the Council failed to apply properly the principles laid down in the Court's judgments.[101]

[96] Council Common Position 2001/931/CFSP of 27 December 2001 on the application of specific measures to combat terrorism, OJ 2001 L 344/93.

[97] Art 1(4), first part, of Common Position 2001/931/CFSP reads as follows: 'The list in the Annex shall be drawn up on the basis of precise information or material in the relevant file which indicates that a decision has been taken by a competent authority in respect of the persons, groups and entities concerned, irrespective of whether it concerns the instigation of investigations or prosecution for a terrorist act, an attempt to perpetrate, participate in or facilitate such an act based on serious and credible evidence or clues, or condemnation for such deeds. Persons, groups and entities identified by the Security Council of the United Nations as being related to terrorism and against whom it has ordered sanctions may be included in the list.'

[98] Council Regulation (EC) No 2580/2001 of 27 December 2001 on specific restrictive measures directed against certain persons and entities with a view to combating terrorism, OJ 2001 L344/70.

[99] Art 2(3) provides as follows: 'The Council, acting by unanimity, shall establish, review and amend the list of persons, groups and entities to which this Regulation applies, in accordance with the provisions laid down in Article 1(4), (5) and (6) of Common Position 2001/931/CFSP; such list shall consist of: (i) natural persons committing, or attempting to commit, participating in or facilitating the commission of any act of terrorism; (ii) legal persons, groups or entities committing, or attempting to commit, participating in or facilitating the commission of any act of terrorism; (iii) legal persons, groups or entities owned or controlled by one or more natural or legal persons, groups or entities referred to in points (i) and (ii); or (iv) natural legal persons, groups or entities acting on behalf of or at the direction of one or more natural or legal persons, groups or entities referred to in points (i) and (ii).'

[100] Regulation (EC) No 2580/2001 has been regularly updated by Council Decisions. Common Position 2001/931 was last amended by Council Common Position 2009/468/PESC of 15 June 2009, OJ 2009 L 23/37.

[101] Case T-228/02, *Organisation des Modjahedines du peuple d'Iran (OMPI) v Council of the European Union*, CFI judgments of 12 December 2006; Case T-256/07, *People's Mojahedin*

The CFI dealt with a number of legal issues that cannot be dealt with here. Suffice it to recall that the CFI has established the principle of full judicial review of Community measures adopted in implementation of EU autonomous (in the sense outlined above) sanctions. On this premise, it set out the guarantees that should be included in the listing procedure, namely: the rights of the defence, in particular the right to be heard, and the right to effective judicial review. These procedural guarantees require that the listed party be informed of the grounds, together with the supporting information and documents, which justify the imposition of restrictive measures against him or her, if not at the time of their adoption, within a reasonable time therefrom.

The major obstacle to the implementation of these guarantees ultimately turned out to be the French authorities' refusal to make available even to the Court the documents contained in the OMPI file.

Notwithstanding the strict requirements of Common Position 2001/931/CFSP, the effectiveness of the principles laid down by the courts has been put into doubt.[102]

It is a fact that months (almost a year) after the third judgment was given by the CFI in relation to the OMPI, the latter is still listed as a terrorist organization in the EU sanctions list.[103]

2. *The ICC and UN targeted sanctions*

The quest for legitimacy of measures imposed within the framework of UN sanctions regimes could find an—albeit partial—answer in the activities of the ICC.

As is known, the ICC is not only the first permanent international criminal tribunal but also the first criminal court to have been given the power to award

Organization of Iran v Council of the European Union, CFI judgment of 23 October 2008; and Case T-284/08, *People's Mojahedin Organization of Iran v Council of the European Union*, judgment of 4 December 2008. The latter judgment was appealed against by France before the ECJ (see Case C-27/09 P, *People's Mojahedin Organisation of Iran v Council of the European Union*, Appeal brought on 21 January 2009 by the French Republic against the judgment delivered on 4 December 2008 by the Court of First Instance (Seventh Chamber) in Case T-284/08, OJ 2009 C 82/14 (all available at http://curia.europa.eu).

[102] The European Parliament had deplored 'the defiance and non-implementation by the EU of the verdict of the CFI on 12 December 2006 [the first OMPI judgment]', in its Report on the situation of fundamental rights in the European Union 2004–2008. See EP Report on the situation of fundamental rights in the European Union 2004–2008 of 5 December 2008, A6-9999/2008, para 32.

[103] For another example of lack of implementation of these procedural guarantees, see Case T-229/02, *Osman Ocalan, on behalf of the PKK v Council*, Judgment of 3 April 2008, [2008] ECR II-45 (summary), which annulled the decision placing the PKK on the list of terrorist entities. See Cuyvers, 'Case C-229/05 P, *PKK & KNK v. Council*, Judgment of the Court of Justice (First Chamber) of 18 January 2007, [2007] ECR I-439' (2008) 45 CMLR 1487, 1504–5: 'Perhaps there are valid reasons for this delay, but to me it would appear that the right to an effective remedy includes an effective execution of a verdict which is favourable to the applicant'. See also Case T-253/04, *Kongra-Gel & others v Council*, Judgment of 3 April 2008, in which the decision to include Kongra-Gel on the list as an alias of the PKK was also annulled. The CFI found that the Decision did not make actual and specific reference to the reasons underlying PKK's placement on the list.

reparations in favour of the victims.[104] According to Article 57(3)(e), the Pre-Trial Chamber may:

Where a warrant of arrest or a summons has been issued under article 58, and having due regard to the strength of the evidence and the rights of the parties concerned, as provided for in this Statute and the Rules of Procedure and Evidence, seek the cooperation of states . . . to take protective measures for the purpose of forfeiture, in particular for the ultimate benefit of victims.

In the *Lubanga* case, Judge Steiner, acting as a single judge of Pre-Trial Chamber I, addressed to the DRC as well as to all states parties of the Statute a request for the identification, tracing, and freezing or seizure of the property and assets of Mr Lubanga 'in the best interests of the victims'.[105] This request is binding upon the DRC and all other states parties to the Statute in accordance with Part 9 thereof. It restates, however, an obligation already existing for all member states of the UN, by virtue of Security Council Resolution 1596 (2005), adopted on 18 April 2005.[106]

Paragraph 15 of Resolution 1596 (2005) mandates all states to 'immediately freeze the funds, other financial assets and economic resources which are on their territories from the date of adoption of this resolution, which are owned or controlled, directly or indirectly, by persons designated by the [Sanctions] Committee . . . or that are held by entities owned or controlled, directly or indirectly, by any persons acting on their behalf or at their direction'. At the time of Judge Steiner's request, Mr Lubanga's name was already included in the list of individuals and entities subject to these measures.[107] The obligation to identify, trace, and freeze Mr Lubanga's property and assets therefore does not bind only the states parties to the Statute as a treaty obligation, but extends to all members of the UN under Article 25 of the UN Charter and prevails over any conflicting treaty obligation by virtue of Article 103 of the latter.

In principle, this overlapping between the ICC's request for other forms of assistance and Security Council Resolution 1596 (2005) removes doubts about the possible infringement of the rights of the targeted individual. Before the ICC, in fact, Mr Lubanga is a person in relation to whom there were, at the time his assets

[104] Under Art 75 of the Rome Statute, the Court may make an order directly against a convicted person or through the Trust Fund established by decision of the Assembly of states parties for the benefit of victims of crimes within the jurisdiction of the Court, pursuant to Art 79 of the Statute. See Rome Statute of the International Criminal Court of 17 July 1998, available on the Official Journal of the ICC at www.icc-cpi.int/NR/rdonlyres/EA9AEFF7-5752-4F84-BE94-0A655EB30E16/0/Rome_Statute_English.pdf (last accessed 10 February 2011).

[105] Request to States Parties to the Rome Statute for the Identification, Tracing and Freezing or Seizure of the Property and Assets of Mr Thomas Lubanga Dyilo of 31 March 2006, ICC-01/04-01/06-62, available on the website of the ICC at www.icc-cpi.int.

[106] SC Res 1596, 18 April 2005.

[107] The list is administered by the Sanctions Committee instituted in accordance with para 13 of the same resolution. See Security Council Sanctions Committee established under Res 1533 (2004) concerning the Democratic Republic of Congo's 'List of individuals and entities subject to the measures imposed by paragraphs 13 and 15 of Security Council resolution 1596 (2005)', last updated on 6 February 2007, at www.un.org/Docs/sc/committees/DRC/1533_list.htm (last accessed 10 February 2011).

were frozen, not only 'reasonable grounds to believe that [he] committed a crime within the jurisdiction of the Court'—as required for the issuance of an arrest warrant under Article 58 of the Statute—but there was also 'sufficient evidence to establish substantial grounds to believe that [he] committed each of the crimes charged' (in accordance with the probatory standard for the confirmation of charges before the trial set out by Article 61(7) of the Statute).[108] Moreover, the decision to freeze Mr Lubanga's property and assets may be subject to judicial review upon request of the accused, once the trial has started, thus overcoming the lack of judicial review of Security Council resolutions in relation to human rights law.

The Lubanga case—the first case initiated before the ICC—presented a rare, although not necessarily unique,[109] situation for harmony of solutions between the Court and the Security Council.

Should the Court decide at a later stage that the circumstances of the case no longer warrant the freezing of Lubanga's property and assets, all member states of the UN—including the parties to the Rome Statute—would remain subject to the obligation arising under Resolution 1596 (2005). However, if this was the case, it would be difficult for the Security Council to ignore the ICC's ruling.

Finally, and most importantly, even the judicial control of restrictive measures imposed by the Security Council against Lubanga is more apparent than real. Security Council Resolution 1596 (2005) mandated the relevant committee to impose sanctions against those 'acting in violation of the measures taken with resolution 1493', ie those violating the arms embargo established thereunder. The ground which justifies the listing, therefore, has little, if anything, to do with the crimes within the jurisdiction of the ICC for which Lubanga has been charged.[110]

3. *Targeting sanctions through the international independent investigation Commission for Lebanon*

The sanctions regime provided for under Resolution 1636 (2005),[111] in relation to the 14 February 2005 terrorist bombing in Beirut that killed former Lebanese Prime Minister Rafiq Hariri and 22 others, gives instead grounds for suggesting some improvements to the UN procedures on targeted sanctions.

In Resolution 1636 (2005), paragraph 3, the Security Council decided to impose a travel ban and financial sanctions 'as a step to assist in the investigation of this crime and without prejudice to the ultimate judicial determination of the guilt or

[108] Judge Steiner's decision followed the Pre-Trial Chamber's determination that there were not only substantial grounds to initiate an investigation but also to issue an arrest warrant against Thomas Lubanga Dyilo, with a view to prosecuting him and committing him to trial.

[109] Katanga and Ngudjolo, whose names are included in the List of 1533 Sanctions Committee, are also accused before the ICC in relation to the situation of the DRC (see www.icc-cpi.int/Menus/ICC/Situations+and+Cases/Situations/Situation+ICC+0104 (last accessed 10 February 2011)).

[110] Lubanga is allegedly responsible for the enlisting and conscripting of children under the age of 15 years. Similar remarks could be extended to Katanga and Ngudjolo, who are charged with sexual slavery as a crime against humanity and a war crime and destruction of property and inhuman treatment as war crimes.

[111] SC Res 1636, 31 October 2005.

innocence of any individual', on 'all individuals designated by the Commission or the Government of Lebanon as suspected of involvement in the planning, sponsoring, organizing or perpetrating of this terrorist act, upon notification of such designation to and agreement of the Committee established [by the same resolution]'. The 'Commission' is the international independent investigation Commission, established under paragraph 1 of Resolution 1595 (2005),[112] 'to assist the Lebanese authorities in their investigation of all aspects of this terrorist act, including to help identify its perpetrators, sponsors, organizers and accomplices'.

Individuals designated by the Commission or the government of Lebanon would be registered as subject to the measures so decided, provided that within two working days of receipt of such designation no member of the Committee objects (in which case the Committee shall meet within 15 days to determine the applicability of the measures). Removal of an individual's name from the list would also be subject to notification from the Commission or the government of Lebanon (that the individual is no longer suspected of involvement in this terrorist act) and the agreement of the Committee pursuant to the same no-objection procedure.

No individual has been registered by the Security Council Committee established pursuant to Resolution 1636 (2005).[113] The Commission's mandate ended on 28 February 2009, as it was superseded by the Special Tribunal for Lebanon on 1 March 2009.[114]

It is submitted, however, that had this sanctions regime been implemented, it would have proven to be one with a clearer and fairer procedure than that administered by the 1267 Committee (and the other sanctions committees so far established by the Security Council).

The basis for the designation was the suspicion of involvement in the terrorist act of 14 February 2005. Although no evidentiary requirement was defined, therefore, the substantive ground that justified the imposition of sanctions related to one—specific—terrorist act.

Moreover, insofar as the proposal for listing emanated from the Commission, the designation would have been the result of a decision taken by an independent body having as its primary task the investigating of the terrorist act at the origin of the designation, including the identification of the individuals responsible thereof.

Listing and de-listing would ultimately have remained subject to the veto power of each member of the sanctions committee, in accordance with the general rule. A clear definition of the grounds for both listing and de-listing, however, would have resulted in fairer procedures. It would have ensured a solid base for discussion for the purposes of the committee's determinations as to both the applicability of the restrictive measures upon a listing proposal and the removal of a name because the individual 'is no longer suspected of involvement in this terrorist act'.

[112] SC Res 1595, 7 April 2005.

[113] See the website of the Security Council Committee established pursuant to Res 1636 (2005) at www.un.org/sc/committees/1636/index.shtml (last accessed 10 February 2011).

[114] For an analysis of the establishment of the Special Tribunal, see Fassbender, 'Reflections on the International Legality of the Special Tribunal for Lebanon' (2007) 5 *Journal of International Criminal Justice* 1091–5.

Moreover, individuals subject to these measures, provided that they were duly informed of these grounds at least within a reasonable time from the inclusion of their name on the list, would have found themselves in a better position to challenge their applicability.

4. The current proposal for review by a panel of independent experts

The possibility for the Security Council and the relevant sanctions committee to base their determinations on the findings of an independent body of experts is in line with some of the options currently under discussion.

Past practice of the Security Council offers a variety of possible forms the process might take.[115] Among those, some appear more realistic than others.

The introduction of judicial or quasi-judicial review of listing and de-listing decisions by a specially constituted tribunal (to be established as a subsidiary body of the Security Council along the lines of the ad hoc international criminal tribunals for the former Yugoslavia and Rwanda) seems hardly feasible. The same applies to the various ideas of creating a form of administrative review comparable to the UN Compensation Commission, a confidential review panel (on the model of the Detention Review Commission established by the UN Mission in Kosovo in 2007) or an Ombudsman institution (comparable to those established in Kosovo and East Timor) whose decisions would be binding on the Security Council and its sanctions committees.[116]

Drawing inspiration from the World Bank inspection panels, a proposal by Denmark, Liechtenstein, Sweden, and Switzerland of the end of 2007 suggested the establishment of a review panel for the purpose of reviewing listing decisions, composed of three independent, impartial, and judicially qualified persons to be proposed by the Secretary General out of a list of candidates submitted by the UN member states and appointed by the Security Council for a non-renewable term of five years. The panel would be endowed with the power to recommend to the sanctions committees either de-listing or the rejection of a petition for removal of a person's name from the list. The recommendations of the panel would be made public. The final decision, however, would rest with the sanctions committees.[117]

To a certain extent, the Security Council followed that suggestion when it established in Resolution 1904 (2009) the Office of the Ombudsperson and requested the Secretary General 'to appoint an eminent individual of high moral character, impartiality and integrity with high qualifications and experience in

[115] Chesterman (n 3 above) 72.

[116] For a full discussion thereof see Watson Institute for International Studies, *Strengthening UN Targeted Sanctions Through Fair and Clear Procedures* (2006), available at www.watsoninstitute.org/TFS (last accessed 10 February 2011).

[117] See *Discussion Paper on Supplementary Guidelines for the Review of Sanctions Committees' Listing Decisions and Explanatory Memorandum* (presented by Professor Michael Bothe at a Roundtable in New York on 8 November 2007, available at www.regierung.li/uploads/media/pdf-fl-aussenstelle-newyork-explanatory-memorandum-prof-bothe-delisting-workshop-2007-11-8.pdf (last accessed 5 June 2011)).

relevant fields, such as legal, human rights, counter-terrorism and sanctions, to be Ombudsperson' (paragraph 20).[118]

It is submitted, however, that until clear substantive standards and minimum evidentiary requirements are set at the stage of listing, no review mechanism, whatever its independence and expertise, will ever result in real and effective protection of the human rights of individuals and entities targeted by UN sanctions.

In this respect, while the need for disclosure of supporting evidence and documents has to be balanced with the legitimate national security interests of the designating states, no general important interest should outweigh the need to overcome the vagueness of substantive grounds such as that provided for under the 'association with' criterion (or its even vaguer specification of the 'otherwise supporting' criterion).[119] An ombudsperson, or a body of independent experts, should not only have the power to review the relevant information in order to determine whether it justifies the listing (or the maintenance thereof). It should also be given the authority to identify which documents in the file of the designating state actually require to be protected from disclosure.

Obviously, an ombudsperson with the mere power to make recommendations to the Sanctions Committee, whose decisions remain subject to consensus rule, only contributes to an enhanced protection of human rights to a limited degree. The consensus rule, in fact, tends to give the designating state (or eventually any other committee member) a real power of veto in relation to de-listing requests, while the same rule is unlikely to result in a state objecting to another state's proposal for listing. However, if more information were provided at the listing stage by the state proposing the inclusion of a new name on the list, this, together with the recommendation for listing made by the Ombudsperson, could arguably correct the imbalance which today makes listing relatively easy and de-listing far too dependent upon political, rather than legal, considerations.

This would enhance the credibility of the Security Council by addressing due process concerns and arguably provide for 'equivalent protection'—in the words of the ECtHR[120]—of human rights at the UN level.

7. Concluding Remarks

The current requirement that proposals for designation be made through the prefixed model and accompanied by 'as much information as possible'[121] is far too timid. Unless more is required from the designating state, any procedural remedy intervening at a later stage will prove inevitably ineffective. The national and international security interests of the state(s) concerned are a legitimate concern

[118] See section 3A2 on *ex post* remedies above.
[119] See SC Res 1822 (2008), n 24 above and the corresponding text.
[120] See n 79 above and the corresponding text.
[121] See SC Res 1904 (2009) para 13.

that ought to be safeguarded. It is a concern, however, that can and must be protected in ways that are different from those prevailing today. Current procedures allow the designating state to withhold the relevant information not only from states outside the Committee (in particular, the state of nationality and/or residence, should it happen not to be a member thereof) but also from the interested person and the Committee itself.

As the preceding analysis has shown, filling the lacuna in human rights protection at the listing phase is hardly possible at a later stage, whether it is attempted by bringing a legal challenge at the regional or national level or by way of improving the mechanism for review of de-listing requests. Until absolute lack of *ex ante* protection is considered acceptable,[122] there can be no effective protection *ex post* either.

Any real improvement in the review of de-listing requests, in fact, will remain unattainable unless some changes are introduced already at the listing phase. These should include clearer substantive standards for listing than those prevailing today (which, notwithstanding recent attempts for improvement, have remained far too vague) as well as minimum evidentiary requirements, which still have to be elaborated in relation to individuals and entities listed by the UN, at least in relation to international terrorism and the financing thereof.

It is hardly controversial to state that effectiveness of UN sanctions should not be pursued at the expense of legitimacy and that 'terrorism can and must be fought effectively with means that respect human rights and the rule of law'.[123] Very few would disagree with the argument that the two objectives of fundamental human rights protection and the safeguard of collective security are not only compatible but interdependent. Appropriate policies can ensure that individual freedoms are not threatened by a repressive approach. Political hurdles, however, lie in the way of an improvement in existing procedures.

The nature of the threat posed by international terrorism, which needs to be fought through prevention rather than being left to a repressive approach, coupled with the fact that individuals responsible thereof are hardly associated or associable with a state or a state entity, however, ought to be contrasted with the potentially devastating consequences of a continuous failure to take into account the law's limits. In the light of the values at stake, the balance between terrorism prevention and the rule of law needs to be recast in a direction closer to the latter, it is submitted, along the lines of improvement indicated above.

[122] With this I revise my opinion (n 18 above) 123.
[123] PACE Res 1597 (2008) (n 91 above).

6

Human Rights Considerations and the Enforcement of Targeted Sanctions in Europe: The Emergence of Core Standards of Judicial Protection

*Erika de Wet**

1. Focus

This chapter analyses judicial decisions primarily from European countries pertaining to targeted sanctions adopted by the United Nations Security Council (hereinafter the Security Council) in Resolution 1267 (1999)[1] and Resolution 1373 (2001).[2] Both resolutions were inter alia directed at combating the financing of international terrorism and generated controversial blacklists, resulting in the freezing of assets of blacklisted individuals and entities—often for an indefinite period of time. The jurisprudence generated by these resolutions brought to the forefront the legal challenges which governments and courts face in balancing international obligations pertaining to peace and security on the one hand, with (international) human rights obligations, on the other hand.

The subsequent analysis focuses in particular on the impact that the respective blacklists had on the right to judicial protection of the listed individuals and entities. This issue was of central importance in almost all cases pertaining to Resolutions 1267 (1999) and 1373 (2001) to date. The chapter attempts to distil the legal standards for blacklisting and de-listing that would satisfy the benchmarks

* The author would like to extend her gratitude to Messrs Clemens Feinäugle, Stephan Hollenberg, Ivan Smyth, and Antonios Tzanakopoulos, for comments on an earlier draft, which was presented at an expert workshop on *Due Process Aspects in the Implementation of Targeted United Nations Security Council Sanctions*, organized by the Finnish and Swedish Missions to the United Nations and the Fourth Freedom Forum and Kroc Institute for International Peace Studies at the University of Notre Dame, in New York on 30 October 2009. The contribution also forms part of a so-called VICI Project of the Netherlands Organisation for Scientific Research entitled: *The Emerging International Constitutional Order: the Implications of Hierarchy in International Law for the Coherence and Legitimacy of International Decision-making.*

[1] SC Res 1267, 15 October 1999.

[2] SC Res 1373, 28 September 2001.

for effective judicial protection before courts in the European Union (EU). An analysis of the decisions indicates that the legal obligations pertaining to judicial protection mainly concern the post-blacklisting phase (as opposed to the pre-blacklisting phase). A further distinction can be drawn between decisions concerning the judicial protection granted to blacklisted persons and entities, and the judicial protection of third parties incidentally affected by the blacklisting.

The analysis also indicates that the principles of judicial protection regarded as being applicable to blacklisted persons (and third parties incidentally affected by the blacklisting) were distilled primarily from EU or domestic law, despite the fact that international human rights instruments such as the European Convention on Human Rights (ECHR)[3] were also applicable to the respective cases. Only in one instance, namely in regard to a complaint against Belgium before the United Nations Human Rights Committee (HRC), did international human rights law (in the form of the International Covenant on Civil and Political Rights (ICCPR))[4] constitute the basis of the decision.

2. The Legal Protection of Listed Persons and Entities

The cases of seminal importance for determining the scope of judicial protection applicable to listed persons and entities were decided by the courts of the European Union (also known as the Community courts), namely the General Court (EGC), known until November 2009 as the Court of First Instance of the European Communities (CFI), and the European Court of Justice (ECJ). The seminal cases to date are *Yassin Abdullah Kadi and Al Barakaat International Foundation v. Council and Commission*[5] (decided by the ECJ) and the three *Organisation des Modjahedines du Peuple d'Iran* (*OMPI*) (decided by the CFI) cases.[6] Whereas the *Kadi* case concerned the blacklist adopted by the Al-Qaida and Taliban Sanctions Committee of the United Nations (UN) itself (in accordance with Security Council Resolution 1267 (1999)[7] and its follow-up resolutions), the *OMPI* cases concerned the blacklist adopted within the EU pursuant to Security Council Resolution 1373 (2002).[8]

[3] European Convention on Human Rights, as amended (adopted 4 November 1950, entered into force 3 September 1953) (ECHR).

[4] International Covenant on Civil and Political Rights (adopted 16 December 1966, entered into force 23 March 1976) 999 UNTS 171 (ICCPR).

[5] Joined Cases C-402/05 P and C-402/05 P, *Kadi and Al Barakaat International Foundation v Council and Commission*, OJ 2008 C 285/2 (*Kadi (ECJ)*). The reasoning of this decision was subsequently confirmed on 30 September 2010 in a follow-up decision by the EGC, Case T/85/09, *Yassin Abdullah v European Commission* (*Kadi EGC*), available at http://eur-lex.europa.eu/LexUriServ/LexUriServ.do?uri=CELEX:62009A0085:EN:HTML (last accessed 30 May 2011).

[6] Case T-228/02, *Organisation des Modjahedines du Peuple d'Iran v Council* [2006] ECR II-4665 (*OMPI (I)*); Case T-256/07, *People's Mojahedin Organization of Iran v Council* [2008] ECR II-03019 (*OMPI (II)*); Case T-284/08, *People's Mojahedin Organization of Iran v Council*, Judgment of 4 December 2008, not yet published (*OMPI (III)*).

[7] SC Res 1267 (1999).

[8] SC Res 1373 (2001).

However, as will be illustrated below, one can conclude from the *Kadi* case that the ECJ insists on the same level of protection to be provided for all blacklisted individuals and entities in the EU—regardless of whether these individuals or entities were listed under the Security Council Resolution 1267 (1999) regime (hereinafter the Al-Qaida and Taliban Sanctions Regime), or the Security Council Resolution 1373 (2002) regime (hereinafter the Counter Terrorism Sanctions Regime). This was subsequently confirmed by the EGC in its most recent *Kadi* decision in September 2010. In the subsequent analysis, the *Kadi* and *OMPI* cases will constitute a point of departure, whilst additional case law from the Community and other (European) courts will serve a supplementary role. Since the EGC's most recent *Kadi* decision essentially reaffirms the reasoning of the ECJ of 2008, the 2008 *Kadi* decision remains the central point of reference, while the 2010 EGC decision constitutes supplementary authority.

A. An introduction to the *Kadi* and *OMPI* disputes

1. *The Kadi dispute*

As is well known, the dispute in the *Kadi* case[9] is rooted in Security Council Resolutions 1267 of 15 October 1999[10] and 1333 of 19 December 2000,[11] and the measures subsequently adopted within the EU in order to implement those resolutions uniformly in all member states.[12] The Security Council adopted the resolutions following the attacks on the American embassies in Kenya and Tanzania, and the suspected involvement of Usama Bin Laden in those acts. These resolutions, geared towards pressuring the (then) de facto Taliban regime in Afghanistan into extraditing Usama Bin Laden to the United States, authorized the Al-Qaida and Taliban Sanctions Committee to identify and blacklist individuals and entities associated with the Taliban, Usama Bin Laden, and al-Qaida (the Al-Qaida and Taliban Sanctions Regime). The assets of blacklisted individuals and entities were to be frozen by the state of residence of those individuals and entities until such time as the Al-Qaida and Taliban Sanctions Committee might remove them from the list. In the period directly after the attacks on the United States of 11 September 2001, the Al-Qaida and Taliban Sanctions Committee was very active in expanding the list of targeted persons and entities. Although the Security Council lifted the sanctions against Afghanistan in Security Council Resolution

[9] Case T-315/01, *Kadi v Council and Commission* [2005] ECR II-3649 (*Kadi (CFI)*); see also Case T-306/01, *Yusuf and Al Barakaat International Foundation v Council and Commission* [2005] ECR II-3353.

[10] SC Res 1267 (1999).

[11] SC Res 1333, 19 December 2000.

[12] See, *inter alia,* Council Common Position 2002/402/CFSP of 27 May 2002 Concerning Restrictive Measures against Usama bin Laden, members of the Al-Qaida organisation OJ 2002 L 139/4; see also Council Regulation 881/2002 of 27 May 2002 imposing certain specific restrictive measures directed against certain persons and entities associated with Usama bin Laden, the Al-Qaida network and the Taliban OJ 2002 L 139/9. Both measures implemented the targeted sanctions of SC Res 1267 (1999), SC Res 1333 (2000), and SC Res 1390, 28 January 2002.

1390 of 16 January 2002,[13] following the fall of the Taliban regime, sanctions have been maintained against the Taliban, Usama Bin Laden, and al-Qaida. Neither Resolution 1267 (1999)[14] nor subsequent resolutions have explicit provisions for independent judicial review for the targeted individuals and entities. Instead, the Al-Qaida and Taliban Sanctions Regime merely provides for a political procedure in the form of de-listing.[15]

The EU implemented Resolution 1267 (1999) and subsequent resolutions through Common Positions and Council Regulations in order to ensure uniform application in all member states.[16] The respective Council Regulations had direct effect, and as the Regulations did not explicitly provide for an independent review mechanism, the issue of the right to a fair trial was bound to arise before the Community courts, beginning with the CFI. This court was confronted with a request for annulment of the Council Regulations that implemented the black-listing regime of the Al-Qaida and Taliban Sanctions Committee. Inevitably however, the legal question before the CFI implicitly raised the additional issue of the legality of the Security Council measures, although the claimant had not directly challenged this point. As the Council Regulations had transposed the relevant Security Council resolutions almost word for word, any review of the substance of the challenged Regulations would necessarily amount to indirect review of the legality of the relevant Security Council measures.[17] The CFI concluded that it would not have the right to engage in such a review, except where violations of peremptory norms (*jus cogens*) of international law were at stake.[18] It further concluded that obligations under Article 103 of the United Nations Charter[19] (UN Charter)—which include binding Security Council decisions—took precedence over all other international obligations, with the exception of *jus cogens* obligations. In accordance with the CFI's reasoning, the Security Council had the competence to suspend the right to a fair trial (as guaranteed by EU law and international law) of the blacklisted persons for an unlimited period of time. The CFI reasoned that since this right does not (yet) belong to the corpus of

[13] SC Res 1390 (2002).

[14] SC Res 1267 (1999).

[15] This remains the case, despite the introduction of an independent Ombudsperson in SC Res 1904, 17 December 2009, para 20. Although the Ombudsperson can contribute to improving the flow of information between the Al-Qaida and Taliban Sanctions Committee and the listed persons and entities, his or her functions do not amount to an independent and impartial judicial review. First, states will still be able to withhold any information which they prefer to keep confidential during the information exchange process. Moreover, the Ombudsperson has no direct influence on any de-listing decision, as his or her formal role is limited to the gathering and presenting of information. The de-listing decisions are still taken confidentially and by consensus by the Sanctions Committee. See also Lord Hope, Joint Appeal of *A,K,M,Q and G* and *Hay* (n 110 below) para 78; *Kadi EGC* (n 5 above) para 128.

[16] Common Position 2002/402/CFSP (n 12 above) and Regulation 881/2002 (n 12 above).

[17] Tomuschat, 'Primacy of United Nations Law—Innovative features in the Community Legal Order' (2006) 43 CMLR 543.

[18] *Kadi (CFI)* (n 9 above) paras 221, 225–6.

[19] Charter of the United Nations, adopted 26 June 1945, entered into force 24 October 1945, 993 TS (UN Charter).

peremptory norms recognized in public international law, it could be overridden by a conflicting Security Council decision.[20]

The CFI *Kadi* case was subsequently followed by the Swiss Federal Tribunal in the *Nada* case, which also concerned the blacklisting of an individual in accordance with the Al-Qaida and Taliban Sanctions Regime.[21] The Swiss Federal Tribunal effectively copied the reasoning of the CFI, despite the fact that Switzerland is not a member of the EU and is therefore not bound by the jurisprudence of its courts. The Swiss Federal Tribunal reiterated this position in two subsequent decisions. Whereas one of the cases also concerned the Al-Qaida and Taliban Sanctions Regime,[22] the other decision concerned the freezing of assets of individuals and entities who were associated with the Iraqi regime of Saddam Hussein, as well as the immediate transfer of those assets to the Development Fund of Iraq in accordance with Resolution 1483 of 22 May 2003.[23] These individuals and entities were directly identified by the Sanctions Committee set up under Security Council Resolution 1518 of 24 November 2003[24] and—as in the case of the Al-Qaida and Taliban Sanctions Regime—the Resolution did not provide for judicial protection. As with its reasoning in the *Nada* case, the Swiss Federal Tribunal readily accepted that the procedure outlined in the Security Council resolution was clear and left no room for interpretation.[25]

However, it is important to note that the aforementioned cases were handed down prior to the September 2008 ECJ ruling that overturned the *Kadi (CFI)* case, and that Mr Nada has also lodged a complaint against Switzerland before the European Court of Human Rights (ECtHR), which is currently still pending.[26] It therefore remains to be seen whether or not the Swiss Federal Tribunal will change its position in the future, as it tends to follow developments in the EU closely.

[20] See also extensively De Sena and Vitucci, 'The European Courts and the Security Council: Between Dédoublement Fonctionnel and Balancing Values' (2009) 20 EJIL 193, 206 *et seq*; the same approach was taken by the ECtHR in the joined cases *Agim Behrami and Bekir Behrami v France* and *Ruzhdi Saramati v France, Norway and Germany*, ECHR, Judgment of 2 May 2007, not yet published, as well as in *Berić and Others v Bosnia and Herzegovina*, ECHR, Judgment of 16 October 2007, not yet published.

[21] *Youssef Mustapha Nada v Staatssekretariat für Wirtschaft*, Case No 1A 45/2007 BGE 133 II 450; See also ILDC 461 (CH 2007) at www.oxfordlawreports.com.

[22] *A v Federal Department of Economics*, Swiss Federal Tribunal, Judgment of 22 April 2008.

[23] *A v Federal Department of Economics*, Swiss Federal Tribunal, Judgment of 23 January 2008; SC Res 1483, 22 May 2003, paras 19, 23.

[24] SC Res 1518, 24 November 2003.

[25] *A v Federal Department of Economics* (n 23 above) paras 9.1–9.2. Similarly, the Turkish Council of State held that the Council of Ministers had an obligation to implement the Security Council resolution, and that the only place to seek redress was the UN, see *Yassin Abdullah Kadi v The State* (2007) Appeal Judgment, E.2824/K.115 (Council of State of Turkey, Board of Administrative Cases); see also Nollkaemper, 'The European Courts and the Security Council: Between Dédoublement Fonctionnel and Balancing of Values: Three Replies to Pasquale De Sena and Maria Chiara Vitucci' (2009) 20 EJIL 853,864, 868.

[26] See the enclosure ('Improving the implementation of the sanctions regime through "fair and clear procedures"') of the identical letters of 23 June 2008 from the Permanent Representative of Switzerland to the UN. The letters are addressed to the President of the UNGA and the President of the UNSC, UN Docs A/62/891 and S/2008/428, para 4; See also Keller and Fischer, 'The UN Anti-Terror Sanctions Regime under Pressure' (2009) 9 *Human Rights Law Review* 257, 265.

Moreover, it remains to be seen whether or not the ECtHR will take a position similar to that of the ECJ in the *Kadi (ECJ)* case (albeit on the basis of the ECHR). Although Mr Nada was de-listed by the Al-Qaida and Taliban Sanctions Committee in September 2009, it is uncertain at the time of writing whether he will nonetheless pursue the case before the ECtHR, notably in order to claim damages.

When confronted with the *Kadi* case on appeal, the ECJ came to the conclusion that—based on the fundamental principles of EU law—those individuals and entities blacklisted under the Al-Qaida and Taliban Sanctions Regime were entitled to full judicial protection in accordance with EU law.[27] The ECJ took what can be described as a strict dualist approach: it held that the EU constitutes an autonomous legal order within which fundamental rights form an integral part of the general and constitutional principles.[28] These principles, one of which is effective judicial protection, could not be prejudiced by an international agreement, be it the UN Charter or otherwise, despite the fact that the treaty in question, in this case the UN Charter, maintains its primacy under the international law.[29]

2. *The OMPI dispute*

By coming to the conclusion that Mr Kadi was entitled to full judicial protection, the ECJ implicitly concluded that he was entitled to the same standards of protection within the EU as those individuals affected by the Counter Terrorism Sanctions Regime, which constituted the basis of the dispute in the *OMPI* decisions.[30] These cases, which were decided by the CFI, concerned the freezing of assets of the organization that was blacklisted by the EU itself, pursuant to Security Council Resolution 1373 (2001). This resolution, which was adopted in the wake of the attacks of 11 September 2001, obliged states to freeze, without delay, funds and other financial assets or economic resources of persons involved in terrorist acts.[31] Unlike the list instituted by the Al-Qaida and Taliban Sanctions Regime,

[27] *Kadi (ECJ)* (n 5 above) paras 299, 303–4, 326; Herik and Schrijver, 'Eroding the Primacy of the UN System of Collective Security: The Judgment of the European Court of Justice in the Cases of Kadi and Al Barakaat' (2008) 5 *International Organizations Law Review* 329, 336.

[28] *Kadi (ECJ)* (n 5 above) para 288; Gattini, 'Joined Cases C-402/05 P & 415/05 P, Yassin Abdullah Kadi, Al Barakaat International Foundation v. Council and Commission, judgment of the Grand Chamber of 3 September 2008' (2009) 46 CMLR 213, 221; Kunoy and Dawes, 'Plate Tectonics in Luxembourg: the *Menage a Trois* between EC Law, International Law and the European Convention on Human Rights Following the UN Sanctions Cases' (2009) 46 CMLR 73, 101; in December 2009 the ECJ confirmed its *Kadi*-reasoning in two very similar cases, Case C-399/06 P, *Faraj Hassan v Council*, Judgment of 3 December 2009, not yet published; and Case C-403/06 P, *Chafiq Ayadi v Council of the European Union*, Judgment of 3 December 2009, not yet published.

[29] See also *Kadi EGC* (n 5 above) para 119; De Búrca, 'The European Courts and the Security Council: Between Dédoublement Fonctionnel and Balancing of Values: Three Replies to Pasquale De Sena and Maria Chiara Vitucci' (2009) 20 EJIL 853; see also De Búrca, 'The ECJ and the International Legal Order after Kadi' (2010) 51 *Harvard International Law Journal* 1. She views the *Kadi* decision in light of a pluralist understanding of the international legal order, in which a multiplicity of distinct and diverse normative systems give rise to clashes of authority-claims and competition for primacy in specific contexts.

[30] SC Res 1373 (2001).

[31] Ibid para 1(c).

Resolution 1373 (2001) does not envisage a central list. Instead, it relies on autonomous lists established by states or the EU. The independent responsibility of states and/or the EU in the creation and maintenance of these lists gave them more (obvious) discretion in balancing potential human rights conflicts with the duty to implement Security Council obligations, since the Security Council had neither ordered that specific assets of specific individuals or entities be frozen nor prescribed a listing or de-listing procedure for this purpose.[32] The adoption of the measures resulting in the freezing of funds thus involved the exercise of discretionary powers by the EU, which is bound to observe the right to judicial protection.[33] However, in the *Kadi* case, the ECJ had insisted that full judicial protection also be granted in situations where the EU implemented a sanctions list compiled at the level of the UN. In doing so, the ECJ rejected the notion that different levels of judicial protection and review were applicable within the EU depending on the degree of discretion or autonomy the EU had in implementing Security Council resolutions directed at the freezing of assets.[34]

The *Kadi* and *OMPI* decisions all underscored the essential importance of a fair hearing before the administrative body ordering the freezing of assets, followed by judicial review (the right to a remedy) before the Community courts. Although the concepts of fair hearing and judicial review are closely related, the former is primarily directed towards the executive, whereas the latter involves the Community judicature. The subsequent analysis will reflect the more detailed account of the benchmarks of a fair hearing and judicial review given in the *OMPI* decisions. However, since the ECJ has indicated that the same level of protection should be provided in relation to all sanctions regimes applicable in the EU, these benchmarks would be analogously applicable to the Al-Qaida and Taliban Sanctions Regime.[35] Recently, the implications of this approach by the ECJ have also started to have an impact on the reasoning of domestic courts in the EU, notably in the United Kingdom.

B. The right to a fair hearing

Within the EU legal order the right to a fair hearing applies to all decisions that can culminate in a measure adversely affecting the person in question. It requires notifying those persons of the evidence against them, providing them with a statement of reasons for the adverse decision, and the opportunity to make their views known. However, under certain circumstances the right is triggered only after

[32] Halberstram and Stein, 'The United Nations, the European Union, and the King of Sweden: Economic Sanctions and Individual Rights in a Plural World Order' (2009) 46 CMLR 13, 31.

[33] *OMPI (I)* (n 6 above) para 24.

[34] Kunoy and Dawes (n 28 above) 100.

[35] The European Commission has submitted an amendment to Regulation 881/2002 (n 12 above), to the European Parliament for consultation. The amendment is aimed at taking account of the *Kadi (ECJ)* decision (n 5 above), and provides in general terms for a statement of reasons and the opportunity to be heard. See COM/20090187 final—CNS 2009/0055. The amendment was forwarded to the Council on 22 April 2009.

the adverse decision has been taken, implying that the reasons for the decision do not necessarily have to be communicated to the affected person or entity in advance.

1. The timing of the right to a fair hearing

Both the *Kadi* and *OMPI* cases underscored that, where a first decision to freeze the funds of a particular person or entity is concerned, the notification of evidence and the right to be heard are only triggered after the blacklisting has taken place. To expect the authorities to notify the affected persons or entities prior to the blacklisting would undermine the very objective and effectiveness pursued by the Regulation, which is based on the element of surprise and must apply with immediate effect. As such, the nature of the freezing mechanism necessarily implies a limitation to the right to a fair hearing.[36]

However, both the ECJ and CFI also underscored that the authorities had to communicate the grounds for the contested decision concomitantly with, or as soon as possible after, the adoption of the initial decision to freeze funds in order to enable the person or entity concerned to be heard regarding that decision, and to consider exercising the right to bring action before the CFI in the matter.[37] A failure to provide this so-called 'statement of reasons' cannot be remedied by the fact that the person concerned learned of the reasons for the decision during the proceedings before the Community courts.[38] Moreover a subsequent decision to prolong the freezing of funds must be preceded by the notification of any new evidence (including exculpatory evidence) and the possibility of a further hearing.[39] In that case the element of surprise is no longer relevant, nor would the efficacy of the measures be threatened as the freezing of assets had already been effectuated for some time.[40]

In the case filed against Belgium by Mr Nabil Sayadi and his wife Ms Patricia Vinck (*Sayadi & Vinck* case),[41] the HRC found Belgium in breach of Article 12 ICCPR as the travel restrictions resulting from the Al-Qaida and Taliban Sanctions Regime prevented the plaintiffs from travelling within or leaving Belgium.[42] The HRC did not consider this restriction on the right to freedom of movement necessary for the protection of national security or public order as provided for in Article 12(3) ICCPR. In reaching this decision, the HRC gave due consideration to the fact that Belgium transmitted the plaintiffs' names to the Al-Qaida and

[36] *Kadi (ECJ)* (n 5 above) para 339; *OMPI (I)* (n 6 above) para 128; Gattini (n 28 above) 222.
[37] *Kadi (ECJ)*, ibid para 336; *OMPI (I)*, ibid para 131; Gattini, ibid 222.
[38] *OMPI (I)*, ibid para 139.
[39] Ibid para 131.
[40] Ibid para 131; *OMPI (III)* (n 6 above) para 41.
[41] CCPR, *Sayadi and Vinck v Belgium*, UN Doc CCPR/C/94/D/1472/2006 (*Sayadi & Vinck*).
[42] Art 12(1) ICCPR, determines: 'Everyone lawfully within the territory of a State shall, within that territory, have the right to liberty of movement and freedom to choose his residence', whereas Art 12(2) states that: 'Everyone shall be free to leave any country, including his own.'

Taliban Sanctions Committee before the couple could be heard.[43] In addition, the Brussels Court of First Instance exonerated the plaintiffs of any suspected criminal activities and dismissed the case in February 2005. It further ordered Belgium to initiate a de-listing request with the Al-Qaida and Taliban Sanctions Committee.[44] Although Belgium ultimately gave effect to the order, the de-listing was blocked within the Sanctions Committee.

It should be noted that this decision can be interpreted as obliging states parties to the ICCPR to institute and await the outcome of criminal proceedings prior to participating in the blacklisting of individuals in the territory of those states. However, such an interpretation seems to have been rejected by the CFI in the *El Morabit* case, decided in September 2009, concerning the freezing of assets in accordance with the Counter Terrorism Sanctions Regime.[45] The claimant submitted that the freezing of his assets by the Council prior to a decision on his appeal against a conviction for participation in a criminal organization with terrorist objectives violated the presumption of innocence protected in Article 6(2) ECHR. The CFI rejected this argument, noting that the freezing measures as such were not a sanction, and did not pre-determine the innocence or guilt of persons they affected. Delaying the freezing measures until after the appeal had been decided would severely undermine the efficacy of measures aimed at combating terrorism, which by their nature had to be taken swiftly. (However, the subsequent *Kadi EGC* decision did indicate that protracted freezing of assets that last up to ten years can turn into punitive measures. This point will be taken up again below in section C2).[46]

In essence, therefore, the HRC's decision seems to imply that by transmitting the names of Mr Sayadi and Ms Vinck to the Al-Qaida and Taliban Sanctions Committee without awaiting the outcome of the national criminal investigation, Belgium is responsible for the resulting infringement of their right to liberty of movement as protected by Article 12 ICCPR. It is difficult to reconcile this position with that of the ECJ and CFI in the *Kadi* and *OMPI (I)* cases, as it was concluded in those cases that a pre-listing-hearing would compromise the purpose of the blacklisting procedure. Had Belgium indeed awaited the outcome of the criminal investigation—which commenced two months before the transmission of the names of Mr Sayadi and Ms Vinck and were only completed three years later—the purpose of 'swift and effective action' would certainly have been undermined.[47]

[43] *Sayadi & Vinck* (n 41 above) para 10.7. The CCPR also attached weight to the fact that no other state had forwarded the names of any of the other employees of the charitable organization in question to the Al-Qaida and Taliban Sanctions Committee.

[44] *Sayadi & Vinck*, ibid paras 2.5, 10.8. At para 10.13, the CCPR further found that the stigmatization involved combined with the publicity attached to the blacklisting resulted in an unlawful attack on the honour and reputation of the plaintiffs in terms of Art 17 ICCPR; Keller and Fischer (n 26 above) 261, 264.

[45] Joined cases T-37/07 and T-323/07, *Mohamed El Morabit v Council*, Judgment of 2 September 2009, not yet published (*El Morabit* case) paras 40, 51, 52.

[46] *Kadi EGC* decision (n 5 above) para 150.

[47] Individual dissenting opinion of Committee member Mr Ivan Shearer in *Sayadi & Vinck* (n 41 above).

2. *The notification of evidence and the right to be heard*

The *OMPI (I)* decision explicitly stated that the right to a fair hearing applies to all acts or decisions in the EU, which can culminate in measures adversely affecting a person, including administrative decisions taken by the Council of the EU (the Council).[48] Any person upon whom a penalty (such as the freezing of funds) may be imposed must be placed in a position in which he or she can effectively make his or her view of the matters on which the penalty is based known.[49] This implies that the person affected has to be notified of the evidence against him or her, and must be given the reasons for that decision; these two criteria are closely intertwined. The statement of reasons becomes all the more important in a situation where persons are not afforded the opportunity to be heard prior to their placement on the sanctions list (which is the case with all persons listed for the first time), as it constitutes the sole safeguard that enables them to challenge the lawfulness of that decision before the Community courts.[50] Thus, there is a close link between the obligation to provide a statement of reasons and the right to an effective remedy in the form of judicial review. On the one hand, the affected individual must be able to determine whether the blacklisting was justified, or whether there was an error that justifies an action before the Community courts. At the same time, the courts themselves must be enabled to exercise review, which is not possible in the absence of a statement of reasons.[51]

In the case of Mr Kadi, the ECJ concluded that he would not be able to defend his rights satisfactorily during judicial review, as the disputed Council Regulation did not provide for any procedure by which the evidence justifying the inclusion of the names of the persons concerned on the list could be communicated. Moreover, the Council did not take any step in that direction in the specific case.[52] The CFI came to a similar and significantly more detailed conclusion in the *OMPI (I)* case (which predated the ECJ's *Kadi* judgment). Some of the elaboration concerned the fact that the *OMPI* cases resulted from the Counter Terrorism Sanctions Regime, which left the identification of the individuals and entities to the national authorities. The second phase of that regime involves action undertaken at the EU level, whereby the Council must decide whether or not to include the party concerned in the so-called blacklist.[53]

[48] *OMPI (I)* (n 6 above) paras 91–2, 94.
[49] Ibid paras 91–2, 94, 116–17.
[50] Ibid para 139.
[51] Ibid paras 89, 93, 143, 145.
[52] *Kadi (ECJ)* (n 5 above) paras 348–51; Gattini (n 28 above) 222. Subsequently, the CFI was obliged to follow this legal reasoning in Case T-318/01, *Omar Mohammed Othman v Council and Commission*, Judgment of 11 June 2009, not yet published, at paras 94 *et seq*. The facts of the case placed the applicant in a situation in every way comparable to that of the appellants in the *Kadi (ECJ)* case. The CFI also criticized the Council for the fact that it had not provided Mr Othman with a response similar to that provided to Mr Kadi, even though it was known that Mr Othman's situation was comparable to that of Mr Kadi in all respects.
[53] *OMPI (I)* (n 6 above) paras 116–17.

This particular division of labour between the member states and the Council implied that the right to a fair hearing (as well as the right to judicial review) are applicable both on the domestic and EU level.[54] Due to the nature of the cooperation between the EU and its member states in matters relating to terrorism, the substantive assessment of the appropriateness and well-foundedness of the decision to place the person on the sanctions list is reserved for the national judiciary. The same applies to challenges to the seriousness and credibility of evidence on which the decision was based.[55] Subsequently, at the EU level, the Council had to defer to this assessment by the national judicial authorities or equivalent thereof, to the extent that an assessment of the evidence had indeed taken place.[56] Where there has been no such assessment by the competent national judicial authority, the Council must consider such challenges as newly adduced evidence subject to notification and a hearing at the Community level.[57]

Where the assessment had taken place at the national level, the Council's own obligations are more procedural in nature. It has to inform the affected individuals or entities that there is precise information or material in the file indicating that a competent national judicial authority has taken a decision to include the individuals in the sanctions list, based on serious evidence or clues. The statement of reasons must concern each of these issues, more specifically it must state in a clear and unequivocal fashion, based on fact and law, the actual and specific reasons that the Council had followed. That a concise statement of reasons may sometimes suffice was illustrated in the *Melli Bank plc* case, which concerned the EU's imposition of an assets freeze on the applicant (the Melli Bank) pursuant to Security Council Resolution 1737 (2006).[58] This resolution required an assets freeze of persons and entities listed in an annex to it due to the alleged involvement of those parties in nuclear proliferation. The Council motivated the freezing of the applicant's assets by reference to the fact that the Melli Bank was controlled by a company (Bank Melli Iran—BMI) suspected of participation in the funding of nuclear proliferation. The freezing of the applicant's funds was therefore necessary to ensure the effectiveness of the measures against BMI. In the circumstances of the case, the CFI deemed those reasons to be sufficient.[59]

Furthermore, the Council has to review the sanctions list at least once every six months to ensure that there are still grounds for sustaining it.[60] Where the Council

[54] Ibid para 119. The CFI, once again citing the ECtHR, namely *Tinnelly & Sons Ltd & Others and McElduff and Others v United Kingdom*, ECHR (1998-IV) Series A No 79, para 78, acknowledged that certain restrictions to the right to a fair hearing may be necessary in light of security reasons or due to the maintenance of international relations.

[55] *OMPI (I)* (n 6 above) para 121.

[56] Ibid paras 124–5.

[57] Ibid para 125.

[58] Joined Cases T-246/08 and T-332-08, *Melli Bank plc v Council*, Judgment of 9 July 2009, not yet published (*Melli Bank* case); SC Res 1737, 23 December 2006.

[59] *Melli Bank* case, ibid paras 140, 148, 151. The applicant's own line of argument revealed its awareness of the link between the freezing of its funds and the alleged engagement in nuclear proliferation of its parent entity.

[60] *OMPI (I)* (n 6 above) para 116.

decides to maintain a name on the list (a so-called 'subsequent decision'), the Council must indicate the actual and specific reasons why, after re-examination, the freezing of the funds remains justified.[61]

At this point it is important to note that both the ECJ and the CFI, relying on jurisprudence of the ECtHR,[62] acknowledged that not all relevant matters have to be conveyed to the affected persons during the notification of evidence or the statement of reasons.[63] The requirements of public security as well as the maintenance of international relations may justify limitations: (i) on the notification of certain serious and credible evidence or clues on which the national decision was based; (ii) on conveyance of the specific content or grounds of that national decision; or (3) even regarding the identity of the authority that took the decision. Under specific circumstances, those factors may also prevent the identification of the country in which the national authority took the decision.[64] However, to the extent that the competent national authority is relying on evidence that is in the public domain, confidentiality should not be used as a pretext for not notifying the affected person of this fact. For example, where national authorities relied on a domestic court ruling as incriminating evidence, this must be mentioned in the statement of reasons. Since these are official acts adopted at the end of public judicial proceedings to which the affected person had been a party, the communication of those acts to the applicant cannot be prevented by any requirement of confidentiality.[65]

In neither the *Kadi*[66] nor the *OMPI*[67] cases did the respective courts engage in any detail as to what these limitations may imply in the concrete case at hand. What was clear, however, was that neither a complete absence of notification of evidence, nor of a statement of reasons was acceptable. Subsequent to the ECJ's decision, Mr Kadi received a summary of reasons which was provided by the Al-Qaida and Taliban Sanctions Committee. However, this summary merely contained certain general, unsubstantiated, vague allegations. When subsequently challenged before the EGC, it confirmed that this information did not grant Mr Kadi even the most minimal access to the evidence against him. He was not given any indication of how he was involved with any particular terrorist activity, when and with whom. As a result his right to defence was infringed, as he was not given a fair opportunity to refute any of the allegations against him.[68]

[61] *OMPI (I)* (n 6 above) paras 138, 143, 145.

[62] *Chahal v United Kingdom*, ECHR (1996-V) Series A No 22 (*Chahal* case) para 131.

[63] *Kadi (ECJ)* (n 5 above) para 344; *OMPI (I)* (n 6 above) paras 135, 146; Gattini (n 28 above) 222.

[64] *OMPI (I)*, ibid para 136.

[65] Case T-47/03, *Jose Maria Sison v Council* [2007] ECR II-73 (*Sison I* case) paras 212, 217, and 224. The facts of this case were similar to those in the *OMPI (I)* decision (n 6 above). In the *Sison I* case it was also unclear whom or what exactly constituted the competent national authority in the Netherlands. Whereas the Council, in its written pleadings, had indicated that it was a decision by a domestic court of first instance dating from 1997, the oral pleadings of the Council referred to the State Secretary as the competent national authority.

[66] *Kadi (ECJ)* (n 5 above).

[67] *OMPI* cases (n 6 above).

[68] *Kadi EGC* (n 5 above) paras 157, 158, 173. See also Martinez, 'Bad Law for Good Reasons: The Contradiction of the Kadi Judgment' (2008) 5 *International Organizations Law Review* 339, 354.

In the *OMPI (I)* case, no mention of any specific information or material was made either in relation to the initial decision to include the organization on the sanctions list, or in relation to the subsequent decision to extend the period of inclusion. The statement of reasons merely repeated the statutory bases for including the individual in the sanctions list and averred that such an inclusion was 'desirable'.[69] Subsequent to the *OMPI (I)* decision, the Council provided the organization with a statement of reasons essentially relating to the order of the Home Secretary of the United Kingdom of 28 March 2001, which proscribed the applicant as an organization concerned with terrorism. Although the adequacy of this statement was not at issue in the subsequent *OMPI (II)* case, the court criticized the Council for not attaching sufficient weight to the national judicial authority's criticism of the competent national authority for designating an entity as being involved in terrorism.[70] The harsher the criticism of the competent national judicial authority, the more difficult it would be for the Council to legally justify the continued inclusion of the affected person or entity in the sanctions list. In such a case the Council would have to give specific reasons as to why it remained justified to include the applicant on the sanctions list, despite clear findings to the contrary by the national judicial authority.[71] Furthermore, where the decision by a competent national authority to include someone in the list ceases to exist, the Council must either take immediate steps to remove the person from its own list or—citing new evidence—explain why this cannot be done.[72]

The *OMPI (II)* case resulted from the Council's decision to maintain the OMPI on its sanctions list despite the national judiciary's criticism of the competent national authority's decision to proscribe the organization. Subsequent to the *OMPI (I)* case, the Proscribed Organizations Appeal Commission (POAC)—a national quasi-judicial body in the United Kingdom that hears appeals against the Home Secretary's decision pertaining to proscription—sharply criticized the Home Secretary for maintaining the OMPI's proscription under domestic law. It described the Home Secretary's conclusion that the applicant was still an organization concerned with terrorism in the period as 'perverse' as it was not possible to have reached any reasonable conclusion to that effect.[73] The POAC concluded that

[69] *OMPI (I)* (n 6 above) paras 142, 161–6; the same deficits also plagued Case T-253/04, *Kongra-Gel v Council*, Judgment of 3 April 2004, not yet published, paras 97–8 and Case T-229/02, *Osman Öcalan acting on behalf of the Kurdistan Workers' Party (PKK) v Council* [2008] ECR II-45 (*Öcalan* case) para 65. The former decision concerned an initial decision of inclusion in the sanctions list, whereas the latter concerned a subsequent decision.

[70] *OMPI (II)* (n 6 above) para 170.

[71] Ibid paras 179–80.

[72] *OMPI (III)* (n 6 above) para 40; subsequently, in Case T-341/07, *Jose Maria Sison v Council*, Judgment of 30 September 2009, not yet published (*Sison II*), at paras 113 *et seq*, the CFI emphasized that the decision of the national judicial authority on which the Council is relying has to have a close nexus with terrorism. In this particular instance no such nexus existed. A decision determining whether Mr Sison should be granted refugee status and a residence permit did not result in the opening of a criminal investigation against him for alleged involvement in terrorism. The Council, in listing or maintaining the listing, had to give due consideration to domestic acquittals of persons prosecuted for terrorism, or decisions not to pursue an investigation or prosecution due to lack of evidence.

[73] *OMPI (II)* (n 6 above) para 168.

since 2001 the OMPI had not been engaged in any terrorist activity anywhere, its military command structure had ceased to exist (without any evidence to the contrary), it had ceased to glorify terrorism, and it had been disarmed. Therefore, the organization no longer satisfied any of the criteria necessary for the maintenance of the proscription as there was no involvement in, preparation or encouragement of terrorism.[74]

The POAC further refused to grant leave to appeal, based on the lack of a reasonable chance of success regarding any of the grounds forwarded. Although the Home Secretary expressed an intention to ask for leave to lodge an appeal with the Court of Appeal, this had not taken place at the time the CFI decided the case.[75] In spite of being in possession of the POAC's letter, the Council ignored the very clear exculpatory findings outlined therein,[76] merely claiming that 'the reasons for continuing to include the applicant in the list at issue were still valid'.[77] This obviously amounted to insufficient justification for continuing to freeze the applicant's funds.

Subsequently on 7 May 2008 the Court of Appeal of England and Wales dismissed the appeal of the Home Secretary against the POAC's decision, as a result of which the Home Secretary removed the OMPI's name from the domestic list of proscribed organizations on 24 June 2008.[78] However, in July 2008 the Council retained OMPI's name on the EU's sanctions list, relying on an ongoing judicial investigation by the Parisian anti-terrorist prosecutor of March 2007 to bring charges against certain OMPI members. The Council considered this action to be 'a decision by a competent national authority'.[79] The Council did not inform OMPI before taking the subsequent decision to maintain it on the blacklist, thereby depriving the organization of the opportunity to make its views on the matter known. According to the court, the Council had not in any way substantiated why such action was necessary under the circumstances. In particular, no urgency was established since the Council had allowed more than two months to lapse after the decision of the Court of Appeal in March 2007 (effectively removing the initial decision by a competent national authority) and identifying another decision by a competent national authority on which it relied to maintain OMPI on the list. Subsequent to the decision of the Court of Appeal, the Council should either have removed OMPI from the sanctions list immediately, or have taken steps on the basis of new evidence to maintain the organization's inclusion on that list.[80]

[74] *OMPI (II)* (n 6 above) para 169.
[75] Ibid paras 174, 184.
[76] Ibid paras 22–3, 141.
[77] Ibid paras 179–80.
[78] *OMPI (III)* (n 6 above) paras 2, 5, 7.
[79] Commission Decision 2008/582 OJ 2008 L 186/39, notified under document number C (2008) 3411; *OMPI (III)* (n 6 above) para 10.
[80] *OMPI (III)* (n 6 above) paras 36, 40.

C. The Right to Judicial Review

The right of the parties concerned to bring an action before the Community courts ensures their right to effective, impartial, and independent judicial protection within the EU. When exercising judicial review, the courts have to strike a balance between deference to the Council's assessment of the evidence, and the level of scrutiny necessary to ensure that the only procedural safeguard ensuring that a fair balance is struck between the need to combat international terrorism and the protection of fundamental rights is maintained.[81] In addition, the right to judicial review applies regardless of whether the freezing of assets amounts to a criminal charge.

1. Balancing counter-terrorism measures with procedural fairness

The Community courts have to give deference to the Council's assessment of the facts in the sense that the courts are not allowed to reassess the evidence, facts, and circumstances justifying the adoption of the respective measures and substitute the judgment made by the Council with its own. In considering the appropriateness of the Council's decision, the judicial review must be restricted to determining whether any manifest error of judgment of the facts or abuse of power has occurred. The review exercised by the courts is primarily procedural in nature. First, compliance with the rules of procedure and the statement of reasons must be verified, and it must be ensured that any claim by the Council that overriding (security) considerations prevents compliance with the right to a fair hearing is well founded.[82] Secondly, the courts must review the material accuracy of the facts, the reliability and consistency thereof, the question whether all the relevant information had indeed been taken into account during the assessment, and whether such information is capable of substantiating the conclusions that were subsequently drawn.[83] As the *OMPI (II)* case revealed, the fact that the Council effectively ignored the exculpatory evidence produced by the applicant to justify removal from the list, constituted a fatal flaw in the Council's decision. Moreover, where the competent national authority has taken a decision against alleged members of an organization as opposed to the organization, the Council will have to provide reasons why the acts of individuals should be imputed to the organization should it decide to list the organization itself.[84]

From this it follows that the Community courts must be able to review the lawfulness and merits of a decision to freeze funds, despite the fact that some information may have to remain confidential when national security is at stake.[85]

[81] *OMPI (I)* (n 6 above) para 155.
[82] Ibid paras 154, 159.
[83] *OMPI (II)* (n 6 above) paras 138–39.
[84] *OMPI (III)* (n 6 above) paras 64–5.
[85] *OMPI (I)* (n 6 above) paras 155–6. The CFI referred to the *Chahal* case (n 62 above), as well as to *Öcalan v Turkey*, ECHR, Judgment of 12 March 2003, not yet published, para 106.

It is the task of the court itself, in the course of judicial review, to adopt suitable techniques for striking a balance between security concerns pertaining to the nature and sources of the information and the provision of justice for the affected individual.[86] The *Kadi* and *OMPI* cases did not elaborate in any detail on whether the applicants and/or their lawyers must be provided with (all) the evidence and information alleged to be confidential, or whether such information must be provided only to the court in accordance with a procedure which remains to be defined.[87]

Nonetheless, the *OMPI (II)* and the most recent *Kadi* case before the EGC indicated that the Council is not allowed to base its fund-freezing decisions entirely on confidential materials received from a member state unwilling to authorize the communication of the materials to the Community judicature.[88] Apart from identifying the nature of the offences under investigation and the details concerning the date that the inquiry commenced in a general manner,[89] the French authorities did not convey any information pertaining to the inquiry. The authorities did not convey the identity of the affected individuals apart from noting that the inquiry concerned certain persons who were alleged to be members of OMPI. The CFI concluded that the refusal of the French authorities to communicate evidence adduced against OMPI—even to the court alone—prevented the court from reviewing the lawfulness of the contested decision as required by EU law.[90] The EGC in the *Kadi* decision subsequently confirmed that under such conditions the right to effective judicial protection is infringed.[91]

The line of reasoning that (at a minimum) the court itself must have access to the gist of the evidence was also identifiable in some jurisprudence pertaining to the combating of international terrorism in the United Kingdom. The *Control Orders* decision of the House of Lords of 2007 concerned so-called non-derogating control orders that were imposed under the Prevention of Terrorism Act 2005[92] and which confined the affected individuals to their homes for 18 hours per day. The orders were adopted vis-à-vis such individuals on the basis of a 'reasonable suspicion of their involvement in terrorism'.[93] The House of Lords emphasized that the thrust of the argument that led to the restriction of the civil rights or obligations of a person had to be conveyed to the affected person. Anything less would amount to a

[86] *Kadi (ECJ)* (n 5 above) para 344; *Kadi (EGC)* (n 5 above) para 134; *OMPI (I)* (n 6 above) para 135; Gattini (n 28 above) 222.

[87] *OMPI (I)* (n 6 above) para 158.

[88] *OMPI (III)* (n 6 above) para 73; *Kadi (EGC)* (n 5 above) paras 145, 176.

[89] The offences concerned a series of offences under French law all of which had a principal or subsidiary link with 'a collective undertaking whose aim is to seriously disrupt public order through intimidation or terror' as well as 'laundering the direct or indirect proceeds of fraud offences against particularly vulnerable persons' and 'organized fraud having a link with a terrorist undertaking', *OMPI (III)* (n 6 above) para 58.

[90] Ibid paras 58, 76. France has appealed the CFI's ruling, see Case C-27/09P, appeal lodged 21 January 2009, announced in OJ 2009 C 82/14.

[91] *Kadi (EGC)* (n 5 above) paras 144–5.

[92] Prevention of Terrorism Act 2005 (United Kingdom).

[93] *Secretary of State for the Home Department v MB and Secretary of State for the Home Department v AF* [2007] UKHL 46 (*Control Orders* decision) para 65 (Baroness Hale of Richmond).

violation of the irreducible minimum core of Article 6(1) ECHR.[94] Such would be the case where the affected individuals were effectively confronted by a bare, unsubstantiated assertion, which they could only deny. In the particular case of the *Control Orders* decision, the individuals had the right to challenge the legality of the order before the courts, but neither the individuals nor the special advocates whom the state had appointed on their behalf had access to the evidence that had led to the imposition of the order in the first place.[95] The justifiability of the control orders depended exclusively on closed (inaccessible) materials, which could not be effectively challenged by the persons those orders controlled. Such a situation was unacceptable and had to be distinguished from cases in which the thrust of the case was conveyed to the controlled person by a summary of statements that was made anonymous.[96]

Subsequently, the ECtHR and (in its wake) the House of Lords refined this line of argument in a manner that casts doubt on the acceptability of procedures by which core evidence is revealed only to the court and special advocates, but not to the affected individual himself. The *A* case before the ECtHR concerned the compatibility of long-term detention of foreign nationals due to their suspected involvement in international terrorism with the fair trial guarantees laid down in Articles 5(4) and 6(1) ECHR.[97] The ECtHR confirmed that the special advocate could perform an important role in counterbalancing both the lack of full disclosure, and the absence of a full, open adversarial hearing by gauging the evidence and forwarding arguments on behalf of the detainee during closed hearings. However, the special advocate could not perform this function in any useful way unless the detainee was provided with sufficient information about the allegations against him so as to enable him to give effective instructions to the special advocate. This would be impossible if the open material consisted purely of general assertions, and the court's decision to uphold detention was based solely—or to a decisive degree—on closed material.[98]

In this particular case open evidence was available that large sums of money passed through the applicants' bank accounts, and in some instances the evidence even showed that this money had been raised fraudulently. However, the evidence allegedly linking the money raised to terrorism was not disclosed to the applicants.

[94] Ibid paras 28–30 (Lord Bingham of Cornwall); see also paras 32, 43.

[95] Ibid para 65 (Baroness Hale of Richmond).

[96] Ibid paras 41, 43 (Lord Bingham of Cornwall), 85 (Lord Carswell of Killeen), and 46 (Lord Brown of Eaton-Under-Heywood).

[97] *A and Others v United Kingdom*, ECHR, judgment of 19 February 2009, not yet published (*A* case); ECHR (n 3 above).

[98] Ibid paras 220, 215. On the domestic level the Special Immigration Appeals Commission (SIAC), which functioned like a full court, considered both open and closed material. Neither the applicants nor their legal advisers could see the closed material. Instead, the closed material was disclosed to one or more special advocates, appointed by the Solicitor General to act on behalf of each applicant. During the closed sessions before the SIAC, the special advocate could make submissions on behalf of the applicant, both as regards procedural matters, such as the need for further disclosure, and as to the substance of the case. However, from the point at which the special advocate first had sight of the closed material, he was not permitted to have any further contact with the applicant and his representatives, save with the permission of the SIAC.

Under such circumstances the applicants were not in a position to effectively challenge the allegations against them.[99] Subsequently, in the *AF* case, the House of Lords interpreted the *A* case decision as implying that no matter how cogent the case based on the closed materials may be, the person against whom the control order applies must always be provided with sufficient information about the allegations against him so as to enable him to give effective instructions to a special advocate.[100]

The question of course arises if and to what extent this line of reasoning would apply to individuals affected by binding Security Council resolutions under Chapter VII of the UN Charter and in particular by the Al-Qaida and Taliban Sanctions Regime. Subsequent to the ECJ's *Kadi* judgment a similar line of reasoning initially emerged in a decision of the Court of Appeal for England and Wales in *A, K, M, Q & G v Her Majesty's Treasury*.[101] This case concerned the review of the legality of a domestic measure in the form of the Al-Qaida and Taliban (UN Measures) Order 2006 (AQO)[102]—which was designed to give domestic effect to Resolution 1267 (1999) and follow-up resolutions, as well as the Terrorism (UN Measures) Order 2006 (TO)[103]—which was designed to give domestic effect to Resolution 1373 (2001). These domestic measures were adopted parallel to the relevant EU legislative measures that had been adopted as a consequence of the respective Security Council Sanctions Regimes. Of importance is also the fact that the authority to adopt executive orders of this kind stems from domestic legislation in the form of section 1(1) of the UN Act of 1946 (the UN Act).[104] According to this section, the government can give effect to decisions of the United Nations Security Council by Order in Council (ie executive order), which is 'necessary or expedient for enabling those measures to be effectively applied'.

The Court of Appeal stated that it had the power to exercise judicial review regarding the underlying basis of a particular blacklisting. This competence applied both in relation to blacklistings resulting from the TO and the AQO. It noted that persons listed under the AQO should be placed, as far as possible, in the same position as those listed in accordance with the TO. This implied that in relation to both categories, listed persons had to be placed in a position to discover the case against them and have the opportunity to challenge that case. In some instances the discovery of the facts necessary for engaging in a merits-based review may be more difficult, notably where the United Kingdom was not the designating state that initiated the particular blacklisting before the Al-Qaida and Taliban Sanctions Committee. However, in this particular instance that problem was not present as

[99] *A and Others v United Kingdom*, ECHR, judgment of 19 February 2009, not yet published (*A* case); ECHR (n 3 above) para 223.

[100] *Secretary of State for the Home Department v AF and another and one other action* [2009] UKHL 28 (*AF* case) paras 59 (Lord Philips of Worth Matravers), 81 (Lord Hope of Craighead), and 116 (Lord Brown of Eaton-Under-Heywood).

[101] *A, K, M, Q & G v Her Majesty's Treasury* [2008] EWHC 869 (*A, K, M, Q & G* case).

[102] Al-Qaida and Taliban (United Nations Measures) Order 2006 (United Kingdom) (AQO); SC Res 1267.

[103] Terrorism (United Nations Measures) Order 2006 (United Kingdom) (TO); SC Res 1373 (2001).

[104] United Nations Act 1946 (United Kingdom).

the United Kingdom, the designating state in the case, was in possession of all or most of the facts that had led to the respective blacklistings. The Court of Appeal further noted that it might be necessary to appoint a special advocate who could protect the interest of the individual in instances where the government relied exclusively on closed material. The court may even need to appoint a special advocate in situations where some of the information (the gist) can be conveyed to the affected person. Where the court cannot ensure a fair procedure, the direction for a blacklisting under the TO would have to be discharged. Where a fair procedure cannot be ensured in relation to an AQO blacklisting, directed by the Al-Qaida and Taliban Sanctions Committee itself, the government would be obliged to submit a de-listing request to that committee.[105]

The concrete implications of this ruling for AQO blacklistings were at issue in the subsequent *Hay* case, which was decided before the English High Court in July 2009.[106] The High Court determined that judicial review would only amount to an effective review on the merits if the full factual basis of the blacklisting was accessible. A lack of disclosure effectively amounted to a denial of the right of access to court in a manner not authorized by the UN Act. Nowhere does section 1 of that Act expressly, or by necessary implication, empower the executive to remove the right of access to courts.[107]

The court was willing to assume that in instances where the United Kingdom was the designating state (as was the case in the *A, K, M, Q & G* case) and therefore had access to all the facts, judicial review with a positive outcome for the complainant would also lead to de-listing on the international level and could therefore be regarded as effective. In particular, the court assumed that where the United Kingdom, as designating state in possession of all the facts, initiated a de-listing request to the Al-Qaida and Taliban Sanctions Committee—subsequent to a merits-based review before a domestic court—the Sanctions Committee would honour the de-listing request.[108] However, in instances such as the *Hay* case, where the Foreign and Commonwealth Office acknowledged that it was not privy to the entirety of the materials put before the Al-Qaida and Taliban Sanctions Committee by the designating state, effective judicial review was inherently impossible. As the full facts upon which the designation was made were not known to the United Kingdom, the claimant would be unable to discover or confront the case against him, nor would the court be able to exercise a merits-based review. Even if a de-listing request by the United Kingdom were to follow from a review based on the limited information accessible, there was no way of knowing whether the review would result in a de-listing in the absence of knowledge of the factual basis on which the Sanctions Committee relied.[109] The High Court concluded that in such

[105] *A, K, M, Q & G* case (n 101 above) paras 74–5, 113–14, 119–20.

[106] *Hay v Her Majesty's Treasury and Secretary of State for Foreign and Commonwealth Affairs* [2009] EWHC 1677 (*Hay* case).

[107] Ibid para 44.

[108] Ibid para 28.

[109] Ibid paras 27, 30, 31, 33.

a case the AQO effectively precluded the claimant's access to the court in a manner that was ultra vires the UN Act and had to be quashed in relation to the claimant.

This reasoning seems to assume that the Al-Qaida and Taliban Sanctions Committee should defer to a domestic court decision in which all relevant facts pertaining to the blacklisting were reviewed and which concluded that the blacklisting was unjustified. Whether such deference can indeed be expected seems highly unlikely, as the Al-Qaida and Taliban Sanctions Committee is neither legally bound to the decisions of domestic courts of UN member states, nor politically inclined to give deference to such decisions. The *Sayadi & Vinck* case illustrated that any member within the Sanctions Committee can still block a de-listing request by the designating state after a merits-based review before a domestic court which exonerated the individuals, without stating reasons for doing so.

In the subsequent joint appeal dealing with both the *A, K, M, Q & G* and *Hay* cases, the United Kingdom Supreme Court did not address this particular reasoning of the Court of Appeal or High Court at great length. Lord Hope merely stated that neither *G* nor *Hay* had access to a merits-based review under the Al-Qaida and Taliban Sanctions Regime which did not provide for basic procedural fairness. He did not draw any particular distinction between those situations in which the United Kingdom was the designating state and those in which it was not.[110] The Supreme Court also underscored that, as long as the 2007 decision of its predecessor the House of Lords in the case of *Al-Jedda* was valid law,[111] it had to depart from the premise that obligations under Article 25 of the UN Charter were, by virtue of the supremacy clause in Article 103 of the Charter, to prevail over any other international obligations including those stemming from the ECHR.[112] The absence of a merits-based review within the Al-Qaida and Taliban Sanctions Regime would thus not be in violation of international law, given that this situation was the result of binding Security Council resolutions.

[110] See Lord Hope in *Her Majesty's Treasury (Respondent) v Mohammed Jabar Ahmed and others (FC) (Appellants); Her Majesty's Treasury (Respondent) v Mohammed al-Ghabra (FC) (Appellant); R (on the application of Hani El Sayed Sabaei Youssef) (Respondent) v Her Majesty's Treasury (Appellant)* (hereinafter Joint Appeal of *A,K,M,Q and G* and *Hay*) 2010 UKSC 2, 27 January 2010, paras 81–2. See also Lord Roger, ibid, paras 203–4.

[111] *R (on the application of Al-Jedda) v Secretary of State for Defence* [2007] UKHL 58 (*Al-Jedda* decision). See in particular the opinion of Baroness Hale of Richmond, at paras 126 *et seq*. This case was pending before the ECtHR at the time the Supreme Court was dealing with the joint appeals, with oral hearings scheduled for 9 June 2010. The *Al-Jedda* decision concerned the issue whether the detention without trial of a British/Iraqi national by British forces in Iraq in 2004, on the basis of SC Res 1546 of 8 June 2004, violated Art 5(1) ECHR. The House of Lords accepted the argument of the British government that the authorization to use 'all necessary means' against Iraq in SC Res 1546 (2004) served as a legal basis for internment, despite the fact that this ground of detention was not covered by the exhaustive list contained in Art 5(1) ECHR. SC Res 1546 (2004) would therefore constitute a justification for deviating from the ECHR. The ECtHR found this reasoning to be in violation of Art. 5(1) ECHR in its decision of *Al-Jedda v United Kingdom*, ECHR judgment of 7 July 2011, not yet published, paras 101ff. Although the ECtHR seemed to accept that obligations under the United Nations Charter prevailed over conflicting obligations under any other international agreement, it did not accept that in this instance such a conflict indeed existed.

[112] Lord Hope, Joint Appeal of *A,K,M,Q and G and Hay*, para 71. See also Lord Phillips, ibid, para 98.

Noteworthy is the rather formalistic manner in which the Supreme Court discarded the relevance of the *Kadi* decision. It distinguished the *Kadi* decision from the case at hand due to the fact that the EU's institutions were not members of the United Nations. As a result, they were bound by Article 103 of the UN Charter like member states such as the United Kingdom. The Supreme Court seemed to have derived this different legal status of the EU vis-à-vis the United Nations from the ECJ's emphasis on the autonomous nature of the EU legal order (even though the ECJ did not expressly address the issue of the EU's non-membership of the United Nations).[113] By relying on the obligations stemming from Article 103 of the UN Charter for member states, as interpreted by the *Al-Jedda* decision as it stood at the time, the Supreme Court circumvented the consequences of the *Kadi* decision in the domestic legal order. It implicitly accepted that the government could adopt parallel measures alongside directly applicable Regulations which were intended to ensure a uniform application of Resolutions 1267 (1999) and 1390 (2002) within its member states. In addition, it accepted that such uniformity could be sacrificed where the domestic measures deviated from the Regulations in order to give effect to obligations for the United Kingdom under the UN Charter. Whether this approach is acceptable from the perspective of EU law is questionable. One may recall that Advocate General Maduro, in his opinion pertaining to the *Kadi* case, stressed that if the ECJ were to annul a contested regulation on the ground that it infringed EU law concerning the protection of human rights, member states could not adopt the same measures without acting in breach of fundamental rights as protected by the ECJ.[114]

However, despite its deferential attitude towards Security Council resolutions, the Supreme Court quashed the AQO on the basis of the principle of separation of powers within domestic law. The Supreme Court emphasized that a drastic limitation of the right to peaceful enjoyment of property and the right to unimpeded access to a court in the manner foreseen by the Al-Qaida and Taliban Sanctions Regime had to be authorized by Parliament in clear and unambiguous language. As these rights were embraced by the principle of legality in domestic law, which lay at the heart of the relationship between Parliament and the citizen, they could not be overridden by the general wording of section 1(1) of the UN Act. Stated differently, it could not be assumed that Parliament intended to include such drastic measures in the generally formulated powers it delegated to the Executive under this Article.[115]

Given the Supreme Court's emphasis on the supremacy of Parliament and its submission that Article 103 of the UN Charter allowed for deviations from the United Kingdom's international human rights obligations when implementing Security Council resolutions, it seems that Parliament could in principle suspend

[113] Ibid para 71. See also Lord Mance, ibid, para 244.

[114] Opinion of Advocate General Poiares Maduro, Case C-402/05 P, *Yassin Abdullah Kadi v Council of the European Union and Commission of the European Communities*, 16 January 2008, para 30.

[115] Lord Hope, Joint Appeal of *A,K,M,Q and G and Hay* (n 110 above) paras 75, 80, 81. See also Lord Phillips, ibid, paras 111, 154, 157. In reaching this conclusion Lord Phillips drew attention to the reference to human rights in the Preamble and Art 1(3) of the UN Charter. He therefore relied on the text of the Charter itself as a guideline for inferring the presumed intention of Parliament. See also Lord Mance, ibid, para 245.

any and every aspect of a merits-based judicial review in order to give effect to the Al-Qaida and Taliban Sanctions Regime. Such a suspension would however have to be undertaken by means of explicit and unambiguous language. It remains to be seen if and to what extent the *Al-Jedda* decision of the ECtHR would change this approach. The decision does seem to acknowledge that obligations under the United Nations Charter trump obligations stemming from any other international agreement (including the ECHR). However, it also departs from a presumption that the Security Council does not intend to impose obligations on member States that would result in human rights violations—a presumption that could only be overcome with clear, unambiguous language to the contrary.

In essence, therefore, the judicial protection provided by the domestic law of the United Kingdom vis-à-vis individuals affected by Security Council sanctions would potentially be less than what is provided for by EU law. Whereas the jurisprudence of the ECJ and CFI have emphasized that effective judicial review, including a sufficient disclosure of the factual evidence on which a particular blacklisting was based, was indispensable within the European legal order, domestic law in the United Kingdom seems to be less absolute on this point. Legislative measures designed to give effect to Security Council resolutions that suspend the right to a fair trial of certain individuals could be accommodated within domestic law, if and to the extent that they were couched in clear and unambiguous terms that survived parliamentary scrutiny.[116]

2. *Judicial review and the nature of the adverse decision*

EU courts were initially at pains to comment on the non-punitive, precautionary nature of asset freezing, as illustrated by the *El Morabit* decision. However, in its September 2010 *Kadi* decision the EGC did caution that measures which have been in place for more than ten years can hardly be described as temporary and precautionary. After such a period of time it is open to question whether the measures have not since become punitive or even amount to a criminal sanction.[117]

The above-mentioned decisions in the United Kingdom have also not made the existence of a (domestic) right to judicial review dependent on whether an adverse decision such as the freezing of assets would amount to a criminal charge. Rather, what is decisive is the gravity of the consequences of the decision for the affected person. In the *Control Orders* decision, the majority of the House of Lords did not accept that the (cumulative effect of) the control order constituted a criminal charge as there was no assertion of criminal conduct but merely a foundation of suspicion. Additionally, the purpose of the order was preventative rather than punitive or retributive. The House of Lords confirmed that the proceedings fell within the civil

[116] *Al-Jedda* case (n 161 above), paras 101–102, 109. The ECtHR did not find that any of the applicable Security Council resolutions either explicitly or implicitly required the United Kingdom to subject an individual to indefinite detention without charge.

[117] *Kadi EGC* (n 5 above) para 150.

limb of Article 6(1) ECHR.[118] In addition, it relativized the difference (as far as the consequences are concerned) between the criminal and civil limbs of that article by emphasizing the need for procedural protection commensurate with the gravity of the potential consequences—regardless of whether one is dealing with the criminal or civil dimension of Article 6(1).[119] The *A, K, M, Q & G* and *Hay* decisions essentially followed a similar approach even though these decisions turned on domestic law and the applicability of Article 6(1) ECHR was not directly at issue.

Unfortunately, the *Sayadi & Vinck* case before the HRC passed up on the opportunity to follow a similar line of reasoning in relation to Article 14(1) ICCPR.[120] The HRC merely confirmed that although the sanctions involved had serious consequences for the complainants, they were of a preventive rather than punitive nature and could therefore not be characterized as criminal for the purpose of Article 14(1) ICCPR.[121] The HRC did not, however, analogously apply the reasoning of the *Control Orders* decision in relation to Article 6(1) ECHR, despite sufficient similarity in the wording of Article 6(1) ECHR and Article 14(1) ICCPR.[122] As a result, it remains uncertain whether the protection provided under the civil limb of Article 14(1) ICCPR is as comprehensive as that of Article 6(1) ECHR.

3. Techniques of Interpretation

As indicated above, there is very limited case law at present that explicitly distils fair trial criteria applicable to the Al-Qaida and Taliban Sanctions Regime and the Counter Terrorism Sanctions Regime from the ICCPR or ECHR. In the *Abdelrazik* case, the Canadian court *en passant* described the Al-Qaida and Taliban Sanctions Regime as untenable under international human rights standards. However, the court did not elaborate on or explicitly refer to any articles in a particular human rights treaty. It merely indicated that the procedure had to ensure that at the very least, the affected individual received a narrative summary of the reasons leading to the blacklisting, as well as (limited) rights to a hearing that met the

[118] *Control Orders* decision (n 93 above) para 15 (Lord Bingham of Cornwall). The relevant sentence of Art 6(1) ECHR reads as follows: 'In the determination of his civil rights and obligations or of any criminal charge against him, everyone is entitled to a fair and public hearing within a reasonable time by an independent and impartial tribunal established by law.'

[119] Ibid paras 24 (Lord Bingham of Cornwall) and 657 (Baroness Hale of Richmond).

[120] The relevant sentence of Art 14(1) ICCPR reads as follows: 'All persons shall be equal before the courts and tribunals. In the determination of any criminal charge against him, or of his rights and obligations in a suit at law, everyone shall be entitled to a fair and public hearing by a competent, independent and impartial tribunal established by law.'

[121] *Sayadi & Vinck* (n 41 above) para 8.1. However, in *Abousfian Abdelrazik v The Minister of Foreign Affairs and the Attorney General of Canada* [2009] FC 580 (*Abdelrazik* case), para 53, the Canadian Federal Court seemed to have assumed that the sanctions resulting from the Al-Qaida and Taliban Sanctions Regime do constitute a criminal charge. It stated that 'it is a fundamental principle of Canadian and international justice that the *accused* does not have the burden of proving his *innocence*, the accuser has the burden of proving guilt' (emphasis added).

[122] See n 118 above.

requirements of impartiality and independence.[123] The United Kingdom Supreme Court has not yet been willing to draw a similar conclusion. According to the reasoning in the *Al Jedda* case (which it reaffirmed in the joint appeals in the *A, K, M, Q & G* and *Hay* cases), fair trial standards under international law could be suspended by Security Council decisions. Whether the Supreme Court will sustain this position will depend on how extensively it applies the presumption articulated by the ECtHR in *Al-Jedda* that Security Council resolutions were not intended to result in human rights violations by member States.

This decision of the ECtHR is the most recent and most prominent in a series of cases, indicating that courts are reluctant to assume that the Security Council intends to limit human rights disproportionately (let alone suspend them) through sanctions regimes or other restrictive measures. This technique of human rights-friendly interpretation of Security Council resolutions is inspired by both domestic and international human rights standards. In the *Abdelrazik* case,[124] the Canadian Federal Court relied on the right of Canadian citizens to enter their country as guaranteed in Article 6(1) of the Canadian Charter of Rights and Freedoms[125] in order to limit the impact of the travel ban contained in Security Council Resolution 1822 (2008);[126] a follow-up to Resolution 1267 (1999).[127] In this instance the exception to the travel ban in paragraph 1(b) of Resolution 1822 (2008) permitted a state to allow entry into its territory of its own nationals, while prohibiting the transit of blacklisted persons through any territory. The Canadian Federal Court nonetheless concluded that Mr Abdelrazik (a Canadian citizen) would not be violating the travel ban if he returned to Canada by airplane. In reaching this conclusion, the court relied on an interpretation of the term 'territory' that did not include airspace.[128] Moreover, the court also interpreted the resolution in question in a manner that allowed Canada to pay the airfare for Mr Abdelrazik's return to Canada, even though the text of the resolution did not provide for this possibility.[129]

In the joint appeal of the *A, K, M, Q & G* and *Hay* cases, Lord Mance drew attention to the support for human rights expressed in the preamble and Article 1 (3) of the UN Charter, as well as the fact that the Security Council itself requested states to implement resolutions aimed at combating international terrorism in

[123] *Abdelrazik* case (n 121 above) para 51.
[124] *Abdelrazik* case (n 121 above) para 51.
[125] Canadian Charter of Rights and Freedoms RS 1982 c C-00 (Canada).
[126] SC Res 1822, 30 June 2008.
[127] SC Res 1267 (1999).
[128] *Abdelrazik* case (n 121 above) para 127. The Canadian Federal Court also described the respondent's interpretation of the travel ban as leading to a nonsensical result, as it only permits a Canadian citizen to enter the country if he happens to be standing at the Canadian border crossing. That same citizen would, however, not be allowed to reach the border crossing if it means he would have to travel across land or air to do so; see also Tzanakopoulos, 'An Effective Remedy for Josef K: Canadian Judge "Defies" Security Council Sanctions through Interpretation', EJIL:Talk!, available at www.ejiltalk.org/an-effective-remedy-for-josef-k-canadian-judge-defies-security-council-sanctions-through-interpretation (last accessed 1 March 2011). It is also worth noting that within the EU, measures implementing sanctions do cover airspace in their scope of application, but travel bans remain an area of member state competence.
[129] *Abdelrazik* case, Ibid para 127; Tzanakopoulos, ibid.

conformity with international human rights obligations.[130] He consequently raised (but left unanswered) the question whether the Security Council resolutions could have intended to require member states to enact domestic legislation that would violate fundamental principles of human rights under their domestic regimes.[131]

A similar position was maintained in some of the individual opinions in the *Sayadi & Vinck* decision by the HRC. Sir Nigel Rodley in particular outlined four criteria for interpreting the UN Charter.[132] The first overarching criterion is the presumption that the Security Council did not intend actions pursuant to its resolutions to violate international human rights standards. The remaining criteria concretize this presumption: namely, in any event there would be no intention to violate a peremptory norm of international law; there would be no intention to violate non-derogable rights, regardless of whether these rights have peremptory status;[133] and all limitations of human rights have to be in accordance with a strict proportionality principle.[134]

If a domestic or regional court were to apply this technique to a UN sanctions regime such as the Al-Qaida and Taliban Sanctions Regime, that court would depart from the premise that a suspension of individual human rights by a Security Council sanctions regime cannot be assumed unless provided for explicitly.[135] This approach would imply that a sanctions regime such as the one resulting from Resolution 1267 (1999) necessarily (implicitly) allows states the discretion needed to enforce the respective sanctions regime in accordance with international human rights standards—including those guaranteed in Articles 14(1) ICCPR and 6(1) ECHR, even though this may not be self-evident from the resolution at first sight. However, this still leaves the problem that in instances where a domestic court

[130] SC Res 1456, 20 January 2003, para 6; see also SC Res 1822 (2008); see also Lord Mance, Joint Appeal of *A,K,M,Q and G* and *Hay* (n 110 above) para 245.

[131] Joint Appeal of *A,K,M,Q and G* and *Hay* (n 110 above) para 86.

[132] See the individual concurring opinions of Committee member Sir Nigel Rodley and Mr Yuri Iwasaw in *Sayadi & Vinck* (n 41 above).

[133] Note that in *A v Federal Department of Economics*, 22 April 2008 (n 22 above) para 8.3, the Swiss Federal Tribunal explicitly determined that non-derogability is the only element that can be taken into account in determining whether a right is of *a jus cogens* character.

[134] On 3 February 2010, the Court of First Instance in The Hague was reluctant to accept that SC Res 1737, 23 December 2006 required states to refuse access of Iranian nationals to certain specialized areas of education and training in member states. According to the government of the Netherlands, this restrictive measure was required by para 17 of the resolution, which called on 'all States to exercise vigilance and prevent specialized teaching or training of Iranian nationals, within their territories or by their nationals, of disciplines which would contribute to Iran's proliferation sensitive nuclear activities and development of nuclear weapon delivery systems'. The Court concluded that the implementing measure constituted discrimination on the basis of nationality and therefore violated Art 26 ICCPR. Although it accepted that a Security Council resolution would trump the states' human rights obligations in cases of irreconcilable conflict, it was unwilling to accept that such a conflict existed in the present case. The Court determined that para 17 did allow sufficient room to states for reconciling the Security Council obligations with its human rights obligations. The differentiation on the basis of nationality was not appropriate for preventing the transfer of specialized nuclear knowledge to Iran, as it was both over and under-inclusive. An effective measure would require a risk analysis of each and every individual in the relevant Dutch educational institutions. In addition, there were less restrictive measures available such as more thorough screening of individuals. See Case No 334949/HA ZA 09-1192, *A,B,C, Actiegroep Iraanse Studenten v The Netherlands*, Court of First Instance, The Hague, decision of 3 February 2010.

[135] Alvarez, 'The Security Council's War on Terrorism: Problems and Policy Options' in E. de Wet and A. Nollkaemper (eds), *Review of the Security Council by Member States* (2003) 119 at 134.

concludes that the listing is not justified, it cannot order the Al-Qaida and Taliban Sanctions Committee to de-list the particular person or entity. While the court may be able to prevent the effects of the listing (eg the freezing of assets), on the domestic or regional level it would still be up to the Sanctions Committee to decide whether the person or entity should formally be de-listed.

4. The Impact of the Blacklisting Mechanism on Third Parties

Security Council sanctions regimes can also have an impact on the human rights of innocent third parties. The *Möllendorf* decision of the ECJ,[136] as well as the reference by the House of Lords in *R (on the application of M) v Her Majesty's Treasury and two other actions* (*R (on the Application of M)* case)[137] to the ECJ (currently pending),[138] indicate a tendency to interpret Security Council obligations that limit the human rights of third parties in accordance with a strict proportionality test.

In the *Möllendorf* case, a sales contract concerning immovable property was concluded between the Möllendorfs (the sellers) and buyers who were subsequently blacklisted under the Al-Qaida and Taliban Sanctions Regime. At the time of the blacklisting, the buyers were already in possession of the immovable property, and the sellers had already received (and spent) the sales price. However, ownership had not yet been transferred since the transaction was not yet, as required by German law, registered in the Land Register.[139] Since registration was no longer possible once the buyers were blacklisted, the question arose whether the sales transaction had to be reversed. This would have been the normal procedure under German civil law when a legal impediment arose against the transfer of property.[140] The sellers objected to repaying the sales price that would result from such a reversal of the transaction, arguing that it would disproportionately limit their right to property.[141] The ECJ supported this position to the extent that it ordered the national authorities to apply the national law to the sellers in a manner that gave effect to EU fundamental rights protection as far as possible.[142]

It is important to note that the legality of the sanctions regime itself was not at stake in this case. Rather, the case concerned the scope of the EU implementing measures and in particular the impact ('collateral damage') of those measures on third parties. Moreover, the case has since been withdrawn from the relevant domestic court roll, as a result of which it remains unclear what the concrete

[136] Case C-117/06, *Gerda Möllendorf and Christiane Möllendorf-Niehuus* [2007] ECR I-08361 (*Möllendorf* case).
[137] *R (on the application of M) v Her Majesty's Treasury and two other actions* [2008] UKHL 26 (*R (on the Application of M)* case).
[138] Case C-340/08, *The Queen (on the application of M) v Her Majesty's Treasury and two other actions*, pending, announced in OJ 2008 C 260/8.
[139] *Möllendorf* case (n 136 above) para 24.
[140] Ibid para 52.
[141] This money would then have to remain in a frozen account for as long as the buyers remained blacklisted. See ibid para 70.
[142] Ibid paras 76, 81.

implications for proportionality in this case would have been. Even so, the case potentially provides an interesting example of how elements of proportionality and human rights protection can be interpreted in a sanctions regime. Neither Resolution 1267 (1999)[143] and subsequent resolutions, nor the EU implementing measures explicitly provide for such protection in instances where the sanctions regime affected the rights of non-listed third parties. The ECJ was nonetheless prepared to read such protection into the sanctions regime.[144]

In the case of *R (on the application of M)*, an Appellate Committee of the House of Lords was confronted with the interpretation of paragraph (a) of Resolution 1390 (2002)[145]—a follow-up to Resolution 1267 (1999)—and the relevant implementing measures at the EU level. These measures determined that no funds may directly or indirectly be made available 'for the benefit of' a person listed by the Sanctions Committee.[146]

In the United Kingdom, a blacklisted person would need a licence from Her Majesty's Treasury (the competent national authority) to obtain any basic funds in order to provide for basic humanitarian needs. Similarly, the spouses of blacklisted persons or any other persons would need a licence in order to make funds or convertible assets available to a listed person. None of these issues were disputed before the court. Instead, the question arose whether a licence was needed to make social security benefits available to the spouse herself. This would imply that the social security benefits had to be paid into a bank account from which she could only draw up to £10 in cash for each member of her household per week. All other payments would have to be made by debit or credit card. In addition, the spouse would have to send a monthly report containing receipts for goods purchased to the Treasury, as well as a copy of her monthly bank statement.

This question boiled down to whether the phrase 'for the benefit of' should have a wide meaning that covered any application for money from which a blacklisted person derived some form of benefit, or whether the phrase applied only to cases in which funds, financial assets, or economic resources were made available in a manner which enabled blacklisted persons to choose how to use them (such as for the advancement of terrorism).[147] In referring the case to the ECJ, the Appellate Committee favoured the latter, less intrusive interpretation. It followed a teleological approach according to which the resolution in question intended to prevent funds from being diverted for terrorist activities. It was difficult to see how the expenditure of money for domestic expenses such as food, from which a blacklisted person derived a kind of benefit, could create the risk that he or she may divert

[143] SC Res 1267 (1999).

[144] Some might question whether the situation of third parties who are indirectly affected by the sanctions regime would at all be comparable with that of persons forming the direct object of the sanctions regime. However, this author submits that the *Möllendorf* case (n 136 above) remains an interesting example of how a court can read some human rights protection into a sanctions regime.

[145] SC Res 1390 (2002).

[146] SC Res 1390 (2002) para 2(a); Art 2.2 of Council Regulation 881/2002.

[147] *R (on the application of M)* case (n 137 above) para 9.

the funds for terrorism.[148] Moreover, it regarded the wider interpretation as disproportionate and oppressive towards the non-blacklisted spouse, who would effectively be unable to spend any of her own money without accounting to the Treasury for every item of her expenditure. According to the Appellate Committee this would constitute an extraordinary invasion of the privacy of someone who is not blacklisted.[149]

This position was upheld by the ECJ, which attached significant weight to the object and purpose of the contested regulation, in light of the fact that the different language versions of the regulation gave rise to divergent interpretations.[150] The ECJ confirmed that in the case in question there was no danger that the funds paid to the spouses could be diverted to support terrorist activities, nor would the benefits in kind that the designated person may derive indirectly from social payments have this effect. The ECJ also underscored the importance of legal certainty in relation to measures that restricted significantly the rights and freedoms of individuals. Legal certainty required clear and precise language so that all involved, including third parties, may know their rights and duties unambiguously and act accordingly. In this particular instance an interpretation of Regulation 881/2002 that included payments of social security or social assistance to the spouses would result in legal uncertainty in triangular situations in which funds are made available to a person associated with the designated person and the latter indirectly benefited in some way from those funds.[151]

5. Conclusion

From the above analysis one can conclude that courts confronted with targeted sanctions in the form of the Al-Qaida and Taliban Sanctions Regime and the Counter Terrorism Sanctions Regime, are increasingly staking out a role for themselves to ensure that a fair hearing for the affected individuals is guaranteed. This applies in particular to the ECJ and CFI/EGC. After a cautious start during which courts were very deferential towards the Security Council, they have become more assertive and unwilling to accept that issues of national or international security fall outside the scope of their competence to conduct judicial review. However, it is also important to note that in most cases the question was not whether the Security Council had the powers to impose a stringent sanctions regime or whether a sanctions regime as such was legal. Instead, the courts were concerned with a review of the legality or factual basis of a particular blacklisting. In most instances under discussion the respective decision turned on domestic law

[148] Ibid para 12.

[149] *R (on the application of M)* case (n 137 above) para 15. This view of the House of Lords was essentially confirmed by the Opinion of Advocate General Mengozzi in Case C-340/08, *M (FC) and Others v Her Majesty's Treasury*, delivered on 14 January 2010.

[150] ECJ, Preliminary Ruling, Case C-340/08, *M and others v Her Majesty's Treasury*, Judgment of 29 April 2010, paras 49, 56, 62.

[151] Ibid paras 64, 65, 66.

(with EU law being treated by the CFI/EGC and ECJ as a domestic legal order). In several instances these decisions were also informed by the ECHR.

The courts have further demonstrated a reluctance to accept that the maintenance of international peace and security can result in a complete suspension of human rights (including the right to a fair hearing), given that they both constitute purposes of the UN. Instead, there is a tendency to interpret Security Council decisions pertaining to sanctions in a human rights-friendly manner—mostly with reference to domestic human rights obligations. This tendency is also noticeable in situations where the consequences of the blacklisting practices have an invasive impact on the rights of innocent third parties, in which case the courts tend to uphold a strict proportionality principle.

The courts confronted with the question of review of a particular blacklisting acknowledged that the administrative organs responsible for blacklisting have a wide degree of discretion in determining whether a person or entity should be blacklisted in accordance with the categories defined by the respective UN sanctions regime. Moreover, authorities are only required to notify affected individuals of the blacklisting and initial freezing of assets after such acts are effected in order to ensure the necessary surprise effect thereof. However, the ECJ and CFI/EGC in particular have insisted that individuals must be informed about the thrust of the factual basis of the case against them as soon as possible thereafter. They must be provided with an opportunity to refute the claims against them, and this must include a judicial review before (the equivalent of) a court of law.

In the relevant cases decided by the CFI/EGC and ECJ, the administrative organs were initially highly uncooperative, refusing to provide any information of significance to either the affected individual or the court reviewing the case. As a result, the courts had no choice but to determine that the exercise of judicial review was impossible, and that the right to a remedy had been violated. From this jurisprudence it is clear that the courts of the European Communities must be placed in a position to determine whether the administrative body has carefully applied its mind to all the relevant facts, whether the facts actually support the conclusions drawn by the administrative body, and whether the administrative authorities have given sufficient consideration to any exculpatory evidence. The courts have also underscored the importance of expediting action on the part of the administrative organs. In those instances where the courts have discharged a decision to list a person or entity, the administrative organ has to act immediately to give effect to the ruling, or to provide credible evidence regarding why this cannot be done.

It remains to be seen how the CFI/EGC and ECJ (and in their wake domestic courts throughout Europe) will react to situations where the administrative organs are more cooperative and willing to provide information about the thrust of the case to the court, the affected individuals, or both. Depending on the circumstances of the case, jurisprudence of the ECJ and CFI/EGC indicates that they may be willing to accept that certain evidence should be revealed only to the court; or that only part of the evidence be revealed to the court and the affected individual. For the time being it remains unclear what exactly this would imply and whether, for example, these courts would accept the appointment of special advocates or other procedures designed to defend the interests of the individual.

The extent to which the ECJ and CFI/EGC (as well as domestic courts) will be able to exercise effective judicial review will not only depend on better cooperation with administrative organs within the EU itself, but also on the willingness of the Al-Qaida and Taliban Sanctions Committee (and similar sanctions regimes) to provide these courts with the factual basis on which a particular blacklisting is based. In addition, the Sanctions Committee would have to be willing to give deference to regional (or domestic) court decisions that support a de-listing of the person affected. For the time being, the jury is still out on whether the attempts of the ECJ and domestic courts will encounter (extensive) cooperation at the level of the Sanctions Committees.

Elsewhere, this author has argued that the position taken by domestic and regional courts may over time result in a 'bottom-up spill-over effect' on UN sub-organs. Sanctions regimes such as the Al-Qaida and Taliban Sanctions Regime would be forced to give better recognition to human rights standards as a matter of practical reality, as anything else may lead to the non-observance of their decisions.[152] For example, in the future these regimes might become willing to introduce judicial protection in accordance with international human rights standards at the UN level. If this were to occur, it is likely that domestic and regional courts will refrain from exercising extensive judicial review if and to the extent that the centralized procedure provides for judicial protection equivalent to the standards developed by those domestic and regional courts. This was also alluded to in the most recent *Kadi* decision before the EGC. This court noted that it will engage in judicial review as long as the de-listing procedure of the Al-Qaida Sanctions Committee clearly fails to guarantee effective judicial protection, as is currently the case.[153]

However, for the time being, individuals affected by the Al-Qaida and Taliban Sanctions Regime, or similar sanctions regimes, have to rely on domestic or regional courts for judicial protection which, as indicated, tend to provide such protection on the basis of domestic or EU law. In addition, such protection can at most prevent the (full) implementation of the sanctions regime within a certain jurisdiction. The formal de-listing can only be undertaken by the respective sanctions committee.

At this point it should also be emphasized that it is still unclear if and to what extent domestic courts will give full effect to the line of reasoning developed by the ECJ and CFI/EGC in the *Kadi* case. The decision of the United Kingdom Supreme Court in the *A, K, M, Q & G* and *Hay* cases illustrate that domestic courts may find creative (albeit formalistic) ways to circumvent the implications of decisions of the ECJ and CFI/EGC in the domestic legal order. In this particular instance the circumvention may result in less legal protection vis-à-vis Security Council resolutions within the domestic legal order than what is required under EU law.

[152] De Wet, 'The Role of European Courts in the Development of a Hierarchy of Norms within International Law: Evidence of Constitutionalisation?' (2009) 5 *European Constitutional Law Review* 284, 284 *et seq.*

[153] *Kadi (ECG)* (n 5 above) paras 127–8.

However, it is also theoretically possible that other domestic courts within the EU may deviate from ECJ and CFI/EGC jurisprudence in a manner that provides a higher level of domestic judicial protection, based on domestic constitutional considerations.

The unwillingness of domestic and regional courts to engage with international law when providing judicial protection to individuals and entities faced with targeted sanctions further implies that courts are unwilling to consider whether the UN and its organs are bound by international human rights standards. In addition, they avoid the question whether states that do not implement Security Council resolutions that infringe international human rights standards are actually in violation of a Security Council resolution.[154] A more active engagement by domestic and regional courts with these questions could contribute significantly to the international debate. Although the interpretations of international law made by these courts are not binding on the UN, they do carry significant judicial authority and also shape the debate at the international level. The reluctance of domestic and regional courts to engage in this debate may inter alia relate to their understandable desire to avoid an open conflict with the Security Council. However, the approach carries with it the risk of devaluing and marginalizing international law. In addition, it fuels the perception that an irreconcilable normative conflict exists between the UN legal regime and domestic or regional regimes that value the protection of human rights—a conflict which could only be resolved by protecting either one of the regimes at the expense of the other.[155]

[154] De Wet, 'Holding the United Nations Security Council accountable through human rights violations through domestic and regional courts: a case of "be careful what you wish for"?', in J Farrall and K Rubenstein (eds), *Sanctions, Accountability and Governance in a Globalized World* (2009) 143 *et seq*; see also De Búrca (EJIL) (n 29 above) 857.

[155] For a recent debate concerning the implications of decisions such as *Kadi (ECJ)* (n 5 above), for the relationship between different legal orders, see De Sena and Vitucci (n 20 above) 206 *et seq*; see also De Búrca (EJIL) (n 29 above) 857 *et seq*; Nollkaemper (n 25 above) 864 *et seq*; and Canor, 'The European Courts and the Security Council: Between Dédoublement Fonctionnel and Balancing of Values: Three Replies to Pasquale De Sena and Maria Chiara Vitucci' (2009) 20 EJIL 870, 870 *et seq*.

7

Reviewing Security Council Measures in the Light of International Human Rights Principles

Salvatore Zappalà

1. Lexicon and Context

At the outset, a few words of caution are necessary to clarify the scope of the topic dealt with in this article, which is entitled 'Reviewing Security Council measures in the light of international human rights principles'. What is meant by Security Council *measures* can be determined with relative ease, restricting the meaning to those measures adopted by the Council under Chapter VII of the UN Charter.[1] On the other hand, the broad notions of '*reviewing*' and of '*international human rights principles*' may indeed be the source of some misunderstandings. Therefore, it is worth clarifying that, for the purpose of this contribution, the notion of 'reviewing' will be considered in its broadest meaning as ranging from judicial review to other forms of quasi-judicial assessment of the consistency between Security Council (hereafter 'SC' or 'Council') action and human rights, as well as more broadly any form of control and evaluation of SC activities, even from a merely academic standpoint. At the same time, the concept of 'international human rights principles' will be used by essentially referring to the fundamental components of human rights law rather than specific rights, and will be assigned both a normative and a *lato sensu* 'political' dimension. Against this background, the present article will not discuss whether or not the Council has violated specific human rights, nor what kind of reactions the affected individuals might resort to (including the institution of judicial proceedings before national or regional courts). Many other contributions in recent years, including in this very volume, have

[1] The term 'measures' is explicitly used in Art 39 of the UN Charter and the notion of Security Council measures clearly has strong ties with Chapter VII of the Charter; in general see B Simma et al (eds), *The Charter of the United Nations. A Commentary*, 2 vols (2002); B Conforti, *Le Nazioni Unite* (2006) (and the English translation *id*: *The Law of the United Nations* (2005, 3rd edn)). On the specific point of UN Sanctions and Chapter VII see V Gowlland-Debbas (ed) *United Nations Sanctions and International Law* (2001); and also E de Wet, *The Chapter VII powers of the United Nations Security Council* (2004).

tackled the issue in much more depth.[2] What really matters from our perspective is whether in general terms SC measures have contributed to enhancing human rights principles or whether they have been detrimental.

It is well known that in the last two decades (1990–2010) the SC has experienced a significant increase in its activities. And, as part of these activities, human rights crises have become increasingly relevant. The Council has been confronted with several situations where massive human rights violations occurred and its reactions may have often determined improvement of the situation.

In contexts such as the Iraq–Kuwait conflict, the situations in Somalia and Haiti, in Angola and Sierra Leone, the civil wars in the former Yugoslavia and the genocide in Rwanda, the operations and establishment of UN administrations in Kosovo and East Timor, the situation in DRC, the commission of inquiry to investigate crimes in Darfur (and to a certain extent the referral of that situation to the ICC[3]), the referral of the crimes in Libya to the ICC, and in several other situations, the Council has shown a great deal of activism and creativity in its interventions, and arguably increased attention to human rights principles. Nonetheless, the results are not entirely persuasive, including from a human rights perspective.

In all these interventions the Council took action which in one way or another affected human rights principles and broadly speaking may be considered as having brought about some improvement in human rights protection.[4] Human rights violations were, at least in part, one of the concerns that the Council hinted at or mentioned explicitly when adopting measures under Chapter VII. In addition, the relationship between the notion of a threat to peace and security and human rights violations became more stable. At the same time, however, in more or less the same years (and sometimes focusing on the same situations), the Council has also progressively resorted to sanctions specifically directed against named individuals.

These measures, which have been called 'targeted' or 'smart' sanctions, were originally seen as a positive development.[5] Contrary to what had happened in the past, these measures would no longer indiscriminately affect the whole civilian

[2] See Bothe, 'Security Council's Targeted Sanctions against Presumed Terrorists. The Need to Comply with Human Rights Standards' (2008) *Journal of International Criminal Justice* 541–55; Lavranos, 'Judicial Review of UN Sanctions by the European Court of Justice' (2009) 78 *Nordic Journal of International Law* 343–59; Tzanakopoulos, 'United Nations Sanctions in Domestic Courts: from Interpretation to Defiance in Abdelrazik v. Canada' (2010) 8 *Journal of International Criminal Justice* 249–67. For a different approach, supporting UN SC measures in this area, with specific reference to the ECJ judgments see Stenhammar (2010) 79 *Nordic Journal of International Law* 113–40.

[3] The Council, however, has been by far less coherent in ensuring appropriate follow-up by supporting the ICC in its endeavour. No follow-up has been given to the ongoing non-compliance by Sudan with the orders of the ICC (in particular the arrest warrants which have been issued by the Court).

[4] Aznar-Gómez, 'A Decade of Human Rights Protection by the Security Council: A Sketch of Deregulation?' (2002) 13 *European Journal of International Law* 223–41; see also the contributions by Ciampi, De Wet, and Fassbender in this volume.

[5] See, eg, Hufbauer and Oegg 'Targeted Sanctions: a Policy Alternative?' (2000) 32 *Law and policy in international business* 11–20.

population, but rather focus on individuals bearing the greatest responsibilities within the power structure of the state (or of rebel groups). Hence, in terms of human rights principles these measures were supposed to be judged positively and attract support (which is what happened, at least in part, at the outset).[6] Nonetheless, in the long run—particularly in the framework of the fight against terrorism[7]—these measures assumed proportions which were too vast and created a mechanism that constituted a source of concern for human rights principles.[8] Furthermore, there has been a shift in perspective, since these measures target individuals qua individuals without any link to a governmental structure or rebel group.

It is undeniable that towards the end of the 1990s the debate focused on how to make these measures more effective by trying to spare suffering to the civilian populations in the affected states.[9] Today, mainly on the basis of the practice of the 1267 (1999) al-Qaida and the Taliban anti-terrorism Sanction Committee of the past ten years, the discussion is more concerned with the inevitable human rights violations which arise from these measures.[10] Arguably these violations do not necessarily depend on the measures per se, but are rather due to the procedure leading to their adoption and to the heavy use that has been made of a tool which was already per se borderline, and of an exceptional nature. It must be admitted that the nature of the measures and the fact that they are adopted by a political organ represent a major weakness. Moreover, when the exception becomes the rule, the criteria for its assessment cannot but change, and measures which may have been tolerable sporadically in the interests of international peace and security, can no longer be acceptable when they become systematic.[11]

In this contribution an attempt is made to provide an overview of the interplay between Security Council measures and human rights principles by recognizing the often positive effects that SC measures and increased activism may have on the strengthening of human rights on a global scale, without, however, turning a blind

[6] It is generally accepted that these measures began with travel restrictions and financial sanctions against UNITA leaders and their family members through SC Res 1127 (1997), 1173 (1998), and 1176 (1998). They then continued with measures against individuals in the context of the Sierra Leone civil war, and subsequently with the regime against al-Qaida and the Taliban on the basis of SC Res 1267 (1999). For a broader picture with specific reference to anti-terrorism measures, see Bianchi, 'Assessing the Effectiveness of the UN Security Council's Anti-terrorism Measures: The Quest for Legitimacy and Cohesion' (2006) 17 EJIL 881–919, and the abundant literature cited therein.

[7] Fassbender, 'The UN Security Council and International Terrorism', in A Bianchi (ed) *Enforcing international law norms against terrorism* (2004) 83–102.

[8] See Cameron, 'UN Targeted Sanctions, Legal Safeguards and the European Convention on Human Rights' (2003) 72 *Nordic Journal of International Law* 159 at 165–8.

[9] See the numerous and excellent contributions which appeared in (2002) 13 *European Journal of International Law* 1–321.

[10] See also Fassbender, 'Targeted Sanctions Imposed by the UN Security Council and Due Process Rights: A Study Commissioned by the UN Office of Legal Affairs and Follow-up Action by the United Naions' (2006) 3 International Organizations Law Review 437.

[11] However, in all fairness, one must recognize that there had already been pleas in favour of the establishment of review mechanisms over Security Council decisions even prior to their becoming so frequent as they did in the last 10 years, cf Dugard, 'Judicial Review of Sanctions', in Gowlland-Debbas (n 1 above) 83–91.

eye to the potentially disruptive consequences that human rights violations somehow attributable to the Council may have both on human rights principles as well as on the effectiveness and credibility of SC decisions.[12]

First, I will address the broader issue of review mechanisms of Security Council measures. Subsequently, attention will be paid to assessing the current role of the SC, starting with the recognition that for at least 20 years it has been operating with a great deal of 'creativity' and outside the legal framework of the Charter, as originally conceived, and thus in a radically new and unknown setting, often with unpredictable consequences. In addition, it will be argued that human rights law and the enforcement of human rights principles are strictly linked to the idea of a balancing exercise of competing interests.[13] An examination of the differences between political and judicial balancing of competing interests will be carried out, and the suggestion that the SC can hardly carry out such appropriate balancing with regard to specific natural or legal persons, especially when individual human rights are concerned, will be put forward. Finally, the conclusion will be drawn that the Council, should it wish to continue resorting so massively to targeted sanctions in the fight against terrorism (which would not seem such a wise option), will have either to agree to adopt further procedural and/or institutional improvements (which is more likely) or eventually accept the idea, which would also be useful with regard to other settings (such as the ad hoc Tribunals or the UN Territorial Administrations), of establishing appropriate human rights monitoring within the system (which, at this stage, is to a large extent unrealistic).

2. Possible Avenues for Reviewing Security Council Measures

A broader issue that goes far beyond the specificity of the interplay between Security Council action and human rights principles is the problem of whether or not, in the first place, SC measures are amenable to review by external bodies.

This is a somewhat classic issue which recurrently comes under scrutiny and creates controversy.[14] Depending on the general feelings surrounding SC action, views on whether or not to submit Council measures to review tend to change. At the moment, the feeling that the action of the Security Council in the field of anti-terrorism measures has impinged on human rights has created a new 'trend' of theories on the possible mechanisms for reviewing SC measures. A few observations are thus apposite.

First of all, it is worth specifying that the Charter as such does not contain specific review mechanisms for SC measures (nor does it exclude them explicitly).

[12] For a thorough study on human rights and UN sanctions cf, eg, A Ciampi, *Sanzioni del Consiglio di Sicurezza e Diritti Umani* (2007).

[13] With specific reference to the cases involving the interplay between Security Council measures in the context of the fight against terrorism and human rights see De Sena and Vitucci, 'The European Courts and the Security Council: Between *Dédoublement Fonctionnel* and Balancing of Values' (2009) 20 EJIL 193–228.

[14] M Bedjaoui, *Nouvel ordre mondial et contrôle de la légalité des actes du Conseil de sécurité* (1994).

There are no provisions in the Charter which indicate the existence of a system for reviewing SC measures. The discussion then turns on whether or not, in the absence of such a system for review, there might be interpretative theories which could lead to some sort of review of SC measures.

In order to address the question it is necessary to discuss whether or not the primacy given to the decisions of the SC under the Charter through the interpretative construction of Articles 25 and 103 also entails that no review at all of SC measures is possible. Certainly, there is a powerful argument to affirm that SC action is broadly covered by the principle of non-interference of judicial organs with political determinations: one could apply to the SC the doctrine of the 'Act of State' largely resorted to in national jurisdictions.[15] This option essentially entails that political actions by governments are not amenable to judicial review to avoid undue interference of one branch of the public powers (eg the judicial v the executive or parliament) over the other. Adapting this theory to international law is not so easy, given its structure and the absence of the notion of separation of powers, but the underlying assumption may find some justification in the UN Charter system. However, one must also note that these doctrines of judicial unaccountability of political organs receive less and less support at the national level. In particular, when human rights are at issue they have become barely acceptable. Moreover, one cannot but take into account the fact that at the international level state sovereignty is still central and it enjoys protection from the action of international organizations. Although the Council possesses broad powers, these must be exercised in keeping with the Charter (Article 24) and, given that all international organizations must operate on the basis of the principle of attribution, it should be possible, at least in theory, to verify whether or not the organization respects the scope of competences and powers attributed by member states. Hence, the conclusion could be drawn that it is not only possible, but to a certain extent, necessary to establish a principle whereby SC measures are amenable to review.

The second aspect of the problem, however, is the determination of the type of review and the identification of the competent organs to carry out such a review. In this respect, it is often argued that review of SC measures is indeed possible and that states can exercise it at a decentralized level in various contexts:[16] when they implement the measures with the scrutiny of their governments or parliaments, or more simply through proceedings before their national courts. Although the argument has some appeal, national review does not seem to be so desirable since it may end up weakening the system, for it allows individual states to unilaterally

[15] See, eg, the famous Sabbatino case, *Banco National de Cuba v Sabbatino,* 376 US 398 (1964), or even more specifically focusing on this argument and more recently in Italy the *Markovic* case (Italian Supreme Court order of 8 February 2002), in which the Italian Court of Cassation held that 'con riferimento ad alcuni tipi di atti (che costituiscono manifestazioni di una funzione politica) nessun giudice ha il potere di controllare il modo in cui la funzione è esercitata', which entails that with regard to certain classes of actions (that are a manifestation of political power) no judge disposes of the power to verify the way in which power has been exercised.

[16] E de Wet, A Nollkaemper and P Dijkstra (eds), *Review of the Security Council by Member States* (2003).

double-check SC determinations. One thing is the political dissent, which can certainly be voiced and recorded within the Organization; another thing is to allow each and every member state unilaterally to review SC measures (see section 6 below) and potentially refuse implementation in contrast to Article 25 of the Charter. Certainly, it would be preferable to organize mechanisms for an international centralized review process. To date, however, no such institutionalized mechanism exists. Nonetheless, there are some indications by international judicial bodies that suggest that some form of review is indeed possible.

For example, as is well known, in 1995 the Appeals Chamber of the ICTY had to decide on a motion by the defendant arguing that the Tribunal was unlawfully established.[17] The Chamber refrained from dismissing the motion for lack of jurisdiction—as the Trial Chamber had done in the impugned first instance decision—but it took up the issue and made its decision on the basis of the principle known as Kompetenz-Kompetenz (or 'compétence de la compétence'), ie a judicial organ always has the inherent power to determine whether or not its jurisdiction is well founded.[18]

[17] ICTY Appeals Chamber Decision on Jurisdiction, Case No IT-94-1 AR 72, 2 October 1995.

[18] At the time it had been argued by the Prosecutor, and upheld by the Trial Chamber that: '[T]his International Tribunal is not a constitutional court set up to scrutinize the actions of organs of the United Nations. It is, on the contrary, a criminal tribunal with clearly defined powers, involving a quite specific and limited criminal jurisdiction. If it is to confine its adjudications to those specific limits, it will have no authority to investigate the legality of its creation by the Security Council.' (Decision at Trial, at para 5; see also paras 7, 8, 9, 17, 24, passim). 'There is no question, of course, of the International Tribunal acting as a constitutional tribunal, reviewing the acts of the other organs of the United Nations, particularly those of the Security Council, its own "creator." It was not established for that purpose, as is clear from the definition of the ambit of its "primary" or "substantive" jurisdiction in Articles 1 to 5 of its Statute. But this is beside the point. The question before the Appeals Chamber is whether the International Tribunal, in exercising this "incidental" jurisdiction, can examine the legality of its establishment by the Security Council, solely for the purpose of ascertaining its own "primary" jurisdiction over the case before it.' The Trial Chamber has sought support for its position in some dicta of the International Court of Justice or its individual Judges (see Decision at Trial, at paras 10–13), to the effect that: 'Undoubtedly, the Court does not possess powers of judicial review or appeal in respect of decisions taken by the United Nations organs concerned.' (*Legal Consequences for States of the Continued Presence of South Africa in Namibia (South-West Africa) Notwithstanding Security Council Resolution 276 (1970)*, ICJ Reports (1971) 16 at para 89 (Advisory Opinion of 21 June, hereafter the *Namibia Advisory Opinion*).) All these dicta, however, address the hypothesis of the Court exercising such judicial review as a matter of 'primary' jurisdiction. They do not address at all the hypothesis of examination of the legality of the decisions of other organs as a matter of 'incidental' jurisdiction, in order to ascertain and be able to exercise its 'primary' jurisdiction over the matter before it. Indeed, in the *Namibia Advisory Opinion*, immediately after the dictum reproduced above and quoted by the Trial Chamber (concerning its 'primary' jurisdiction), the ICJ proceeded to exercise the very same 'incidental' jurisdiction discussed here: '[T]he question of the validity or conformity with the Charter of General Assembly resolution 2145 (XXI) or of related Security Council resolutions does not form the subject of the request for advisory opinion. However, in the exercise of its judicial function and since objections have been advanced the Court, in the course of its reasoning, will consider these objections before determining any legal consequences arising from those resolutions' (ibid at para 89). The same modality of examination was undertaken by the ICJ, inter alia, in its Advisory Opinion on the *Effect of Awards* Case: '[T]he legal power of the General Assembly to establish a tribunal competent to render judgements binding on the United Nations has been challenged. Accordingly, it is necessary to consider whether the General Assembly has been given this power by the Charter' (*Effect of Awards* at 56). 'Obviously, the wider the discretion of the Security Council under the Charter of the United Nations, the narrower the scope for the International Tribunal to review its actions, even as a matter of

It must, however, be clarified that such a review was *incidental* and has often been criticized as unrealistic. Could the Tribunal have pronounced a death sentence for its own existence?

For our ends it is not necessary to engage in such a discussion. What is important is that the ICTY precedent (echoed by the ICTR in *Kayishema and Ruzindana*) proves that there has been an authoritative statement that there is a possibility of reviewing SC measures, at least as far as the inherent powers of an International Tribunal, required to determine whether or not it has jurisdiction, are concerned. More broadly, one can derive from this precedent an incidental power of international judicial bodies to review the legality of SC measures. However, this power, at least *de lege lata*, should be considered as being restrained by the following factors: (i) it can only be exercised by *international judicial bodies*; (ii) it can only have an *incidental nature*; and (iii) it can only be exercised to the *limited extent* that it is indispensable for making a decision on the specific proceedings pending before the judicial organ concerned.[19] Moreover, its effects are to be considered as limited to the said proceedings. This form of review could, of course, also take place in the framework of contentious or advisory proceedings before the ICJ, provided of course that these are not intended as substitutes for the exercise of a form of primary jurisdiction over the legality of SC measures, which does not exist in positive international law. Naturally, if the principal judicial organ of the United Nations in the course of contentious or advisory proceedings needs to review some SC measures, there is nothing in the Charter or in other provisions of international law that prevents it from doing so.

This situation is not entirely satisfactory in terms of respect for the rule of law and for the principle that there must exist appropriate scrutiny over decisions of any authority. However, there seems to be little doubt that in terms of judicial review, this is the current standing. Nor would it be necessarily appropriate to try to expand by interpretation the system of judicial review of SC measures. Nonetheless, as mentioned earlier, there are various forms of review which do not necessarily involve immediate effects on the measures examined, but do create a movement of opinion that cannot easily be ignored by the Council.

To a certain extent, this is a broader form of social review of SC measures which is highly possible and which has been exercised, in particular with regard to anti-terrorism measures. This review may assume different forms and is carried out by a variety of entities: first of all by states in the implementation of the measures, but also by way of declarations and policies through which they can make their opinion on SC measures broadly known. In addition, the review can be indirectly exercised

incidental jurisdiction. Nevertheless, this does not mean that such power disappears altogether, particularly in cases where there might be a manifest contradiction with the Principles and Purposes of the Charter . . . In conclusion, the Appeals Chamber finds that the International Tribunal has jurisdiction to examine the plea against its jurisdiction based on the invalidity of its establishment by the Security Council' (paras 20–2 of the 2 October decision).

[19] The case law of other courts, such as the European Court of Justice and the European Court of First Instance with regard to the anti-terrorism measures, seems to confirm this trend of caution in directly tackling the decisions of the Security Council.

by national judicial bodies and regional courts. These courts—even though they do not pronounce on SC measures per se as they generally lack jurisdiction—may, by reviewing the acts implementing at the domestic or regional level the decisions of the Security Council, end up expressing a view on SC measures. These views could (and indeed have) subsequently become relevant in the debate. Finally, there is a much broader review by monitoring agencies, NGOs, academics and other interested actors, which also contribute to a reflection on SC measures and can lead to change.

All these mechanisms just mentioned have had an influence, at least to a certain extent, on the debate over SC measures in the fight against terrorism, which have been considered as posing problems in terms of consistency with human rights principles and which brought about some change. In order to verify whether or not such a perspective is justified, it seems necessary to take a closer look at the developments in SC measures which have signalled an increased (and unprecedented) activism on the part of the Security Council and a social reaction in the international community.

3. The Security Council Acting as a Sovereign Power: The Inevitable Risks of a Global Leviathan Operating in Uncharted Waters

Undoubtedly, one of the distinctive traits of the measures adopted by the SC in the past 20 years is the broad reference to Chapter VII of the Charter and the tendency to operate in a creative manner. In addition, in many instances, the SC adopted decisions which involved innovative interactions between the Council and individuals.

In theory one could still argue that the relationship between the Council and legal or natural persons is always eventually mediated by states. However, in reality, one must admit that the recent trends increasingly see the Council addressing individuals directly (albeit through subsidiary bodies). This takes place with appropriate (in terms of human rights) filters in some cases (ad hoc Tribunals or UN Territorial Administrations), with little or no filter at all in other cases (the Sanctions Committees). In particular, the latter system, where no filter really exists between the Council and the individuals affected by its measures, is particularly troublesome. Nothing in the system provided for by the UN Charter could have foreseen that the Council would specifically name individuals in its measures, nor that it would establish a whole system whereby natural and legal persons would be individually targeted by the Council itself.[20]

[20] For a broader discussion of the revitalized Security Council practice in resorting to Chapter VII, see Gaja, 'Reflexions sur le rôle du Conseil de sécurité dans le nouvel ordre mondial' (1993) 97 *Revue générale de droit international public* 297–320; Kirgis, 'The Security Council's First Fifty Years' (1995) 89 AJIL 506–39.

In certain circumstances these developments lead the Council to act, in many or some respects, as a sovereign power.[21] Hence, like any potentially worldwide government, the Security Council may also pose a threat to human rights, as all governments do. There are several explanations of why this has occurred and certainly those who have forcefully argued against the SC transforming its role into a world governance authority are proved to be right in many respects.[22] This is not the main object of this article; however, it is clear that whenever the Council attempts to transform itself into a 'global government', human rights violations are most likely to occur, particularly because the system was never conceived to operate in this way, and thus does not contain appropriate safeguards.

Admittedly, had the Council limited its activities to those provided for in the UN Charter, the risks of jeopardizing human rights principles through its measures could have been mitigated; their protection too however. In this respect, it is true that had the Council remained within the boundaries of its competences under the Charter, or at least under an orthodox reading of the Charter, it would not have contributed to the protection and development of human rights principles, particularly in the field of international criminal law.[23]

From a legal perspective, the current situation can be considered as resting on dubious legal foundations, although at the same time it must be recognized that SC action has received widespread support in the international community and by member states. Some of the problems are linked to the fact that the Council is operating beyond the letter of the Charter and since it moved into somewhat uncharted waters, the existing checks and balances provided by the system (which are already minimal and essentially political) are not really suitable. In particular, when it comes to dealing with the rights of individuals, which the Council should not be dealing with in the first place, there are no appropriate mechanisms for the Council to take into account human rights in situations concerning specific individuals. This is simply because there was nothing in the Charter that could have led to expect that the Council would directly seek to impose limitations on the rights of specific individuals listing them by name, which is what is done through the Sanction Committees.

The argument that the SC is not directly affecting individual rights may be true for the ICTY and ICTR, or the UN Territorial Administrations in Kosovo or East Timor (UNMIK and UNTAET), for these are independent and impartial bodies and when they adopt any decision which may affect individual rights they do so after allowing individuals to participate somewhat in the decision-making process at the administrative level or in the framework of judicial proceedings. On the other hand, when it comes to the Sanction Committees, individuals—although they are

[21] For a general study on the exercise of sovereign powers by international organizations, see D Sarooshi, *International Organizations and Their Exercise of Sovereign Powers* (2005).

[22] Arangio-Ruiz, 'On Security Council Law-Making' (2000) 83 *Rivista di diritto internazionale* 609–725.

[23] For a general appraisal of the contribution of the human rights work of the Security Council, see the contribution of D Shraga to the present volume.

the target of the measure—are not involved in any way. Moreover, states do not possess sufficient margins of discretion in implementing the measures. The practice whereby the Council decides that the assets of given individuals must be frozen and obliges states to do so, originates in a situation which automatically creates risks for human rights. One of the basic implied tenets of any human rights system (a human rights principle we could say) is a functioning mechanism of checks and balances. The move of the SC outside the boundaries of the Charter system created inevitable tensions and an ideal context for human rights violations. A context in which all powers are mixed together, without appropriate mechanisms for ensuring respect for individual rights, is largely unacceptable from the standpoint of human rights principles, irrespective of any specific violation.

Furthermore, while through some measures—such as the establishment of ad hoc Tribunals or of the UN Territorial Administrations—the SC created systems of interactions with the individuals involved that ensure that the relationships are handled by independent and autonomous bodies to which certain human rights obligations have been imposed, in the case of the 'targeted sanctions' systems, individuals are directly affected by SC decisions. In the latter case there is no real filter between the Council's decision and the rights of the individual. True, the Sanction Committees are subsidiary organs of the Council, but they are not composed of independent and impartial members, in that they reflect the composition of the Council itself. Furthermore, while it is true that the measures are formally addressed to states, this is done for the mere purpose of implementation. States, however, are not at all the final target of the sanctions and the measures are not taken to force states to follow a certain course of action (or only as 'intermediaries'). There is no obligation of result, there is rather an obligation of conduct, an obligation merely to enact the measures disposed by the Council, the ultimate goal of which is not so much to determine the action of a state but rather of individuals. Within this framework, states end up being the mere executioners of SC measures adopted under a very broad interpretation of the powers of the Council according to the Charter, which aim at specific individuals as the final targets of the measure.

Of course, one may argue that the Council could expand the boundaries of its powers, but it must be recognized that this would only be possible, apart from the adoption of a formal amendment to the Charter, on the condition that most (all?) UN member states acquiesce to its measures. Acquiescence not only occurs through acts of governments, but also needs the acceptance of domestic (or regional) courts. In other words, it is perfectly conceivable that, although governments may seem to acquiesce to innovative SC measures, states may—through judicial decisions—challenge the legality of SC measures (albeit indirectly)[24] and thus acquiescence cannot be recorded. This somewhat reflects what has recently happened with targeted sanctions against terrorism.

[24] Tzanakopoulos, 'United Nations Sanctions in Domestic Courts: from Interpretation to Defiance in Abdelrazik v. Canada' (2010) 8 *Journal of International Criminal Justice* 249–67; and van den Herik, 'The Security Council's Targeted Sanctions Regimes: In Need of Better Protection of the Individual' (2007) 20 *Leiden Journal of International Law* (2007) 797–807.

Moreover, in terms of human rights principles most of the measures mentioned above, even those whereby the Council created ad hoc Tribunals or established UN Administrations, do create some concerns because they impose on individuals legal settings which are not their 'natural' context (ie the legal order in which they would normally operate) and, in many cases, these measures deprive them of the protections which they could have enjoyed within their national systems. With regard to the ad hoc Tribunals (or the UN Administrations) this does not necessarily refer to their '*primary*' *rights* (since often the effort has been made to replicate appropriate catalogues of rights within each given system—think of Article 21 ICTY Statute which reproduces verbatim Article 14 ICCPR),[25] but certainly it concerns their '*secondary*' *rights*, namely those relating to the mechanisms for monitoring by supranational authorities or potential remedies, where applicable, such as, for example, the right of recourse to the European Court of Human Rights, or other monitoring bodies—which are becoming an increasingly important component of human rights principles.

In the case of targeted sanctions (and in particular those against terrorism), however, the problem of weakening (or infringing) individual rights has become more evident, and requires greater effort to find appropriate solutions. The weakening of human rights principles is more evident because in the context of anti-terrorism targeted sanctions even the 'primary' rights of individuals have not been duly taken into account in setting up the system and through the very process allegedly violated: it is the procedural system per se that does not respect such rights. In the specific context of the targeted sanction regimes what is really at issue is the very right of individuals to have any form of access to justice. Individuals are not heard prior to the adoption of the measures, which is understandable, nor do they have sufficient rights to subsequently obtain a review of the measures.[26] For this reason these measures will be the main underlying object (or target) of the following remarks.

4. The Sword and the Scale. The Difference Between Political and Judicial Balancing of Competing Human Rights Principles

A. Human rights obligations of the Security Council and balancing as an essential component of human rights law

As mentioned above, starting with the fall of the Berlin Wall, the SC has become increasingly active in the field of human rights by considering them a meaningful

[25] In this way human rights are protected in a somehow 'equivalent' way. On the notion of 'equivalent protection' see the judgment of the European Court of Human Rights in the so-called *Bosphorus* case, *Bosphorus Hava Yollari Turizm ve Ticaret Anonim Şirketi v Ireland*, 30 June 2005, available at www.echr.coe.int at para 155 and Conforti, 'Le principe d'équivalence et le contrôle sur les actes communautaires dans la jurisprudence de la Cour européenne des droits de l'homme', in M Breitenmoser, B Ehrenzeller, M Sassòli, W Stoffel, and B Wagner Pfeifer (eds), *Human Rights, Democracy and the Rule of Law. Liber amicorum Luzius Wildhaber* (2007) 173–82.

[26] F Francioni (ed), *Access to Justice as a Human Right* (2007).

part of stable peace. However, almost at the same time, the practice has shown that the Council can also create serious concerns for human rights principles. In this respect, as mentioned above, until relatively recent times few negative reactions had been recorded against 'targeted sanctions' and more generally against the creativity of the SC. In particular, from a human rights perspective, often more activism has been invoked (think, for example, of the situation in Darfur, where some have argued that the Council should do more to obtain the enforcement of the arrest warrants issued by the ICC, or to the recent criticisms over the deadlock in addressing the Syrian situation). Nonetheless, the immensity of SC targeted sanctions against terrorism and the fact that the system did not contain appropriate due process guarantees, led to several criticisms primarily from a human rights perspective.

Broadly speaking, it should be emphasized that there are solid arguments to maintain that the Council must respect a core of human rights principles when it comes to regulating its actions. This somehow flows from the logic of the Charter and some of its provisions. What is more debated, however, is whether or not there can be forms of control over the legality of SC measures.

As far as the first part of the question is concerned, the argument has been made that 'the inter-action of the principle of good faith with articles 1(1) and 1(3) of the Charter . . . would estop the organs of the United Nations from behaviour that violated . . . the core elements of the human rights norms underpinning article 1(3)'.[27] This is certainly a reasonable argument, as are equally reasonable and powerful the arguments revolving around the idea of a category of norms which cannot be violated (the *jus cogens* nature of many fundamental human rights would impose them even on the Security Council).

For the sake of brevity, *let us take for granted that the Council has human rights obligations* without engaging in a precise clarification of the existence and scope of these obligations. The assumption can be made that the Council must respect at least the rights codified in the catalogue contained in the Universal Declaration on Human Rights of 1948.[28] Any of those rights could be taken into account, but, for the purpose of our analysis, insofar as measures against terrorism are concerned, the debate is pretty clear and the confrontation is essentially between due process rights, on the one hand, and the right to security, on the other. Hence, admittedly the SC is pursuing the protection of one class of human rights. However, these rights are not absolute and must be balanced against other relevant rights (due process vs security).

When competing human rights principles are at issue—as is the case in the situation of the fight against terrorism—how should the Council operate? It is submitted that it is extremely difficult for the Council to obtain an appropriate balance and, even when such a balance is created, it is often unclear how the

[27] De Wet, 'The Security Council as a Law Maker: The Adoption of (Quasi)-Judicial Decisions', in R Wolfrum and V Röben (eds), *Developments of International Law in Treaty Making* (2005) 183.

[28] See Condorelli, 'Conclusions générales', in *La soumission des organisations internationales aux normes internationales relatives aux droits de l'homme* (2009) 131 at 145.

decision is reached.[29] Even though in many situations it is clear that human rights played a role in determining SC measures, it is always extremely uncertain what grounds led the Council to adopt a given decision, in the absence of any explicit need to spell out the reasoning.

Continuing with the example of measures against terrorism, one may argue that on both levels—rights (due process vs security) and principles (rule of law vs international peace and security)—there is a need for taking into account potentially conflicting interests and balancing them. The main problem is to understand how the balancing should be made, how the Council can carry out such balancing and, lastly, what reasons are behind its decisions.

It is argued here that while the UN Security Council might be an appropriate body to carry out the abstract balancing between conflicting principles (including human rights principles), and thus decide whether or not in a given situation priority should be given to human rights principles over other relevant principles, is the Council not the most appropriate authority to carry out a concrete and specific balancing of conflicting rights in cases concerning individuals. And this explains why, to a certain extent, the system faced substantial criticism under the new anti-terrorism sanctions regime—in which the rights of specific individuals are targeted by the measures adopted by Council, through the Sanction Committees. Normally, under international law (and under the national Constitutions of many States) prior to the adoption of measures impinging upon the personal liberties of individuals, some due process guarantees must be respected: the right to be heard, the right to be able to obtain review of the measure, the right to know the reasons justifying the measures and so on. In particular, at domestic level measures restricting the rights of individuals can indeed be taken, but they usually imply that the body adopting them takes into account the competing interests at issue and strikes a balance between them: typically it would be individual rights and liberties vs public security. To do so, a balancing of individual rights vs the public interest is to be carried out.

This sort of balancing is more the job of courts or, in some cases, of administrative bodies; it cannot be the task of any political organ (or at least this is very difficult and would imply modifying the nature of the deliberation and mode of functioning of the organ, at least for that very specific purpose).[30] Moreover, the fact that there are no obligations for the Council to provide in any details the reasons and grounds on which a certain decision is based, nor any indication on how the balancing took place, makes it even less adequate, assuming that the Council could exercise judicial or quasi-judicial functions with regard to individuals. Hence, one could argue that the balancing carried out by the Council is not transparent. This institutional lack of transparency—which is necessary in many

[29] Koskenniemi 'The Place of Law in Collective Security' (1996) 17 *Michigan Journal of International Law* 455, 485–8.

[30] At the national level this sometimes occurs with parliamentary bodies that can be tasked with judicial or quasi judicial functions, but operate in those cases under specific rules, eg in cases of impeachment.

respects given the sensitivity of the issues tackled by the Council—hardly makes it possible for the Council to be considered an appropriate balancing body for the purposes of respecting fundamental human rights principles where the rights of specific individuals are concerned.

B. The normative (and thus abstract) balancing of competing principles

Conflicting interests and competing values may arise in all fields of human activity. Law is essentially aimed at preventing and solving conflicts of interests, and all legal systems possess mechanisms for organizing such potential conflicts. The settlement of these conflicts usually rests on several mechanisms (eg hierarchy, temporal criteria, distribution of competences, and so on). A difference, however, must be drawn between the abstract balancing of conflicting interests and the concrete balancing of the same interests with regard to cases involving specific natural or legal persons. While normally the former is within the purview of the legislator or, to a lesser degree, governments—and is normally expressed through constitutions, laws, and other regulations—the latter is generally in the hands of specific administrative bodies and ultimately the judiciary,[31] because it requires specific techniques and procedures, some of which possess the nature of fundamental rights, such as all the so-called 'due process guarantees'.

The Security Council may be an appropriate body to carry out abstract balancing, by taking into account general public interests and identifying the best political compromise to satisfy them. On the basis of Article 103 of the Charter the Council may even apply a hierarchical supremacy to its decisions vis-à-vis other treaty provisions, on the condition that the Charter is respected. Arguably, when it comes to specific individual cases which need concrete balancing and which concern the rights of natural and legal persons, the Council is by far a less appropriate forum, since it did not receive such a mandate and it does not institute proceedings to which individuals are party.

Under the Charter, the Council may be an appropriate organ to handle interstate disputes, but it lacks the necessary structure, means, procedures, and all the other institutional tools explicitly designed to take into account the specificities of situations involving individuals (or, rather, individuals do not possess under the Charter and the Provisional Rules of Procedure of the Security Council the necessary procedural rights to interact with the Council). Moreover, even the practice shows that so far the Council has proved more successful in the area of abstract balancing of competing values, and in this area, at least to some extent, it has succeeded in promoting human rights principles. By contrast, its measures turned out to be much more problematic where they specifically targeted individuals. In particular, the Security Council has proved effective in contributing to the protection of

[31] Even when administrative authorities carry out the balancing at first, there is normally a right of recourse to have their decisions re-examined by a judicial body.

human rights principles through the creation of UN bodies such as the ad hoc Criminal Tribunals for the former Yugoslavia and Rwanda or the Commissions of Inquiry (eg in Darfur), or where it established UN Territorial Administrations in Kosovo or in East Timor. On the other hand, in other cases, ie when Sanctions Committees were established, the Council eventually targeted individuals directly, in the absence of any meaningful filter or procedural mechanism that would allow these individuals to interact with the Council. One might argue that the filter is ensured by states at the stage of implementation, but this would amount to over-emphasizing a fiction and would create risks of 'disobedience'. In reality states are under an obligation to abide by these measures, which are so detailed that they do not leave any room for discretion in their implementation. Moreover they do not seem to have any discretion in establishing review mechanisms that could lead to providing individuals with detailed information (nor do they necessarily have that information). The conclusion could thus be drawn that it is the Council that created the premises for a system in which human rights could not specifically be taken into account and thus violations may occur and be directly attributable to the Council itself. It ought to be clarified that while the creation of these bodies cannot be viewed per se as a violation of human rights, from the outset their concrete functioning has created problems from the standpoint of human rights principles, in particular since the due process guarantees have not been respected.

The reason for this drawback is that these subsidiary organs adopt measures which impinge upon human rights, specifically targeting determined individuals without even giving them a chance to be heard, nor of being involved in other meaningful ways, and without being in a position to provide them with information on the grounds for which the measures are adopted. Moreover, these bodies do not apply appropriate due process guarantees in their procedures nor are they subjected to any system of judicial overview of their decisions or external monitoring.

In order to carry out a concrete balancing of interests in a specific individual case, it is necessary to have some appropriate procedural devices while the Security Council Committees (despite the laudable amendments which at least for the 1267 Committee have been adopted by Resolutions 1822 (2008) and even more, through 1904 (2009)) still lack such mechanisms. In this respect, it does not seem justified for the Council to continue adopting such measures without further amendments to accommodate the necessary requirements for the system to be in keeping with human rights standards. The problem, however, might be insurmountable. The structure of the Committees and the way in which they operate make it impossible for the Council to deal with cases involving the rights of legal and natural persons in keeping with human rights principles (since there is little or no chance for all targeted persons to be heard).

C. The concrete (judicial?) balancing of interests with reference to individual cases

From the remarks above the conclusion follows that no matter how many changes can be made to the current procedures, the Sanction Committees are simply too similar to the structure of the Council and to its working methods, for a meaningful change to occur. The SC cannot really change its nature, nor is it realistic to expect that the Committees will become truly independent and autonomous bodies from the Council, which, however, without due process guarantees would not per se be sufficient.

The only mechanism which could ensure an appropriate balancing in cases involving the specific rights of given individuals would be the establishment of a judicial or quasi-judicial body to replace the Committees or the adoption of specific review mechanisms that would allow affected individuals to impugn the measures and obtain effective re-examination. There is something in the judicial function and its specificities that make it unique in the area of the exercise of power and in decision-making. The judicial process is an ideal mechanism for comparing competing interests against one another and giving them appropriate weight in *individual cases,* because it carries out a complex balancing exercise and leads to a verifiable decision, with transparent methods, in a given situation involving individuals and not in general and broad terms, which entail political considerations.

In the context of UN SC measures against terrorism, the concrete balancing (which, in theory, could have been operated by the Committees) failed from the outset because the Committees do not act as judicial bodies and probably could not even do so given their structure and the way in which they operate, and the fact that there is no real review mechanism to control the legality of SC measures.[32] To determine that an individual right must be sacrificed in the interest of another individual or collective right, what would be required is the carrying out of an appropriate balancing process which should take into account the specificities of each single case, in light of the relevant rights which come into play. The process would require the active participation of the individual concerned.

It is well known that the procedures for the adoption of UN SC measures against terrorism (but more broadly all targeted sanctions mechanisms) do not respect the fundamental due process rules, because individuals have no opportunity to take part in the proceedings, nor do they properly interact with the bodies adopting the measures, or receive any detailed information on the 'evidence' which the Council relies upon.

A viable option could have been to establish a process which would ensure that the participation of the affected individuals could take place *ex post,* as a form of control against the measures. For example, through the recognition of a right to have the measure re-examined; this re-examination would be useful, however, only if the targeted person were to be placed in a position to effectively challenge the

[32] More broadly on this topic see Bedjaoui (n 14 above).

measure. There would be the need to disclose the reasons for the adoption of the measure and the grounds on which it was adopted (all information that could be, and often probably are, classified).

This brings us to a more general theme underlying the fight against terrorism. It is well known that the kind of information and 'evidentiary' materials which have been used in this fight are unsuited to transparency because they come from a traditionally protected source. Admittedly, in the sphere of anti-terrorism measures a great deal of information comes from confidential sources (often intelligence sources) and this makes it nearly impossible to comply with any information or disclosure process. The choice in this area has not been very wise, both at the national level and at the international level: considerable reliance on information gathered through means that prevent communication to the targeted persons, makes it extremely difficult to fight against terrorism in keeping with several fundamental principles of the rule of law and due process (which include many human rights principles).

To a large extent, the problem goes beyond the activities of the SC. Most of the problems in handling the proceedings related to the detainees in Guantánamo and, in particular, the substantial failure of the laudable attempt to hold proceedings other than before the Military Commissions (in ordinary courts), are linked to the difficulties relating to disclosure of evidence—which are essentially due to the nature of the information used in the fight against terrorism. Arguably in that area a serious mistake has been made in the strategy adopted by the international community in the fight against terrorism; in particular, it was perhaps inappropriate to think that it was possible to react to terrorist threats by military means and by stretching the principles of respect for the rule of law.

Today, what has been agreed upon with the establishment, under Resolution 1904 (2009), of the ombudsperson in charge of examining the requests for de-listing and facilitating the contacts between states and individuals affected by the measures, is probably the best compromise that could be achieved especially in the light of further improvement obtained through resolutions 1988 and 1989 (2011). And yet there are several doubts as to the fact that this is sufficient in terms of compliance with human rights standards, in particular given the relative lack of information that can be provided to the targeted persons, and the weakness of the powers of the Ombudsperson vis-à-vis the Council and member states.

5. Targeted Sanctions as a Threat to Human Rights Principles for the Lack of an Appropriate Balancing

The structure and competences of the SC do not create the appropriate framework to deal with cases concerning the rights of legal and natural persons. The Council is too distant from the individuals concerned and its mandate is essentially to deal with fundamental political choices relating to inter-state scenarios. The Council may well use its powers to settle inter-state disputes (think of Chapter VI of the Charter), but that would in no case be a dispute concerning specific persons; it would be an inter-state dispute. In this regard the Council has all the ability to deal with broader general interests; it may determine whether or not in a given scenario under Article 39 human rights principles can be taken into account and which weight should be given to them in general terms, as well as how to balance them against other general principles. However, if one turns to individual rights and specific persons whose rights are involved, it is very difficult for the Council to achieve satisfactory results, since balancing individual rights against one another, or against general interests, requires that the individual is heard and his or her specific rights are examined in detail at some stage in the proceedings. It is true that the Council has very broad powers, but they are essentially tailored to intervene in crises that have an inter-state dimension or, in any case, that involve states. However, the involvement of states cannot merely occur because they are the geographical location where measures must be implemented (as is the case with anti-terrorism sanctions); states are supposed to be the main targets of SC measures (or at least the end target). With the creation of 'targeted sanctions', states as such have been removed from the scene. In the early days, targeted sanctions were addressed against individuals who represented some sort of public power within a given state and often they were part of the state machinery. The 'old' targeted sanctions, in this respect, were more in line with the Charter in that they were aimed at sanctioning a state, at forcing the state as such to do or not to do something. The 'new generation' of targeted sanctions, namely in the framework of the fight against terrorism, has radically changed the nature of the measure. Individuals are targeted irrespective of any link to a sovereign or quasi-sovereign power, and the aims of the measures are not really to oblige states to follow a given course of conduct. In other words, states are under an obligation to enact the measure but the goal pursued through the measure itself is not (as it should be) to obtain that one or more states (which are ultimately targeted by the measure) change their course of action. Individuals are targeted qua individuals because it has been indirectly recognized that individuals can pose a threat to international peace and security. This radical shift of paradigm probably explains why the phenomenon of targeted sanctions is in conflict with human rights principles and has created much controversy.

Moreover, the Committees in the area of sanctions against terrorism hardly made it possible for the Council to deal with specific concrete cases concerning individuals and to carry out the appropriate balancing necessary to avoid human rights violations in these situations. They are not independent and autonomous bodies, their working methods are essentially political and they function in a way which is very similar to that of the Council itself.

Of course, the Council could try to further adapt its traditional procedures (in the framework of specific subsidiary organs) to the need of addressing the fundamental rights of individuals. However, this would need dramatic changes in the structure of deliberations, the need for an in-depth debate, the need to provide detailed reasoning and the grounds on which a given decision is taken.[33] All these

[33] Some progress in this direction has been made, eg with the statements accompanying the measures and the new procedures set out by SC Res 1822 (2008).

features could find their way in appropriate procedural mechanisms and may enable the Council to move from a general and abstract balancing aiming at the protection of general interests, to a new ability to deal more specifically with the details of cases involving natural and legal persons, but would this be an appropriate development?

In reality, the above-mentioned developments do not seem to be entirely appropriate according to the Charter. In particular, there is little doubt that the Council must respect its statutory function—to preserve peace and security. In this context, it is difficult to find justifications in the Charter to balance international security against the fundamental human rights of one single individual. This cannot be considered a defect of the Charter, since the Charter had never been conceived as a mechanism that would authorize the Security Council to engage in relationships with individuals and to adopt measures against them in their individual capacity.

As is well known, the SC possesses under the Charter enormous powers: it may impose on states wide-ranging obligations, it may decide on the use of armed force or authorize states to use it. And thus, clearly the Council is in a position to determine dramatic sacrifices for the human rights of millions of persons (under Articles 41 and 42 of the Charter), without any need to provide the grounds in terms of human rights principles. However, there is no parallel power to sacrifice the rights of one or more specific individuals. This is not regulated by the Charter and thus the Council can hardly take such decisions without relying on the general rules and principles applicable in international human rights law, which require the respect of due process principles and the involvement of the individuals in the relevant proceedings or in subsequent proceedings entailing a review of the measure with appropriate guarantees.

In reality, there are strong arguments to maintain that the targeted sanctions regime should be drastically revised, and arguably the only way to do it would be to reverse it completely. It is certainly not realistic to suggest that the Council will go back to the Charter and refrain from exceeding its competences. Once a practice is established and states have substantially acquiesced to it, it is very difficult to simply reverse it. However, once the emergency phase is over, such a practice could be abandoned.

6. Tentative Conclusions on How to Review Security Council Measures in the Light of Human Rights Principles

The Council, with its broad powers, does not only act as a legislator,[34] but also in some areas as the executive and the judiciary. In terms of human rights principles this is certainly not satisfactory, since the concentration of power is too intense, and the absence of checks and balances too evident.[35] There is no need to recall that, broadly speaking, human rights were born to protect individuals against abuses of power by authorities. In this regard, the powers concentrated in the hands of the

[34] As it did when it adopted SC Res 1373 (2001).

[35] For a broader picture see Reinisch, 'Governance Without Accountability?' (2001) 44 *German Yearbook of International Law* 270–306.

Security Council are too vast and largely unrestrained to be acceptable from a human rights perspective. The main restraints are the largely unknown political negotiations within the Council for the approval of measures. The problem is thus to try to understand what mechanisms of control are possible. Assuming that external control is not possible, nor desirable, there must be some sort of self-control within the system which, however, allows the protection of human rights principles more effectively.

The suggestion can be (and has been) made to leave it to member states to determine when SC measures are affected by illegality. The Charter contains a textual indication that could be used to counterbalance SC power. The wording of Articles 24(2) and 25 of the Charter indicates that 'the Security Council shall act *in accordance with the Purposes and Principles of the United Nations*' and that, on their side, '[the] Members of the United Nations agree to accept and carry out the decisions of the Security Council *in accordance with the present Charter*'.[36] A solution that may seem practicable is that states are to be considered responsible for verifying whether or not the Council has respected the Charter, including human rights principles, and determine to what extent and how to implement the Council's measure.

However, the real problem is to what extent and under which circumstances could SC measures be second guessed by national authorities? The issue is then to understand which organs would be entitled to do it and on which basis? There are a few points that are worth examining. Some have argued that there is nothing in the Charter that prevents national jurisdictions to examine the legality of SC measures.[37] As mentioned above, the measures of the Council to be legally binding must be lawful (and there must be ways in which their legality can be assessed). The reasoning is very well argued and indeed apparently persuasive. However, there is a fundamental problem with the possible consequences of such a reasoning. If international organizations ought to be independent and autonomous from states, if they have to be effective despite states' tendencies to obstruct their activities, how could this be reconciled with a right (or even a duty) of national judges to verify the lawfulness of their measures? If even the UN Security Council can be the object of second guessing by national authorities, other international organizations will find it extremely difficult to impose their decisions onto recalcitrant states.

Moreover, another concern could be that this line of reasoning would not only apply to the UN Security Council, but could expand to all international organizations which would ultimately remain unprotected from obstructions in their activities by national jurisdictions. This would eventually mean that national jurisdictions would be in a position to prevent international organizations from carrying out their mandates. Let me just give an example: if the idea of national judicial scrutiny was a reality, the Supreme Court of any state would have been in a position to review the legality of the UN SC Resolution establishing the ICTY or ICTR and would have potentially been able to determine that the Tribunals were

[36] Emphasis added.

[37] Condorelli (n 28 above). For an in depth study cf. Reinisch, *Challenging Acts of International Organization Before National Courts*, Oxford, OUP, 2010.

illegally created and thus no cooperation was indeed necessary, including the courts of the countries targeted by the measure. What would happen if the Supreme Court of Sudan were to determine that the SC resolution whereby the Council referred the case of Darfur to the ICC, is in contrast with fundamental human rights principles, such as, for example, the principle of equality before the law, in the part where it contains a clause that treats the nationals of Sudan differently from the nationals of other states not parties to the ICC?

In this context, two competing interests are at issue: on the one hand, the ambition to establish accountability for international organizations and their organs (including ultimately their officials); on the other, the need to ensure that the organization discharges its functions in full autonomy without the risk of undue interference.

A national review of SC measures should only be considered possible under very stringent circumstances—e.g. in the case of anti-terrorism measures—given that the system set up by the Council is not sufficiently autonomous and independent, and that the decisions taken by the Council through its subsidiary bodies (the Committees) directly affect the fundamental rights of specific individuals. Now the problem is that if states start to have a say on how to implement these measures and how to tailor them to the need to respect human rights principles, the risk is very strong that this margin of evaluation left in the hands of individual states could jeopardize the action of the Council. On the other hand, of course, if states can't do what they should in order to protect human rights principles, they may be responsible for the violations. Ultimately, if the Council wants to avoid states 'double checking' its measures, it must ensure that all necessary guarantees for human rights principles are put in place at the Council's level or it should go back to the Charter and refrain from engaging in activities which directly involve impinging upon the fundamental rights of individuals.

Conversely, in other cases no review should be admissible. For example, in cases such as the ad hoc Tribunals, or the UN Territorial Administrations (cases in which violations of human rights may occasionally occur, but are not systematic—in the sense of being linked to the system established by the Council) one could argue that there is a sufficient degree of independence and impartiality in the bodies which assume the decisions that directly affect individual rights. Moreover, individuals are entitled directly to interact with these bodies, to have their views heard and argue in support of their position. Generally speaking, the rules governing the proceedings before these bodies (either of a judicial or administrative nature) are in keeping with human rights standards and human rights principles have been respected. Hence, the conclusion can be drawn that in these cases, the systems as such are not in conflict with human rights principles (on the contrary, these measures can be seen as a contribution to human rights protection).

A problem still exists in these cases: how can we react to sporadic and isolated human rights violations which are always possible? This problem more broadly refers to the issue of the existence of human rights obligations binding on international organizations and of the establishment of human rights monitoring over the activity of organizations. In particular, when potentially conflicting rights are at issue, it seems hardly deniable that it is necessary to rely on judicial authorities to carry out the appropriate balancing.

Not only has progress in the area of establishing the human rights obligations of international organizations been rather slow, but it is also a reality that very often the involvement of international organizations ends up removing responsibility from the member states. Thus there is often a situation where neither the state nor the organizations are clearly responsible, which is obviously extremely worrying in terms of human rights principles.[38]

This leads us to another possible alternative (though largely utopian), which could help address both the problem of violations of human rights principles due to the system that has been put in place (the anti-terrorism sanctions) and the issue of occasional violations by UN SC bodies that in principle respect human rights: the establishment of an international human rights monitoring body or even better a *human rights world court* with jurisdiction over international organizations and their measures. Indeed, this could be an appropriate answer. Although at this stage such an idea does not seem realistic and there are no prospects for the institution of such a body, in the future the establishment of such a jurisdiction would be highly desirable.

In the long run, however, it is clear that should the Council wish to continue to heavily interfere with state sovereignty by exercising the functions of states (judicial, administrative, and so on, as is the case with ad hoc Tribunals or UN territorial administrations) or by using domestic legal systems uniquely as cogs for the transmission of its measures (anti-terrorism sanctions), there will be an increased need for some sort of monitoring within the system.

7. Conclusions

Finally, a few words on the broader assessment of the relationship between SC measures and human rights principles. As indicated above there may be different ways of reviewing Security Council measures through the prism of human rights principles. At the general, abstract and political level, the evaluation is rather positive;[39] on the other hand, at the level of individual cases—when the need to operate a concrete balancing of rights is necessary—the assessment is less positive. The Council lacks the instruments to carry out such concrete balancing in that substantially it does not interact with individuals and it is very difficult to carry out the balancing when individual rights are concerned without offering individuals a real opportunity to interact (including by receiving detailed information). There is

[38] On these problems see Mégret and Hoffmann. 'The UN as a Human Rights Violator? Some Reflections on the United Nations Changing Human Rights Responsibilities' (2003) 25 *Human Rights Quarterly* 314–42.

[39] See Cohen-Jonathan, 'Le Conseil de sécurité et les droits de l'homme', in JF Flauss and P Wachsman (eds), *Le droit des organisations internationales: recueil d'études à la mémoire de Jacques Schwob* (1997) 19–70.

such a huge gap between isolated individuals and the SC that one can hardly conceive of any system to bridge such a gap. It is not only the traditional dichotomy which involves the relationship of individual vs authority—it is a much broader dimension: the world vs one individual. While in the first cases of targeted sanctions, the individuals affected often were leaders and, to a certain extent, represented state sovereignty, in the current sanction systems, individuals or targeted entities are often devoid of any link with states and do not operate at the same level of states in international relations.

There is little doubt that the SC is entitled to take policy decisions which entail more progressive or more restrictive actions concerning fundamental rights. What it cannot and should not do is to engage directly in actions of concrete and specific balancing of interests (and even less individual rights) in cases concerning individuals. This is due to three reasons: (i) there are no procedures which allow the Council to gather details about the specificities of each individual case; (ii) there is no mechanism whereby individuals can appear before the Council and exercise their rights; and (iii) there is no obligation for the Council to give reasons for its determinations. This makes it impossible for the Council to take informed and transparent decisions respecting the rights of individuals. Moreover, there is no institutionalized review mechanism that would allow the affected individuals to have the measures re-examined after their adoption. Of course, if such mechanisms were to be created the evaluation could be different and the prospects for human rights protection vis-à-vis Security Council measures could improve. However, it does not seem realistic that the Council would adopt such further amendments. Against this background, what would seem more desirable is a return to the Charter and a more traditional interplay between the Council and individuals.

ANNEX

26 January 2011

SECURITY COUNCIL COMMITTEE ESTABLISHED
PURSUANT TO RESOLUTION 1267 (1999)
CONCERNING AL-QAIDA AND THE TALIBAN
AND ASSOCIATED INDIVIDUALS AND ENTITIES

Guidelines of the Committee for the Conduct of its Work

(Adopted on 7 November 2002, as amended on 10 April 2003, 21 December 2005, 29 November 2006, 12 February 2007, 9 December 2008, 22 July 2010[1], and 26 January 2011)

1. The Al-Qaida and Taliban Sanctions Committee

(a) The Committee of the Security Council established by paragraph 6 of Security Council resolution 1267 (1999) of 15 October 1999 is known as the Al-Qaida and Taliban Sanctions Committee. Its functions were modified by resolutions 1390 (2002) of 16 January 2002, 1526 (2004) of 30 January 2004, 1617 (2005) of 29 July 2005, 1730 (2006) of 19 December 2006, 1735 (2006) of 22 December 2006, 1822 (2008) of 30 June 2008 and 1904 (2009) of 17 December 2009. For the purposes of these guidelines, the Al-Qaida and Taliban Sanctions Committee shall hereinafter be referred to as 'the Committee.'

(b) The Committee is a subsidiary organ of the Security Council and will consist of all Members of the Council.

(c) The Chairman of the Committee will be appointed by the Security Council to serve in his/her personal capacity. The Chairman will be assisted by two delegations who will act as Vice-Chairmen, and who will also be appointed by the Security Council.

(d) The Chairman will chair meetings of the Committee. When he/she is unable to chair a meeting, he/she will nominate one of the Vice-Chairmen or another representative of his/her Permanent Mission to act on his/her behalf.

(e) The Secretariat of the Committee will be provided by the Secretariat of the United Nations.

[1] Following the adoption of resolution 1904 (2009), several sections were restructured and redrafted, and Section 9 was added. [Footnote in the original.]

2. Mandate of the Committee

The mandate of the Committee shall be, on the basis of the measures imposed by paragraph 4(b) of resolution 1267 (1999), paragraph 8 (c) of resolution 1333 (2000), and paragraphs 1 and 2 of resolution 1390 (2002) as reiterated in paragraph 1 of resolutions 1526 (2004), 1617 (2005), 1735 (2006), 1822 (2008) and 1904 (2009), to undertake the following tasks and to report on its work to the Council with its observations and recommendations:

Consolidated List

(a) To consider listing submissions, delisting requests and proposed updates to the existing information relevant to the list referred to in paragraph 1 of resolution 1904 (2009) (the 'Consolidated List'), as described in Sections 6, 7 and 8 below respectively;

(b) To update regularly the Consolidated List, as described in Sections 5 and 8 below;

(c) To make accessible on the Committee's website narrative summaries of reasons for listing for all entries on the Consolidated List, as described in Section 9 below;

(d) To review the names on the Consolidated List, as described in Section 10 below;

Measures Implementation

(e) To seek from all States further information regarding the actions taken by them with a view to effectively implement the measures imposed by the resolutions as referred to above;

(f) To consider information brought to its attention by States concerning non-compliance with the measures imposed by the resolutions as referred to above, to identify possible cases of non-compliance with these measures and to determine the appropriate course of action on each case;

(g) To make periodic reports to the Council on information submitted to the Committee regarding the implementation of resolution 1904 (2009), including regarding non-compliance with the measures imposed by the resolutions referred to above;

(h) To keep these guidelines under active review in support of the objectives to continue to ensure that fair and clear procedures exist for placing individuals and entities on the Consolidated List and for removing them as well as for granting humanitarian exemptions;

(i) To amend expeditiously these guidelines and criteria as may be necessary to facilitate the implementation of the measures imposed by the resolutions as referred to above;

(j) To consider requests by Member States for additional information which would facilitate the implementation of the measures referred to above in accordance with Section 8, paragraph (f) below;

(k) To transmit requests by Member States for technical assistance to the Counter-Terrorism Committee and the Counter-Terrorism Implementation Task Force;

Exemptions to the Measures

(l) To consider notifications and requests concerning exemptions from the assets freeze set out in paragraph 1(a) of resolution 1904 (2009), in accordance with resolution 1452 (2002) and 1735 (2006) and as described in Section 11 below;

(m) To consider requests for exemptions from the travel ban set out in paragraph 1(b) of resolution 1904 (2009), in accordance with that paragraph and as described in Section 12 below;

Reports

(n) To examine the reports submitted by Members States pursuant to paragraph 6 of resolution 1455 (2003), reports presented by the Analytical Support and Sanctions Monitoring Team (hereinafter referred to as 'the Monitoring Team') pursuant to Annex I to resolution 1904 (2009), checklists submitted by Member States pursuant to paragraph 10 of resolution 1617 (2005) and information submitted by Member States using the tools provided on the Committee's website (such as the Annual Statements of Information on Updates to the Consolidated List[2] and the Voluntary National Assessment of Implementation Survey[3]);

Outreach

(o) To cooperate with other relevant Security Council Sanctions Committees and with the Committee established pursuant to paragraph 6 of resolution 1373 (2001) of 28 September 2001 and with the Committee established pursuant to paragraph 4 of resolution 1540 (2004) of 28 April 2004 as well as with the Counter-Terrorism Implementation Task Force;

(p) To make publicly available through the appropriate media information it considers relevant, including the Consolidated List;

(q) To consider, where and when appropriate, visits to selected countries by the Chairman and/or Committee members (see Section 15 (c) below);

(r) To report orally, through its Chairman, at least every 180 days to the Council on the state of the overall work of the Committee and the Monitoring Team, and, as appropriate, in conjunction with the reports by the Chairmen of Counter-Terrorism Committee and the Committee established pursuant to resolution 1540 (2004), including briefings for all interested Member States as described in Section 14 below;

3. Meetings of the Committee

(a) Meetings of the Committee, both formal and informal, will be convened at any time the Chairman deems necessary, or at the request of a Member of the Committee. To

[2] http://www.un.org/sc/committees/1267/annualstat.shtml [This reference to the UN website and the following in the original.]

[3] http://www.un.org/sc/committees/1267/pdf/New%20tool%20-%20survey%20-%20English.pdf

the extent possible, four working days notice will be given for any meeting of the Committee, although shorter notice may be given in urgent situations.

(b) The Committee will meet in closed sessions, unless it decides otherwise. The Committee may invite any Member of the United Nations to participate in the discussion of any question brought before the Committee in which interests of that Member are specifically affected. The Committee will consider requests from Member States and relevant international organizations to send representatives to meet with the Committee as described in Section 13, paragraph (e). The Committee may invite members of the Secretariat or other persons to provide the Committee with appropriate expertise or information or to give it other assistance in examining matters within its competence.

(c) The Committee may invite the members of the Monitoring Team to attend meetings as appropriate.

(d) When the Committee considers a delisting request submitted to the Ombudsperson, the Chairman shall invite the Ombudsperson, aided by the Monitoring Team, as appropriate, to present his/her Comprehensive Report and answer Committee Members' questions regarding the request.

4. Decision-making

(a) The Committee shall make decisions by consensus of its Members. If consensus cannot be reached on a particular issue, the Chairman should undertake such further consultations as may facilitate agreement. If after these consultations, consensus still cannot be reached, the matter may be submitted to the Security Council. The Chairman may encourage and facilitate bilateral exchanges between interested Member States in order to clarify the issue prior to a decision.

(b) Where the Committee agrees, decisions may be taken by a written procedure. In such cases the Chairman will circulate to all Members of the Committee the proposed decision of the Committee, and will request Members of the Committee to indicate any objection they may have to the proposed decision within 5 full working days (or in urgent situations, such shorter period as the Chairman shall determine). Listing and delisting requests, together with all relevant information in accordance with the guidelines, as assessed by the Chairman, shall be considered in accordance with paragraph 6 (h) and 7 (g) respectively. If no objection is received within the specified period, the decision will be deemed adopted. Communications submitted to the Committee pursuant to resolution 1452 (2002) shall be considered in accordance with the procedure determined by that resolution, as revised by resolution 1735 (2006).

(c) If a Committee Member requests more time to consider a proposal, the Chairman shall inform the other Committee Members. The Secretariat shall include the matter in the list of pending issues and inform the State(s) concerned or, where appropriate, the Ombudsperson that the matter is still under the Committee's consideration. If the Committee Member concerned requires additional information to resolve the pending matter, it may ask the Committee to request additional information on that specific matter from the State(s) concerned. The Committee Member concerned shall provide updates after three months on its progress in resolving the pending matter.

(d) The Committee shall ensure that no matter is left pending for a period longer than six months. At the end of the six month period the pending matter shall be deemed approved unless

(i) the Committee Member concerned has objected to the proposal; or

(ii) the Committee determines, at the request of the Committee Member concerned, on a case by case basis that extraordinary circumstances require additional time to consider the proposal and extends the time for consideration by up to three months at the end of the six month period. At the end of this additional period, the pending matter shall be deemed approved unless the Committee Member concerned has objected to the proposal.

The Secretariat shall immediately take the necessary steps, including updating the Consolidated List, and inform the State(s) concerned and, where appropriate, the Ombudsperson, about the Committee's decision.

(e) The Committee will review once a month, as necessary, the status of pending issues as updated by the Secretariat, including updates provided by Committee Members.

(f) A hold placed on a matter by a Member of the Committee will cease to have effect at the time its membership of the Committee ends. New Members shall be informed of all pending matters one month before their membership of the Committee begins and shall inform the Committee of their position on relevant matters, including possible approval, objection or hold, by the time they become Members.

5. The Consolidated List

(a) The Committee will update regularly the Consolidated List when it has agreed to include or delete relevant information in accordance with the procedures set out in these guidelines.

(b) The updated Consolidated List will be made promptly available on the website of the Committee. At the same time, any modification to the Consolidated List will be communicated to Member States immediately through Notes Verbales, including an electronic advance copy, and United Nations Press Releases.

(c) Once the updated Consolidated List is communicated to Member States, States are encouraged to circulate it widely, such as to banks and other financial institutions, border points, airports, seaports, consulates, customs agents, intelligence agencies, alternative remittance systems and charities.

6. Listing

(a) The Committee shall consider including new names based on submissions received from Member States.

(b) Member States are encouraged to establish a national mechanism or procedure to identify and assess names for inclusion on the Consolidated List and to appoint a national contact point concerning entries on that list according to national laws and procedures.

(c) Before a Member State proposes a name for inclusion on the Consolidated List, it is strongly encouraged, to the extent possible, to approach the State(s) of residence and/or nationality of the individual or entity concerned to seek additional information. States are advised to submit names as soon as they gather the supporting evidence of association with Al-Qaida and/or the Taliban. A criminal charge or conviction is not a prerequisite for listing as the sanctions are intended to be preventive in nature. The Committee will consider proposed listings on the basis of the 'associated with' standard described in paragraphs 2 and 3 of resolution 1617 (2005), as reaffirmed in paragraphs 2 and 3 of resolution 1904 (2009). When submitting names of groups, undertakings and/or entities, States are encouraged, if they deem it appropriate, to propose for listing at the same time the names of the individuals responsible for the decisions of the group, undertaking and/or entity concerned.

(d) When proposing names for inclusion on the Consolidated List, Member States should use the standard forms for listing available on the Committee's website[4] and shall include as much relevant and specific information as possible on a proposed name, in particular sufficient identifying information to allow for the accurate and positive identification of the individual, group, undertaking or entity concerned by competent authorities, including:

- For individuals: family name/surname, given names, other relevant names, date of birth, place of birth, nationality/citizenship, gender, aliases, employment/occupation, State(s) of residence, passport or travel document and national identification number, current and previous addresses, current status before law enforcement authorities (e.g. wanted, detained, convicted), location;
- For groups, undertakings or entities: name, registered name, short name(s)/acronyms, and other names by which it is known or was formerly known, address, headquarters, branches/subsidiaries, organizational linkages, parent company, nature of business or activity, State(s) of main activity, leadership/management, registration (incorporation) or other identification number, status (e.g. in liquidation, terminated), website addresses;

(e) Member States shall provide a detailed statement of case in support of the proposed listing that forms the basis or justification for the listing in accordance with the relevant resolutions. The statement of case should provide as much detail as possible on the basis(es) for listing, including but not limited to: (1) specific information demonstrating that the individual/entity meets the criteria for listing set out in paragraphs 2 and 3 of resolution 1904 (2009); (2) details of any connection with a currently listed individual or entity; (3) information about any other relevant acts or activities of the individual/entity; (4) the nature of the supporting evidence (e.g. intelligence, law enforcement, judicial, open source information, admissions by subject, etc.); (5) additional information or documents supporting the submission as well as information about relevant court cases and proceedings. The statement of case shall be releasable, upon request, except for the parts the designating State identifies as being confidential to the Committee, and may be used to develop the narrative summary of reasons for listing described in section 9 below.

[4] http://www.un.org/sc/committees/1267/listing.shtml

(f) Member States proposing a new designation, as well as Member States that have proposed names for inclusion on the Consolidated List before the adoption of resolution 1904 (2009), should specify whether the Committee may make known, upon request from another Member State, their status as designating State(s).

(g) Member States may co-sponsor a new designation as long as the listing request is under the Committee's consideration. These States will also be considered designating States and should also specify whether the Committee may make known, upon request from another Member State, their status as designating State(s).

(h) The Committee will consider listing requests within a period of 10 full working days, which may be shortened, if requested, at the Chairman's discretion, for emergency and time-sensitive listings. If a proposal for listing is not approved within the decision-making period, the Committee will notify the submitting State on the status of the request.

(i) Committee Members and the Monitoring Team are called upon to share with the Committee any information available regarding a listing request to help inform the Committee's decision and provide additional material for the narrative summary of reasons for listing.

(j) Upon request of a Committee Member, listing requests may be placed on the Committee's agenda for more detailed consideration. If deemed necessary, the Committee may request additional background information from the Monitoring Team and/or the designating State(s). Following consideration by the Committee, the Chairman shall circulate the listing request under the written decision-making procedure as described in Sections 4 (b) and 6 (h) above.

(k) At the same time a name is added to the Consolidated List, the Committee shall, with the assistance of the Monitoring Team and in coordination with the relevant designating State(s), make accessible on the Committee's website a narrative summary of reasons for listing for the corresponding entry or entries. In addition to the narrative summary, the Secretariat shall, promptly after a name is added to the Consolidated List, publish on the Committee's website all relevant publicly releasable information, where available.

(l) In its communication informing Member States of new entries to the Consolidated List, the Secretariat shall include the narrative summary of reasons for listing.

(m) Unless the Committee decides otherwise, the Secretariat shall request INTERPOL to issue, where feasible, an INTERPOL-United Nations Security Council Special Notice for each name added to the list.

(n) The Secretariat shall, after publication but within three working days after a name is added to the Consolidated List, notify the Permanent Mission of the country or countries where the individual or entity is believed to be located and, in the case of individuals, the country of which the person is a national (to the extent this information is known). The Secretariat shall include with this notification a copy of the narrative summary of reasons for listing, a description of the effects of designation, as set forth in the relevant resolutions, the Committee's procedures for considering delisting requests, including the possibility of submitting delisting requests to the Office of the Ombudsperson in accordance with paragraphs 20 and 21 and annex II of resolution 1904 (2009), and the provisions for available exemptions. The letter shall remind States receiving such notification that they are required to take, in accordance with their domestic laws and practices, all possible measures to notify or inform in a timely manner the newly listed individuals and entities on the Consolidated List of the measures imposed on them, any information on reasons for listing available on the Committee's website as well as all the information provided by the Secretariat in the above-mentioned notification. In addition, in its notification, the Secretariat shall invite States to provide in accordance with national law details on measures taken to freeze assets of the individuals or entities concerned.

(o) Where address is known, and after the Secretariat has officially notified the Permanent Mission of the State(s) concerned, the Ombudsperson shall notify individuals or entities about the status of their listing. The Ombudsperson shall include all additional information as described in paragraph [n] above.

7. Delisting

(a) A petitioner (individual(s), groups, undertakings, and/or entities on the Consolidated List) seeking to submit a request for de-listing can do so either directly to the Office of the Ombudsperson as outlined in paragraph (c) and in the attached annex, or through his/her State of residence or nationality as outlined in paragraph (e) below

(b) A State can decide, that as a rule, its nationals or residents should address their delisting requests directly to the Office of the Ombudsperson. The State will do so by a declaration addressed to the Chairman that will be published on the Committee's website.

(c) In accordance with paragraph 20 and annex II of resolution 1904 (2009) the Office of the Ombudsperson shall receive delisting requests submitted by, or on behalf, of a petitioner following the procedures outlined in annex II of resolution 1904 (2009) (reproduced in the annex to these guidelines).

(d) After the appointment of the Ombudsperson, the Focal Point established in resolution 1730 (2006) shall no longer receive delisting requests regarding individual(s), groups undertakings and/or entities on the Consolidated List. In case the Focal Point continues to receive such delisting requests, it shall forward those requests to the Office of the Ombudsperson and shall inform the individual/entity accordingly. The Focal Point shall continue to process pending delisting requests which it had received prior to the appointment of the Ombudsperson in accordance with the annex to resolution 1730 (2006).

(e) Member States may at any time submit to the Committee requests for delisting of individuals, groups, undertakings, and/or entities inscribed on the Consolidated List, after having bilaterally consulted with the designating State(s), the State(s) of nationality, residence or incorporation, where applicable. The Chairman, with the support of the Secretariat, shall facilitate contacts between the State requesting the delisting and the designating State(s).The Chairman shall circulate the request, including, as appropriate, additional information provided by the Monitoring Team, under the written procedure as described in Section 4 (b) above and 7 (g) below. Upon request of a Member of the Committee, the delisting request shall be placed on the Committee's agenda for more detailed consideration. If deemed necessary, the Committee may request additional background information from the Monitoring

Team and/or the State(s) concerned and may invite these States to submit their views within a period of one month. Following consideration by the Committee, the Chairman shall circulate the delisting request under the written procedure as described in Section 4 (b) above and 7 (g) below.

(f) When submitting a delisting request, the standard form for delisting, available on the Committee's website[5], should be used. The delisting request should explain why the individual or entity concerned no longer meets the criteria described in paragraphs 2 and 3 of resolution 1617 (2005) as reaffirmed in paragraphs 2 and 3 of resolution 1904 (2009). Any documentation supporting the request can be referred to and/or attached together with the explanation of its relevance, where appropriate.

(g) When considering delisting requests, the Committee shall give due consideration to the opinions of designating State(s), State(s) of residence, nationality or incorporation. The Committee will consider delisting requests within a period of 10 full working days, which may be shortened to a minimum of two full working days, if requested and in exceptional circumstances, at the Chairman's discretion, for emergency and time-sensitive delistings after previously informing the Members of the Committee. After this period, the Secretariat shall inform the Members of the committee whether an objection has been received and the Consolidated List will be updated accordingly, where appropriate.

(h) Committee Members are called on to make every effort to provide reasons for objecting to delisting requests. If the Committee decides to reject a delisting request, the Committee shall convey to the petitioner, through the Ombudsperson or the State(s) concerned, its decision following the respective procedures outlined in annex II of resolution 1904 (2009) (reproduced in the annex to these guidelines) or in Section 7 (k) below.

(i) For a deceased individual, the delisting request shall be submitted either directly to the Committee by a State, or to the Office of the Ombudsperson by his/her legal beneficiary, together with official documentation certifying that status. The delisting request shall include a death certificate or similar official documentation confirming the death. The Committee considers any official communication from a State declaring a listed person to be dead as fulfilling the requirement for 'credible information regarding death' as described in paragraph 26 of resolution 1904 (2009), without prejudice to the final decision of the Committee as to the removal of the name from the List. The official communication, such as documentation certifying death, should include, to the extent possible, the full name, permanent reference number, date of birth, and the date and place of death of the individual, as well as any further information about the circumstances of the death. The submitting State or the petitioner should also ascertain and inform the Committee whether or not any legal beneficiary of the deceased's estate or any joint owner of his/her assets is on the Consolidated List, and to the extent possible, inform the Committee about the names of any individuals or entities who would be in a position to receive any unfrozen assets of a deceased individual or defunct entity, in order to prevent unfrozen assets from being used for terrorist purposes. In cases where individuals have no frozen assets, the Committee will accept as sufficient for delisting an official communication from the

[5] http://www.un.org/sc/committees/1267/delisting.shtml

State(s) of nationality and residence declaring the financial status of the individuals in question, without prejudice to the final decision of the Committee.

(j) The Secretariat shall, within three working days after a name is removed from the Consolidated List, notify the Permanent Mission of the country or countries where the individual or entity is believed to be located and, in the case of individuals, the country of which the person is a national (to the extent this information is known). The letter shall remind States receiving such notification that they are required to take measures, in accordance with their domestic laws and practices, to notify or inform the concerned individual or entity of the delisting in a timely manner. The Secretariat will also concurrently, if an INTERPOL-UNSC Special Notice exists for the relevant name, request INTERPOL to cancel that notice as well as provide confirmation when the cancellation is in effect.

(k) If a delisting request submitted by a Member State is rejected, the Secretariat shall, within three working days after the Committee's decision, notify the Permanent Mission of the State submitting the request, the State(s) where the individual or entity is believed to be located and, in the case of individuals, the country of which the person is a national (to the extent this information is known). The notification shall include the Committee's decision, an updated narrative summary of reasons for listing and, where available, any other publicly releasable information about the Committee's decision, as well as other relevant information described in Section 6 (n) above. The letter shall remind States receiving such notification that they are required to take measures, in accordance with their domestic laws and practices, to notify or inform the concerned individual or entity in a timely manner of the decision and as well as all the information provided by the Secretariat in the above-mentioned notification.

8. Updating the Existing Information on the Consolidated List

The Committee shall consider expeditiously, in accordance with the following procedures, any information supplied by Member States, regional or international organizations, or the Monitoring Team, in particular additional identifying information and other information, along with supporting documentation, including updates on the operating status of listed individuals, groups and undertakings, the movement, incarceration or death of listed individuals and other significant events as well as any relevant court decisions and proceedings, as such information becomes available, and shall decide which information would improve the existing information on the Consolidated List.

(a) The Committee will consider any additional information on listed individuals or entities submitted to it by Member States, regional or international organizations or the Monitoring Team. The Committee or the Monitoring Team, at the Committee's request, may approach the original designating State(s) and consult with it on the relevance of the submitted additional information. The Committee may also encourage Member States or regional or international organizations providing such additional information to consult with the original designating State(s). The Secretariat will, subject to the designating State's consent, assist in establishing the appropriate contacts.

(b) The Monitoring Team will, as appropriate, review any and all information received by the Committee in order to clarify or confirm such information. In this connection, the Monitoring Team will use all sources available to it, including other sources than those provided by the original designating State(s).

(c) The Monitoring Team will subsequently advise the Committee, within 4 weeks, if such information could be included in the Consolidated List, or if further clarification is recommended in order to ascertain that the information received can be incorporated in the Consolidated List. The Committee shall decide whether and how such clarification should be obtained and may again call upon the expertise of the Monitoring Team.

(d) The Monitoring Team may also submit to the Committee any information on listed individuals and entities it has obtained from publicly available official sources, or with the help of United Nations agencies, such as the United Nations Assistance Mission in Afghanistan, with their agreement. In such cases, the Monitoring Team shall identify the source of each piece of new information when presenting it for the Committee's consideration.

(e) Upon the decision of the Committee to incorporate additional information into the Consolidated List the Committee will inform the Member State or regional or international organization that submitted the additional information accordingly.

(f) Any additional relevant information submitted to the Committee that is not incorporated into the Consolidated List or the narrative summary of reasons for listing will be stored by the Monitoring Team in a database for the use of the Committee and the Monitoring Team in carrying out their respective mandates. Upon request, the Committee shall share any such additional information with Member States whose nationals, residents or entities have been included on the Consolidated List provided that the information is publicly releasable or the provider of the information has agreed to its release. The Committee may also call on the Monitoring Team to assist in conveying such additional relevant information to the requesting State(s). On a case-by-case basis the Committee may decide to release the information to other parties, with the prior consent of the submitting State.

9. Narrative Summaries of Reasons for Listing

(a) For all entries on the Consolidated List, the Committee, with the assistance of the Monitoring Team and in coordination with the relevant designating State(s), shall continue to make accessible on its website narrative summaries of reasons for listing.

(b) When a new name is proposed for listing, the Monitoring Team shall immediately prepare, in coordination with the relevant designating State(s), a draft narrative summary for the Committee's consideration which shall be circulated together with the corresponding listing request. The narrative summary shall be made accessible on the Committee's website at the same time a name is added to the Consolidated List.

(c) Draft narrative summaries should be based on information provided by the designating State(s), Committee members or the Monitoring Team, including the statement of case, the standard form for listing, any other official information provided to the Committee or any other relevant information publicly available from official sources.

(d) The narrative summary should include: the date of listing; the basis(es) for listing according to relevant resolutions adopted by the Security Council, i.e. specific information demonstrating that the individual or entity meets the criteria for listing set out in the relevant resolutions; information about any acts or activities of the individual/entity indicating an association with Al-Qaida, Usama Bin Laden or the Taliban pursuant to paragraphs 2 and 3 of resolution 1904 (2009); the names and permanent reference numbers of other entries on the List associated with the listed party; any other relevant information available at the date or after the date of listing such as relevant court decisions and proceedings as provided by the designating State(s) or other Member States concerned; the date(s) when the narrative summary was first made accessible on the Committee's website and when it was reviewed or updated.

(e) If the Committee decides to grant a delisting request, the Secretariat shall immediately remove the corresponding narrative summary from the Committee's website. If the Committee decides to reject a delisting request, the Monitoring Team shall prepare an updated draft narrative summary for the Committee's consideration reflecting the date of the Committee's decision to reject a delisting request as well as any relevant new publicly releasable information provided during the Committee's consideration.

(f) When reviewing a list entry in accordance with paragraph 25 of resolution 1822 (2008) and paragraphs 26, 31 and 32 of resolution 1904 (2009), the Committee shall also review the corresponding narrative summary. Upon completion of the review, the Monitoring Team shall prepare an updated draft narrative summary for the Committee's consideration reflecting the date of the Committee's review as well as any relevant new publicly releasable information provided during the Committee's consideration.

(g) At any time the Committee may consider updating narrative summaries based on new information, proposed changes or additions as well as information about any relevant court decisions and proceedings submitted by Committee Members, the Monitoring Team, Member States or relevant international organizations.

10. Review of the Consolidated List

(a) The Committee was directed by the Security Council in resolution 1822 (2008) to conduct a one-time review of all names that were inscribed on the Consolidated List as at 30 June 2008, in order to ensure the Consolidated List is as updated and accurate as possible and to confirm that listing remains appropriate. For the purposes of this review the following procedure has been applied:

i. Each trimester, the Committee shall circulate a subset of these names to the designating State(s), together with the original statement of case and cover sheet, as applicable. At the same time, the Monitoring Team shall provide these States with the corresponding draft narrative summary of reasons for listing. The Committee shall also circulate those names to the State(s) of residence and/or nationality, where known, together with the publicly releasable portion(s) of the statement of case. Each subset should comprise, to the extent possible, a balanced selection of names from the different sections of the Consolidated List.

ii. The Committee shall ask the designating State(s) and the State(s) of residence and/or nationality to submit to the Committee within 3 months any updated information on the reasons for listing, as well as any additional identifying and other information, along with supporting documentation, on these listed individuals and entities, including updates on the operating status of the listed entities, the movement, incarceration or death of the listed individuals and other significant events. The Committee shall also urge these States to indicate whether they deem the listing remains appropriate.

In cases where any of the States reviewing the names in accordance with subparagraph ii. above determines that a listing is no longer appropriate, that State may submit a de-listing request following the same relevant procedures set out in Section 7 of these guidelines.

iii. At the latest at the end of the 3 months period referred to in subparagraph ii. above or when the designating State(s) and the State(s) of residence and/or nationality have provided the sought information when they had reported within the 3 months on their progress in reviewing the names, the Chairman shall circulate each name with all the available information to the members of the Committee and to the Monitoring Team. Within one month, which may be shortened, if necessary, at the Chairman's discretion to a minimum of two weeks, after this circulation, any Member of the Committee and/or the Monitoring Team may submit any additional information on the names under review.

iv. At the end of the one month (or shortened) period referred to in subparagraph iii. above, the Chairman shall place each name under review on the Committee's agenda and circulate to the Committee all available information, including information provided by Member States and relevant international organizations informing the Committee of any relevant court decisions and proceedings. On the basis of this information, the Committee shall consider updating the Consolidated List and shall make accessible on its website the narrative summary of reasons for listing, as appropriate.

In cases where a member of the Committee in the course of the review referred to in subparagraph iv. above determines that a listing is no longer appropriate, it may, in close consultations with the designating State(s), State(s) of residence and/or nationality and taking into account their views on the matter as referred to in subparagraph ii. above, submit a de-listing request following the same relevant procedures set out in Section 7 of these guidelines.

If no decision has been taken by the Committee to remove a name under review from the Consolidated List, the listing of that name shall be confirmed to remain appropriate and those names shall remain on the Consolidated List.

v. Upon completion of the review of a name, the Secretariat shall notify the designating State(s) and the State(s) of residence and nationality thereof. The State(s) of residence and nationality shall be encouraged to take, in accordance with their domestic laws and practices, all possible measures to notify or inform the individual or entity accordingly and in cases where listing is confirmed to remain appropriate, provide any information on reasons for listing available on the Committee's website as well as the procedures for considering de-listing requests and the provisions for available exemptions.

(b) Upon conclusion of the review pursuant to paragraph 25 of resolution 1822 (2008) as described in paragraph (a) above the Committee shall conduct an annual review of all names on the Consolidated List that have not been reviewed in three or more years, in which the relevant names are circulated to the designating States and States of residence and/or nationality, where known, in order to ensure the Consolidated List is as updated and as accurate as possible and to confirm that the listing remains appropriate.

(c) The Committee's consideration of a delisting request after the date of adoption of resolution 1904 (2009), pursuant to the procedures set out in annex II to resolution 1904 (2009) (reproduced in the annex to these guidelines), should be considered equivalent to a review of that listing.

(d) Upon conclusion of the review pursuant to paragraph 25 of resolution 1822 (2008), the Monitoring Team shall circulate to the Committee every six months a list of individuals on the Consolidated List who are reportedly deceased, along with an assessment of relevant information such as the certification of death, and to the extent possible, the status and location of frozen assets and the names of any individuals or entities who would be in a position to receive any unfrozen assets. The Committee shall review these listings along with the original listing request, as well as all relevant information pertaining to those entries to decide whether they remain appropriate, and to remove listings of deceased individuals where there is credible information regarding death as described in Section 7 (i) above. To ensure the Consolidated List is as updated and as accurate as possible, any member of the Committee may request a review of these names.

(e) If after the review of a deceased person as described in paragraph (d) above all members of the Committee are of the view that the name should be removed from the list but no Member State proposes delisting, the delegation of the Chairman shall submit a request for delisting to be circulated under the written procedure as described in Section 4 (b) above.

(f) Upon conclusion of the review pursuant to paragraph 25 of resolution 1822 (2008), the Committee will request the Monitoring Team to circulate to the Committee annually a list of individuals and entities on the Consolidated List whose entries lack identifiers necessary to ensure effective implementation of the measures imposed upon them. The Committee shall review these listings to decide whether they remain appropriate.

(g) The procedures for the reviews under paragraphs (b), (d) and (f) shall be based on the procedures described in paragraph (a) above but may be adapted by the Committee according to lessons learned during that review.

(h) The reviews described in this section shall not preclude the submission of de-listing requests at any time, in accordance with the relevant procedures set out in Section 7 of these guidelines.

(i) As directed by the Security Council in paragraph 42 of resolution 1904 (2009), the Committee will conduct a comprehensive review of all issues pending before the Committee as at 17 December 2009, and shall endeavor to resolve all such pending issues, to the extent possible, by 31 December 2010.

11. Exemptions to the Assets Freeze

(a) Pursuant to resolution 1452 (2002), as amended by paragraph 15 of resolution 1735 (2006), the Committee shall receive notifications from Member States of their intention to authorize, where appropriate, access to frozen funds or other financial assets or economic resources to cover basic expenses, as provided for in paragraph 1(a) of resolution 1452(2002). The Committee, through the Secretariat, will immediately acknowledge receipt of the notification. Should no negative decision be taken by the Committee within the requisite 3 working day period, the Committee, through its Chairman, will inform the notifying Member State thereof. The Committee will also inform the notifying Member State if a negative decision has been taken regarding the notification.

(b) The Committee shall consider and approve, if appropriate, requests by Member States for extraordinary expenses, as provided for in paragraph 1(b) of resolution 1452 (2002). Member States are encouraged, when submitting requests to the Committee pursuant to paragraph 1 (b) of resolution 1452 (2002), to report in a timely way on the use of such funds, with a view to preventing such funds from being used to finance terrorism.

(c) Notifications under paragraph 1(a) of resolution 1452 (2002) and requests under paragraph 1(b) of resolution 1452 (2002) should, as appropriate, include the following information:

i. recipient (name and address)
ii. recipient's permanent reference number on the Consolidated List
iii. recipient's bank information (name and address of bank, account number)
iv. purpose of payment and justification of the determination of the expenses falling under paragraph 1(a) or under paragraph 1(b):
  - under paragraph 1(a):
    - basic expenses, including payment for foodstuffs, rent or mortgage, medicines and medical treatment, taxes, insurance premiums, and public utility charges;
    - payment of reasonable professional fees and reimbursement of incurred expenses associated with the provisions of legal services;
    - fees or service charges for routine holding or maintenance of frozen funds or other financial assets or economic resources.
  - under paragraph 1(b):
    - extraordinary expenses (other categories than the ones mentioned under paragraph 1 (a)).
v. amount of installment
vi. number of installments
vii. payment starting date
viii. bank transfer or direct debit
ix. interests
x. specific funds being unfrozen
xi. other information.

(d) Pursuant to paragraph 2 of resolution 1452 (2002) and paragraph 6 of resolution 1904 (2009), States may allow for the addition to accounts subject to the assets freeze of:
i. interest or other earnings due on those accounts, or
ii. payments due under contracts, agreements or obligations that arose prior to the date on which those accounts became subject to the assets freeze, or
iii. any payment in favour of listed individuals, groups, undertakings or entities, provided that any such interest, other earnings and payments continue to be subject to the assets freeze.

12. Exemptions from the Travel Ban

In paragraph 2 (b) of resolution 1390 (2002), as reaffirmed by subsequent relevant resolutions, including paragraph 1 (b) of resolution 1904 (2009), the Security Council decided that the travel ban imposed under the Al-Qaida/Taliban sanctions regime shall not apply where the Committee determines, on a case by case basis only, that entry or transit is justified.[6]

(a) Each request for exemption must be submitted in writing, on behalf of the listed individual, to the Chairman. The States that may submit a request through their Permanent Mission to the United Nations are the State(s) of destination, the State(s) of transit, the State of nationality, and the State of residence. If no effective central government exists in the country in which the listed individual is located, a United Nations office or agency in that country may submit the request for exemption on the listed individual's behalf.

(b) Each request for exemption shall be received by the Chairman as early as possible but not less than five working days before the date of the proposed travel.

(c) Each request for exemption should include the following information:

  i. the permanent reference number, full name, nationality, passport number or travel document number of the listed individual;
  ii. the purpose of and justification for the proposed travel, with copies of supporting documents, including specific details of meetings or appointments;
  iii. the proposed dates and times of departure and return;
  iv. the complete itinerary and timetable, including for all transit stops;
  v. details of the mode of transport to be used, including where applicable, record locator, flight numbers and names of vessels;
  vi. all proposed uses of funds or other financial assets or economic resources in connection with the travel. Such funds may only be provided in accordance with paragraph 1 of resolution 1452 (2002), as modified by paragraph 15 of resolution 1735 (2006). The procedures for making a request under resolution 1452 (2002) can be found in Section 11 of these guidelines.

(d) Once the Committee has approved a request for exemption from the travel ban, the Chairman shall notify in writing the Permanent Missions to the United Nations of: the State in which the listed individual is resident, the State of nationality, the State(s) to which the listed individual will be traveling, and any transit State, as well as any UN office/agency involved as provided for in paragraph (a) above, to inform them of the approved travel, itinerary and timetable.

(e) Written confirmation of the completion of the travel by the listed individual shall be provided to the Chairman within five working days following the expiry of the exemption by the State (or United Nations office/agency as in paragraph (a) above) in which the listed individual has stated he will be resident after completion of the exempted travel.

[6] The Security Council also decided that the travel ban shall not oblige any State to deny entry into or require the departure from its territories of its own nationals and shall not apply where entry or transit is necessary for the fulfillment of a judicial process. [Footnote in the original.]

(f) Notwithstanding any exemption from the travel ban, listed individuals remain subject to the other measures outlined in paragraph 1 of resolution 1904 (2009).

(g) Any changes to the information provided under paragraph (c) above, including with regard to points of transit, shall require further consideration by the Committee and shall be received by the Chairman no less than three working days prior to the commencement of the travel.

(h) Any request for an extension of the exemption shall be subject to the procedures set out above and shall be received by the Chairman in writing, with a revised itinerary, no less than five working days before the expiry of the approved exemption.

(i) The submitting State (or United Nations office/agency as in paragraph (a) above) shall inform the Chairman immediately and in writing of any change to the departure date for any travel for which the Committee has already issued an exemption. Written notification will be sufficient in cases where the time of departure is advanced or postponed no more than 48 hours and the itinerary remains otherwise unchanged. If travel is to be advanced or postponed by more than 48 hours, or the itinerary is changed, then a new exemption request shall be submitted in conformity with paragraphs (a), (b) and (c) above.

(j) In cases of emergency evacuation to the nearest appropriate State, including for medical or humanitarian needs or through force majeure, the Committee will determine whether the travel is justified within the provisions of paragraph 1 (b) of resolution 1904 (2009), within 24 hours once notified of the name of the listed individual traveler, the reason for travel, the date and time of evacuation, along with transportation details, including transit points and destination. The notifying authority shall also provide, as soon as possible, a doctor's or other relevant national official's note containing as many details as possible of the nature of the emergency and the facility where treatment or other necessary assistance was received by the listed individual without prejudice to respect of medical confidentiality, as well as information regarding the date, time, and mode of travel by which the listed individual returned to his/her country of residence or nationality, and complete details on all expenses in connection with the emergency evacuation.

(k) Unless the Committee otherwise decides, all requests for exemptions and extensions thereto which have been approved by the Committee in accordance with the above procedures, shall be posted in the 'Exemptions' section of the Committee's website until expiry of the exemption.

13. Reports Submitted by Members States and Other Information Supplied to the Committee

(a) The Committee will examine reports and checklists submitted by Member States pursuant to relevant resolutions and other relevant information, including through the use of the tools provided on the Committee's website. The Committee may request further information that it considers necessary.

(b) The Committee will consider other information relevant to its work, including possible non-compliance with the measures imposed by the relevant resolutions, received from different sources through Member States, international or regional organizations or the Monitoring Team.

(c) The information received by the Committee will be kept confidential if the provider so requests or if the Committee so decides.

(d) With a view to assisting States in their endeavour to implement the measures set out in paragraph 1 of resolution 1904 (2009), the Committee may decide to supply information forwarded to it relating to possible non-compliance to the States concerned, and ask any such State to report to the Committee subsequently on any follow-up action undertaken.

(e) The Committee will provide Member States and relevant international organizations with an opportunity to send representatives to meet the Committee for more in-depth discussion of relevant issues or to give voluntary briefings on their efforts to implement the measures, including particular challenges that hinder full implementation of the measures.

14. Reports to the Security Council

The Committee, through its Chairman, will report orally to the Security Council at least every 180 days pursuant to paragraph 46 of resolution 1904 (2009) on the state of the overall work of the Committee and the Monitoring Team, and, as appropriate, in conjunction with the reports by the Chairmen of the Counter-Terrorism Committee and the Committee established pursuant to resolution 1540 (2004), including briefings for all interested Member States. In its periodic reports to the Council, the Chairman will also provide progress reports on the Committee's work on the identification of possible cases of non-compliance with the measures pursuant to paragraph 1 of resolution 1904 (2009). The Committee will also submit written reports to the Council in accordance with relevant resolutions. The Committee, through its Chairman, may report to the Council when it deems appropriate.

15. Outreach

(a) In order to enhance the dialogue with Member States and to publicize the work of the Committee, the Chairman will on a regular basis hold briefings for all interested Member States, as well as brief interested Member States and the press following formal meetings of the Committee, unless the Committee decides otherwise. In addition, the Chairman may, after prior consultations and with the approval of the Committee, hold press conferences and/or issue press releases on any aspect of the Committee's work.

(b) The Secretariat shall maintain a website for the Committee which should include all public documents relevant to the Committee's work, including the Consolidated List, relevant resolutions, public reports of the Committee, relevant press releases, reports submitted by Member States pursuant to resolution 1455 (2003), and reports of the Monitoring Group and the Monitoring Team. Information on the website should be updated in an expeditious manner.

(c) The Committee may consider, as appropriate, visits by the Chairman and/or Committee Members to selected countries to enhance the full and effective implementation of the measures referred to above, with a view to encouraging States to comply fully with the relevant resolutions:

i. The Committee shall consider and approve the proposal to visit selected countries, and coordinate such visits with the Counter-Terrorism Committee and other subsidiary organs of the Security Council as appropriate.
ii. The Chairman will contact the selected countries through their Permanent Missions in New York, and will also send letters seeking their prior consent and explaining the objectives of the trip.
iii. The Secretariat and the Monitoring Team will provide the Chairman and the Committee with the necessary assistance in this regard.
iv. Upon his return the Chairman will prepare a comprehensive report on the findings of the trip and will brief the Committee orally and in writing.

(d) The Committee shall consider and approve the six monthly travel plan of the Monitoring Team. Any new travel plans in addition to already approved travel of the Monitoring Team shall be sent to the Committee Members for information on a regular basis as necessary. Unless a Committee Member expressly objects to any proposed travel, the Chairman will take it that the Members of the Committee have no objection to the proposed travel and will advise the Monitoring Team to proceed accordingly.

* * * * *

Annex (Ombudsperson Procedure for Delisting)[7]

In accordance with paragraph 20 of resolution 1904 (2009), the Office of the Ombudsperson shall be authorized to carry out the following tasks upon receipt of a delisting request submitted by, or on behalf of, an individual, group, undertaking or entity on the Consolidated List ('the petitioner').

Information Gathering (two months)

1. Upon receipt of a delisting request, the Ombudsperson shall:

   (a) Acknowledge to the petitioner the receipt of the delisting request;
   (b) Inform the petitioner of the general procedure for processing delisting requests;
   (c) Answer specific questions from the petitioner about Committee procedures; and,
   (d) Inform the petitioner in case the petition fails to properly address the original designation criteria, as set forth in paragraph 2 of resolution 1904 (2009), and return it to the petitioner for his or her consideration;
   (e) Verify if the request is a new request or a repeated request and, if it is a repeated request to the Ombudsperson and it does not contain any additional information, return it to the petitioner for his or her consideration.

2. For delisting petitions not returned to the petitioner, the Ombudsperson shall immediately forward the delisting request to the members of the Committee, designating State(s), State(s) of residence and nationality or incorporation, relevant UN

[7] This annex reproduces annex II of resolution 1904 (2009). See also Section 7 of the guidelines.

bodies, and any other States deemed relevant by the Ombudsperson. The Ombudsperson shall ask these States or relevant UN bodies to provide, within two months, any appropriate additional information relevant to the delisting request. The Ombudsperson may engage in dialogue with these States to determine:

(a) These States' opinions on whether the delisting request should be granted; and,

(b) Information, questions or requests for clarifications that these States would like to be communicated to the petitioner regarding the delisting request, including any information or steps that might be taken by a petitioner to clarify the delisting request.

3. The Ombudsperson shall also immediately forward the delisting request to the Monitoring Team, which shall provide to the Ombudsperson, within two months:

   (a) All information available to the Monitoring Team that is relevant to the delisting request, including court decisions and proceedings, news reports, and information that States or relevant international organizations have previously shared with the Committee or the Monitoring Team;

   (b) Fact-based assessments of the information provided by the petitioner that is relevant to the delisting request; and,

   (c) Questions or requests for clarifications that the Monitoring Team would like asked of the petitioner regarding the delisting request.

4. At the end of this two-month period of information gathering, the Ombudsperson shall present a written update to the Committee on progress to date, including details regarding which States have supplied information. The Ombudsperson may extend this period once for up to two months if he or she assesses that more time is required for information gathering, giving due consideration to requests by Member States for additional time to provide information.

Dialogue (two months)

5. Upon completion of the information gathering period, the Ombudsperson shall facilitate a two-month period of engagement, which may include dialogue with the petitioner. Giving due consideration to requests for additional time, the Ombudsperson may extend this period once for up to two months if he or she assesses that more time is required for engagement and the drafting of the Comprehensive Report described in paragraph 7 below.

6. During this period of engagement, the Ombudsperson:

   (a) May ask the petitioner questions or request additional information or clarifications that may help the Committee's consideration of the request, including any questions or information requests received from relevant States, the Committee and the Monitoring Team;

   (b) Shall forward replies from the petitioner back to relevant States, the Committee and the Monitoring Team and follow up with the petitioner in connection with incomplete responses by the petitioner; and,

   (c) Shall coordinate with States, the Committee and the Monitoring Team regarding any further inquiries of, or response to, the petitioner;

7. Upon completion of the period of engagement described above, the Ombudsperson, with the help of the Monitoring Team, shall draft and circulate to the Committee a Comprehensive Report that will exclusively:

   (a) Summarize and, as appropriate, specify the sources of, all information available to the Ombudsperson that is relevant to the delisting request. The report shall respect confidential elements of Member States' communications with the Ombudsperson;
   (b) Describe the Ombudsperson's activities with respect to this delisting request, including dialogue with the petitioner; and,
   (c) Based on an analysis of all the information available to the Ombudsperson and the Ombudsperson's observations, lay out for the Committee the principal arguments concerning the delisting request.

Committee Discussion and Decision (two months)

8. After the Committee has had thirty days to review the Comprehensive Report, the chair of the Committee shall place the delisting request on the Committee's agenda for consideration.
9. When the Committee considers the delisting request, the Ombudsperson, aided by the Monitoring Team, as appropriate, shall present the Comprehensive Report in person and answer Committee members' questions regarding the request.
10. After the Committee consideration, the Committee shall decide whether to approve the delisting request through its normal decision-making procedures.
11. If the Committee decides to grant the delisting request, then the Committee shall inform the Ombudsperson of this decision. The Ombudsperson shall then inform the petitioner of this decision and the listing shall be removed from the Consolidated List.
12. If the Committee decides to reject the delisting request, then the Committee shall convey to the Ombudsperson its decision including, as appropriate, explanatory comments, any further relevant information about the Committee's decision, and an updated narrative summary of reasons for listing.
13. After the Committee has informed the Ombudsperson that the Committee has rejected a delisting request, then the Ombudsperson shall send to the petitioner, with an advance copy sent to the Committee, within fifteen days a letter that:

    (a) Communicates the Committee's decision for continued listing;
    (b) Describes, to the extent possible and drawing upon the Ombudsperson's Comprehensive Report, the process and publicly releasable factual information gathered by the Ombudsperson; and,
    (c) Forwards from the Committee all information about the decision provided to the Ombudsperson pursuant to paragraph 12 above.
14. In all communications with the petitioner, the Ombudsperson shall respect the confidentiality of Committee deliberations and confidential communications between the Ombudsperson and Member States.

Other Office of the Ombudsperson Tasks

15. In addition to the tasks specified above, the Ombudsperson shall:

 (a) Distribute publicly releasable information about Committee procedures, including Committee Guidelines, fact sheets and other Committee prepared documents, to anyone who requests such information;
 (b) Where address is known, notify individuals or entities about the status of their listing, after the Secretariat has officially notified the Permanent Mission of the State or States, pursuant to paragraph 18 of resolution 1904 (2009); and,
 (c) Submit biannual reports summarizing the activities of the Ombudsperson to the Security Council.

Index

The manufacturer's authorised representative in the EU for product safety is Oxford University Press España S.A. of El Parque Empresarial San Fernando de Henares, Avenida de Castilla, 2 - 28830 Madrid (www.oup.es/en or product.safety@oup.com). OUP España S.A. also acts as importer into Spain of products made by the manufacturer.
Printed and bound by CPI Group (UK) Ltd, Croydon, CR0 4YY
14/09/2026
02216308-0008